ERRATA-- The Greek words at the bottom of
pages 101, 102, 104, 121, 164 should be
read into the text at the blank spaces
reserved for them higher up on each page.

OTHER CHRISTS

The Coming Copernican Christology

OTHER CHRISTS

THE COMING COPERNICAN CHRISTOLOGY

by
WOODBRIDGE O. JOHNSON, PH.D.

Pageant Press International Corp.
New York, N. Y.

Preface and Acknowledgements

To all copyright owners who have given permission to quote from their publications, I wish to express my thanks. They are: Charles Scribner's Sons for use of Alice Meynell's poem "Christ in the Universe" in their publication *The Poems of Alice Meynell;* the Westminster Press for quotations from *Religion and the Christian Faith* by Hendrick Kraemer, published in the U. S. A. in 1957; The Division of Christian Education of the National Council of the Churches of Christ in the U. S. A. for scripture quotations from the *Revised Standard Version Bible,* copyright 1946 and 1952; the University of Chicago Press for quotations from Paul Tillich's *Systematic Theology,* Vols. I, II, and III; The American Academy of Religion for use of my article "Non-Christian Salvation" in the *Journal of Bible and Religion,* issue of July, 1963, copyrighted by what was then the National Association of Biblical Instructors; George Allen and Unwin, Ltd. of London for my article "The Coming Copernican Christology" in *The Hibbert Journal* issue of October, 1960. I would also like to thank the Reverend Taisen Miyata of the Koyosan Buddhist Temple of Los Angeles, California, for the use of a portion of Hymn 210, "Light From the East" in his Temple hymnbook.

I am indebted to Professor Joseph M. Kitagawa of the University of Chicago for his incisive and helpful overall criticism of the manuscript. Especially helpful were the detailed critical analysis of the biblical sections of the manuscript made by Dean Clinton Morrison of Louisville Presbyterian Seminary; the thorough probing treatment of the sections on historical theology and scientific analogy done by Assistant Professor John C. Godbey of Meadville Theological School; the sharp criticism of my handling of comparative religions by Dr. Tyler Thompson, Professor of the Philosophy of Religion at Garrett Theological Seminary; the care with which Dr. Henry N. Wieman, Professor Emeritus of Christian Theology of the University of Chicago Divinity School, has scrutinized the essay from the perspective of his own revolutionary theological thinking; and the suggestions for improved English composition and the secretarial labors of my wife Geraldine. Most of all I am grateful to Dr. Floyd H. Ross, formerly Professor of World Religions at Claremont Graduate School and Southern California School of Theology in Claremont, California, and Director of the Blaisdell Institute for Advanced Study in World Cultures and Religions. It was graduate study under him and his encouragement that were largely responsible for the writing of this book.

Chapter one appeared originally, October, 1960, as the *Hibbert Journal* article, "The Coming Copernican Christology." Chapters Six and Seven constitute a somewhat enlarged version of the article, "Non-Christian Salvation" appearing July, 1963, in *The Journal of Bible and Religion.*

A simplified glossary of foreign words, without their diacritical markings, and some technical words has been added for the benefit of the general reader.

Certain sections of the book presuppose special theological and critical background to be fully appreciated, hence will require more careful reading than the rest and might well be postponed till the other sections have been read. The sections referred to are: Chapter One, "Its support in Current Reappraisals of the Trinity"; Chapter Two, "Tillich's Criteria for an Incarnation" and "The Problem of Historicity"; Chapter Four, "Mystic Union and the Problem of the One and the Many."

INTRODUCTION

New occasions teach new duties
Time makes ancient good uncouth;
They must upward still and onward
Who would keep abreast of truth.

> . . . James R. Lowell
> From Hymn 326
> *The Pilgrim Hymnal*

I have much more to tell you
but you cannot take it in now,
but when the Spirit of Truth comes,
he will guide you into the full truth;
for he will not speak for himself
but will tell you what he hears,
and will announce to you the things that are to come.

> . . . Jesus
> From John 16: 12-13
> Goodspeed's translation

He who is not against us is on our side.

> . . . Jesus
> From Mark 9:40
> *The New English Bible*

TABLE OF CONTENTS

Part One

Page

Chapter I Extraterrestrial Incarnations and Trinity Revision 7

The Thesis Stated: There are other incarnations beside Jesus 7

The Thesis Supported 9

Its historical emergence and growth 9

Its support in Tillich's view of extraterrestrial incarnations 11

Its support in current reappraisals of the Trinity.... 18

Summary 26

Footnotes 27

Part Two

Chapter II Jesus and the Criteria for an Incarnation.. 30

Tillich's criteria for an incarnation 30

Incarnation as total and monopolistic 34

Incarnation as total but selectively pluralistic 34

Incarnation as total and universal 35

Incarnation as partial 38

Tillich's concept of revelation 44

Evidence that Jesus does not meet Tillich's criteria 46

The problem of historicity 46

Was Jesus centered in and transparent to God?.... 55

Is there evidence of Jesus' estrangement from God? 55

Is the question of Jesus' sinlessness irrelevant?...... 57

Footnotes 64

Chapter III The Uniqueness of Jesus' Revelation
of God 68

Can his revelation be duplicated, augmented, or
surpassed? 68
His general ethical and religious teaching 69
His teaching on survival of death 71
His teaching that God is a person 74
His teaching of God's loving fatherhood 74
His teaching that God suffers in his son's death 75
His teaching that salvation depends on his
own death 80
His teaching that men are saved only by
God's grace 90

Footnotes 94

Chapter IV Did Jesus Claim to be God and Man's
Only Saviour? 98

Did he teach that he reveals God because he himself
is God? 98
Did he claim identity with or subordination to God? 98
Is his title "Lord" a deific title? 99
Evidence of alleged self-identification with God 101
Is he the only-begotten son of God? 104
Natural versus adopted or spiritual sonship 106
Does his sonship differ in kind from his disciples'? .. 108
Do his claims to spiritual authority imply
his deity? 110
Do his miracles prove his deity? 120
Did the worship accorded him imply his deity? 121
Do his claims to oneness with the Father prove
his deity? 122
Mystic union and the problem of the one and
the many 127

Footnotes 131

Chapter V Jesus and the Fellowship of Faiths 136
Agreements and differences between the faiths 136
Non-Christian faiths as sharers in the incarnation .. 141

Footnotes 144

Part Three

Chapter VI Salvation as the Enjoyment of
Religious Peace 146

Testimonies to non-Christian religious peace 147

Objections to non-Christian religious peace 149

Footnotes 156

Chapter VII Salvation as Loving Behavior 157

Is love a valid criterion? 157

Testimonies to non-Christian love 160

Kraemer's objection to this criterion based on his
dichotomy between religion and the biblical
revelation 163

The weakness of Kraemer's objection due to his
vague concept of salvation 166

Footnotes 169

Chapter VIII "Saved" vs. "lost" Remythologized
as a Continuum 170

Philosophical and scientific support for a
spiritual continuum 170

The universality of saving grace 179

The logic of the continuum 181

Objections to the continuum considered 184

Spiritual development vs. primordial fall 188

Footnotes 191

Chapter IX Many guides to the One Goal 194

"The only way" vs. relativistic soteriology 194

The impossibility of demonstrating absolute
superiority 198

The one faith within the many religions 201

Footnotes 206

Glossary 207

Author index 214

Subject index 217

PART ONE

The Possibility of Divine Incarnations beyond the Earth and Human History: A Rational-Metaphysical Approach Suggested by Astronomical Theory.

Chapter I

EXTRATERRESTRIAL INCARNATIONS AND TRINITY REVISION

1. THE THESIS STATED

THE COPERNICAN REVOLUTION in astronomy has been over for a long time: it is still going on in theology. The substitution of heliocentrism for geocentrism is no longer disputed by educated persons. But the need for a new center in Christology is only beginning to be generally discussed. What is needed, if we are to keep our theology relevant to the new knowledge of our rapidly expanding universe, is a Christology centered in God as Logos rather than in Jesus of Nazareth.

The present pressure for a new look at Christology comes from two directions—scientific and religious. The scientific stimulus comes from the vastly larger universe given to us by the 200-inch telescope and improved methods of photography, Einstein's general theory of relativity, the development of jet propulsion and nuclear power, popular science fiction correlated with the literature of flying saucer phenomena and the growing probability of intelligent beings living on other planets, the successful launching of man-made moons, and the arrival of space travel.[1] The religious stimulus comes from the amazing resurgence of the great Asian religions and our rapidly growing understanding and appreciation of them. These pressures are forcing us to take a new look at the orthodox doctrine of the Incarnation, a doctrine which at present reflects a static provincialism blind to expanding cultural and sidereal horizons.

This doctrine is provincial in insisting that a remote Creator—God invaded his universe once and once for all, at only one point in space-time, when he assumed the body of a Jewish carpenter some 2,000 years ago in Palestine on the planet Earth. It is provincial also in insisting that in the life of that Jewish carpenter the nature of the ineffable Ground of Being has been fully and finally revealed to all his creatures in all worlds, and that those unfortunate enough not to establish vital connection with that carpenter are predestined to eternal spiritual death.

The carpenter himself proclaimed a universal, not a tribal[2] God, who loves all his children, good and bad alike, "not wishing that any should perish but that all should reach repentence."[3] Yet orthodox Christology teaches that God doomed millions of his children to be eternally lost because they lived in the centuries before the carpenter appeared as savior, and dooms uncounted millions more in succeeding centuries because they either have no means of hearing about the savior or, having heard, don't recognize him as the only savior.

Such provincial Christology is doubly off-center. It is culture-centered rather than humanity-centered, since it restricts God's direct and full concern for men to the Jewish culture of the Near East, allowing him only a belated and seemingly indifferent interest in the rest of mankind. It is also geocentric rather than heliocentric, for it is still postulated on the Ptolemaic world view which holds that Earth is both spatially and axiologically the center of space-time, and which ignores the growing probability that other beings needing spiritual salvation inhabit other planets in other solar systems in other galaxies.

It is the purpose of this study to reappraise the Christian doctrines of the Incarnation, the Trinity, and Salvation, and, in the light of the new evidence, suggest the lines of their reformulation. This reformulation will require a theocentric and logocentric, in place of the present Jesus-centered, Christology. It will require a pluralistic rather than a monistic Christology, for it will show that "Jesus as the Christ" (neo-orthodoxy's formula) is not the absolute center about which all truth and value revolve but is, rather, only one of a number of self-disclosures of God in this and other worlds which revolve around God himself as their collective center. The new Christology will try to show that God has not in the past limited his self-revelation to Jesus of Nazareth, but that there have been other incarnations of God in human flesh, are possibly even now others in other types of flesh and consciousness, and that there may well be, as Rebecca West phrased it, "other and greater Christs" to come on the Earth.

2. THE THESIS SUPPORTED

ITS HISTORICAL EMERGENCE AND GROWTH

The new Christology is not a novelty; it has merely been a long time coming before the theological public and is still, for most conservative Christians, a shocking heresy. The Copernican revolution in astronomy was probably first suggested in the cosmological speculation of Anaximander in the middle of the sixth century B.C., yet was not generally accepted as true until as late as 1835 A.D., when an edition of the Roman Catholic Index appeared for the first time without condemnation of the double motion of the earth. Thus it took more than 2300 years for the minds of orthodox Christians to accommodate to this truth. It met with theological opposition on the ground that heliocentrism vitiated the whole Christian plan of salvation, an opposition epitomized in the words of Father Melchior Inchofer:

"The opinion of the earth's motion is of all heresies
the most abominable, the most pernicious, the most
scandalous; the immobility of the earth is thrice sacred.
Argument against the immortality of the soul, the existence of God, and the incarnation should be tolerated
sooner than an argument to prove that the earth
moves."[4]

General acceptance of the Copernican Christology is
resisted for the reason that it directly challenges what has
been the indispensable theological foundation of Christianity
—the conviction that Christianity is man's only way to God
because only in Jesus has God come to man. Yet the new
Christology is older than the orthodox Christology. Jewish,
early Apostolic, Ebionite, and Pauline denial of full deity
to Jesus was continued by Sabellius and Arius, and their
followers, and was not condemned officially until Nicea in
325, when the "very God of very God" formula became sacrosanct. But anathematization only drove the viewpoint un-
derground—from where it has emerged with growing
strength in Socinianism, Unitarianism, and ecumenical liberalism. In spite of successive reactionary new orthodoxies,
the Copernican Christology is gaining a wider and wider
hearing, with men of other faiths like Baha'u'lla, Suzuki,
and Radhakrishnan speaking earnestly on its behalf.

Acquaintance with Eastern faiths entered Christendom
late, and only gradually, through the travel reports of Marco
Polo and Jesuit missionaries in the thirteenth to sixteenth
centuries. Then, with the help of empirical philosophy and a
rediscovered Hellenism, it produced in the seventeenth and
eighteenth centuries that rethinking of orthodox theology
conventionally known as Deism or, more broadly, the Enlightenment. Here, pioneer work in religions was done by
Reimarus, Lessing, Mendelssohn, and Herder, who helped
to found the comparative-religions school of thought and began to see the mythological character of theology. Added to

theirs was the work of such scholars as Max Müller, Edwin Arnold, Rhys Davids, René Guénon, James Frazer, and Ernst Troeltsch; and the West was forced to a new respect for the non-Christian faiths and the insight that there is a common pattern in all faiths, including Christianity.

Other streams of influence contributory to the concept of universal revelation and the pluralistic Christology of a nascent world faith include the great Protestant missionary movement of the nineteenth and twentieth centuries, which magnified and intensified the interfaith contacts of the earlier Jesuit missions; the new science of Biblical Criticism, culminating in Form and Mythological criticism; Jungian exploration into religious archetypes; and the search, á la Bultmann, for the common existential root of the many-branched mythological interpretation of mankind's religious experience.

Contemporary thinkers sympathetic to the new Christological dawn would include such Americans as J. B. Pratt, Ernest Hocking, C. W. Morris, F. S. C. Northrop, Alan Watts and Floyd H. Ross; such Europeans as Toynbee, Zimmer and Eliade; such Easterners as Baha'u'lla, Vivekenanda, Radhakrishnan, Aurobindo Ghose, Coomaraswamy, Nikhilananda, Das Gupta, Suzuki and Joseph Kitagawa.

More cautious thinkers, but ones also approaching the new insight, would include such men as Söderblom, Temple, Joaquim Wach, Brunner, and Tillich whose inner logic points toward the broader concept in spite of his outer traditionalism. Defenders of traditionalism would include Karl Barth, E. D. Soper, Hendrik Kraemer, Edmund Perry, and their followers.

ITS SUPPORT IN TILLICH'S ADMISSION OF EXTRA-TERRESTRIAL INCARNATIONS

We have selected as our point of departure in presenting evidence for the Copernican Christology a thoughtful,

tradition-breaking statement of Tillich's. But first hear him
absolutizing Jesus in the orthodox manner:

> Jesus as the Christ is the final revelation. This claim
> establishes a Christian Church, and, where this claim
> is absent, Christianity has ceased to exist. . . .[5]

> But final revelation means more than the last genuine
> revelation. It means the decisive, fulfilling, unsurpass-
> able revelation, that which is the criterion of all the
> others. . . .[6]

> [Christ's life] is the ecstatic moment of human history
> and, therefore, its center . . . .[7]

> As its central event, he creates the meaning of human
> history,[8] . . . he who cannot be transcended by anyone
> else who may appear in the course of human
> history.[9] . . .

> The incarnation is an historical event and occurs only
> once in time and space.[10]

Such strictures would seem to leave no loophole for
the infiltration of Christological relativism. But, contradictorily, he goes on to declare that such absolutism

> . . . leaves the universe open for possible divine mani-
> festations in other areas or periods of being . . . In-
> carnation is unique for the special group in which it
> happens, but it is not unique in the sense that other
> singular incarnations for other unique worlds are
> excluded.[11] . . .

> For historical mankind in its unique, continuous de-
> velopment, as experienced here and now, Christ is the
> center. But . . . this existential limitation. . . leaves
> open other ways of divine self-manifestations before
> and after our historical continuum.[12]

By this admission of the possibility of "other singular
incarnations for other unique worlds" does not Tillich
open the door to Christological relativism? It seems to us
that this concession boldly extends the Copernican revolu-

tion into Christology; that it removes Jesus from the role of absolute center round which God's whole creative and redemptive activity revolves, to an off-center position where he and other saviors revolve together, though in diverse orbits, around the central Godhead. Jesus Christ is no longer the one and only, complete and final, creating and saving word of God. His sovereignty is limited to this "wayside planet." He is but one among other instances of the eternal Logos becoming flesh in a divine kenosis. He is not the only supernatural savior, but one of a plurality of saviors, sent forth to save a plurality of intelligent races of beings, in a plurality of worlds throughout the flow of time.

Tillich's theological speculation is, of course, premised on astrophysical data. Beginning with the Greek, Milesian cosmologists, Western thought has witnessed a succession of thinkers believing in the existence of life and intelligent beings on other planets than our own. Several recent evaluations of the hypothesis are of special interest: Iosif S. Shklovsky's book on the universality of intelligent life, published in 1962 by the Soviet Academy of Science; Alastair Cameron's book, *Interstellar Communication;*[13] Thornton Page's *The Origin of the Solar System;*[14] and Walter Sullivan's, *We are not Alone.*[15] Admittedly there are qualified skeptics; but Sullivan cites in support of his own affirmative conviction such outstanding astronomers as Father Angelo Secci, the mid-nineteenth century Jesuit, Hans Bethe, Otto Struve, Carl Sagan and Harlow Shapley. The last named, considering a typical estimate that there are a hundred billion stars with possible planetary systems in each of a hundred billion galaxies, and that "one or two percent of stars may have at one time or another supported intelligent life,"[16] writes:

> As far as we can tell, the same physical laws prevail everywhere. The same rules apply at the center of the

Milky Way, in the remote galaxies, and among the stars of the solar neighborhood. In view of a common physics and chemistry, should we not also expect to find animals and plants everywhere? It seems completely reasonable; and soon we shall say that it seems inevitable.[17]

Edwin Hubble supports Shapley in his well-known statement:

It seems reasonable to assume, doesn't it, that among the myriads of stars that we now know to be in the grand universe there are innumerable ones that have planets associated with them. Many of these planets must be suitable for supporting life. On the whole one is inclined to think that there may be countless other worlds with life, even life such as we do not know or cannot conceive on the basis of our earthly experiences.[18]

And Alastair Cameron asserts even more boldly:

We are now completing the Copernican intellectual revolution and admitting the probability not only that we are not unique in the universe but that there may be millions of societies more advanced than ourselves in our galaxy alone.[19]

As evidence of the seriousness with which the scientific world is considering Cameron's hypothesis, we would point to the Conference on Extra-terrestrial Civilization, held in the Soviet Union the fall of 1964 at the Burakan Astrophysical Observatory.

And so seriously have American astronomers considered the hypothesis that Project Osma was carried out in mid-1960 by Frank D. Drake and associates at the National Radio Astronomy Observatory at Green Bank, West Virginia.

Its purpose was to detect any radio signals coming from intelligent beings in the vicinity of the stars Tau Ceti and Epsilon Eridani. While the results were negative, further experimentation on this frontier are going steadily forward.

With such a distinct possibility as a premise, the traditional Trinity, which conceives of the human nature of Jesus as being taken up into the Godhead and becoming the only case of the infinitization of the finite, must undergo alteration: either it must be relinquished as unrealistic, or it must be metamorphosed into a vast multiplicity or, more accurately, into a trinity whose second member, and possibly also its third, become multiple. Considered historically and geographically, if its three-foldness be retained it would then become a plurality of interlocking trinities, including a different one for each inhabited planet. The Father, constituting the common factor of all the trinities, would be augmented by a different incarnation of the Son, and a different manifestation of the Holy Spirit for each world. God's incarnation through the Son or Logos, and immanence through the Spirit, would be in the type of consciousness peculiar to each separate world, and would effect salvation in that world's peculiar historical context and mythological idiom.

Such extra-terrestrial incarnations of God are acceptable to others beside Tillich.

W. N. Clarke, Protestant theologian, declared:

> If there are other races of creatures that bear the likeness of God, he may have entered them in like manner. It may be his good pleasure then to enter in the fullness of time, every race that he has created in his own image. If there are sinless races he may thus have crowned them with their predestined glory; if there are other sinful races he may have entered them as he entered ours, seeking to save.[20]

It is acceptable also to some Roman Catholic theological thought. For example, Father L. C. McHugh, Associate Editor of *America,* and Father Daniel C. Raible of the Brunnendale Seminary of the Society of the Precious Blood in Canton, Ohio, who is quoted in the pages of that journal as saying, "There is nothing at all repugnant in the idea of the same Divine Person taking on the nature of many human races. Conceivably we may learn in Heaven that there has been not one incarnation of God's son, but many."[21]

The pattern of such a Christology, though strange to most Christians, is not new to mankind. It has long been a theological pattern of Mahayana and Tantrayana Buddhism. For these the ultimate Being, whether conceived supra-personally as in Dharmakaya, or as alaya vijñana in Yogacharya's absolute idealism, or personified as Adibudda or Vairocana, manifests itself for the enlightenment of creatures through a plurality of historical buddhas in a plurality of worlds throughout an infinity of time.[22]

It is a commonplace also in Vedantist thought, where a plurality of divine incarnations, for example of Vishnu, are sent periodically to purify men in successive universes through the infinite Kalpas of time.[23]

In a widely read book on Hindu religious practices, an extra-terrestrial society is described on the planet (albeit an "astral" planet), Hiranyaloka, to which Sri Yukteswar ascended at his death to serve as spiritual leader.[24]

Tillich's view has been expressed poetically by Alice Meynell:

> No planet knows that this
> Our wayside planet, carrying land and wave,
> Love and life multiplied, and pain and bliss,
> Bears, as chief treasure, one forsaken grave.
>
> Nor in our little day
> May His devices with the heavens be guessed,
> His pilgrimage to thread the Milky Way
> Or His bestowals there be manifest.
>
> But in the eternities
> Doubtless we shall compare together, hear
> A million alien gospels, in what guise
> He trod the Pleiades, the Lyre, the Bear.

> O be prepared, my soul,
> To read the inconceivable, to scan
> The million forms of God those stars unroll
> When, in our turn, we show to them a man.[25]

Her thought, like Tillich's, seems to be that there is only one supernatural Son or Logos or Second Person of the Trinity, who is God in his creator-revealer-redeemer aspect, and who incarnates himself in a plurality of planetary saviors or "Christs," whether they appear successively or contemporaneously throughout the space-time continuum. But the foregoing break with the Jesus Christ of orthodoxy would seem to vitiate Tillich's case for the absoluteness of the Christian revelation. In it, as in his doctrine of the "God beyond the God of Theism,"[26] who is beyond but does not exclude the subject-object, person to person, I-Thou polarity, this great Christian thinker arrives at the fundamental insight of Vedantism and Buddhism and stands on common ground with them, thus helping to lay a foundation for a coming interfaith world faith.

But we move too fast. The logic of Tillich's position would seem only to require that if incarnations are admissible for possible extra-terrestrial races as well as for Earthlings, they should be admissible for the Hindus and Chinese as well as for the Jews. The difference between any possible extra-terrestrial and Hindu incarnations is great but not absolute since both, being presumptively intelligent and moral, are made in God's image. The fact that Vedantism actually points to such incarnations in Krishna, Buddha, Ramakrishna, et al., and even in certain sub-human beings, would seem to validate the application of the principle historically. For Hindus and Buddhists testify as well that they do learn the nature of the supreme being, and find religious peace in him, through these intermediaries, these Words of God.

To press the logic still further: If we are prepared, as Alice Meynell and Tillich are, to allow "a million alien gospels" for other worlds which actually save God's creatures there, though none is "the Gospel of our Lord and Savior Jesus Christ" (since lacking the person of Jesus and probably couched in other mythology than "virgin birth," "crucified Messiah," and "atoning sacrificial lamb of God"), then why not allow the alien gospels preached by Zoroaster, Laotse, Gotama, Baha'u'llah, the Upanishads, and the Bhagavadgita which should be culturally closer to the Christian Gospel than any extra-terrestrial mythology could be?

So far, then, Tillich's Christology has replaced the old, once-for-all monopolistic incarnation of God with a plurality of extra-terrestrial incarnations and, as we apply his logic, with a plurality of terrestrial incarnations outside of the Judeo-Christian tradition, thus surmounting the provincial barriers of the Hebrew-Christian "special chosenness" and "only way" theology, to share with the Asian faiths the doctrine of God's saving revelatory universalism. The criteria for identifying an incarnation will be examined in chapter two.

ITS SUPPORT IN CURRENT REAPPRAISALS OF THE TRINITY

We have thus far shown how Tillich's doctrine of multiple incarnations pluralizes the second person of the biblical Trinity and so breaks Jesus' monopoly of it. But other changes in trinitarian thought are afoot. We mention two. There is a fresh attempt to preserve the "essence-ial," or non-contingent, love of God by reformulating the social analogy to the Trinity in such a way as to escape the tri-theism which modern psychological understanding of "person" makes almost inevitable. And there is a surprising attempt to reduce the biblical Trinity to the metaphysical duality so fundamental to neo-Platonism, Gnosticism, Vedantism and Buddhism.[27]

We note first the failure to guarantee the essence-ial love of God by reformulation of the social analogy to the Trinity. Those making this attempt include such writers as Wilfred Richmond, Charles F. D'Arcy, John B. Champion, Charles N. Bartlett, Leonard Hodgson, William A. Brown, Claude Welch, and Dorothy Sayers. The details of their various reformulations are too complex for analysis here. But they all seem to be caught on one or the other horn of a dilemma. On the one hand, to preserve the eternalness of God's love, they are forced to say that God loves himself eternally, which, unless it includes loving others beside himself, is egotism. But if it does include loving others, then God is not absolute and self-sufficient; for such love requires co-eternal objects of his love. Or they must define God as an eternal society of three persons who love each other. But such intramural love requires the tri-theism they abhor, for only independent conscious subjects can be said to love; modes of a single person's being or acting cannot be described as loving each other. Welch is emphatic in his opinion that modern thought should drop the concept of three "persons" altogether and be content with the more meaningful though still heretical three "modes of being" concept.[28] But even granted that the three constituent Gods within God love each other, how can the constituting or collective God be said to love? Whom does he love? If he loves his three parts, we return to the unsatisfactory notion of self-love. However, if the three member Gods exhaust the Godhead, no one is left to love them. And to postulate the Godhead as a fourth person is to enlarge the Trinity to a quadrinity, which is one degree worse than tri-theism. Thus, seeking to preserve God's love, they lose his absoluteness.

But on the other horn of the dilemma, to preserve God's absoluteness they must endow him with a love which is

independent of love for others, for love for others indicates
a need or vulnerability which is a defect in self-sufficiency.
One would think self-sufficient love was a contradiction in
terms; it is certainly contradictory to the biblical description of God, as Charles Hartshorne insists in his major
writings. Nevertheless, the attempt is made to establish it
by drastic reformulation of the social analogy to the Trinity.
The three persons are changed into aspects of God's revelation, of his experience, or of his activity. But since one cannot love aspects of one's own behaviour, which would be nar-
cissism, nor speak of aspects of one's behaviour as loving
each other, which is psychologically impossible, the love
evaporates altogether and the social analogy breaks down.

We note, secondly, a proposal to reduce the biblical
Trinity to a metaphysical duality.

But those seeking this second objective do so as another
solution to the foregoing dilemma. They frankly accept the
paradox as conceptually insoluble. Their thesis is clearly
worked out by Richardson. He insists that the Trinity "is an
artificial construct,"[29] that "there is no necessary three-ness
in the Godhead,"[30] that the Holy Spirit is "logically identical
with the Logos."[31] He then proceeds to transform the traditional religious Trinity of Father (loving creator), Son
(incarnate redeemer) and Holy Spirit (immanent purifier
and empowerer)—all of whom express God's relatedness to
the universe—into the metaphysical duality of God-as-abso-
lute-transcendent-and-ineffable (the Father) and God-as-
related-immanent-and loving-personal-creator (the Son-Holy
Spirit),[32] neither of which is prior to or superior to the
other.

The inadequacy of the biblical Trinity consists in its
ignoring of God's absolute-relative polarity, for all its three
persons are subsumable under "God-as-related." The very
metaphors "Father" and "Son" require relatedness, and
both Judaism and Jesus were metaphysically naive and did

not rise above the anthropomorphic pattern for God. Moreover, for the first disciples there was no Trinity at all—there
was only the three-fold experience of Yaweh, the righteous
creator lawgiver, Jesus, the loving teacher and prophet-
Messiah, and in the Holy Spirit, the felt powerful presence
in their midst of Yaweh, focussed through the lens of Jesus'
life and teaching. These experiences were then, and have
been ever since, normative for Christian living; but they
are not the doctrine of the Trinity. It did not come for 300
years, not until the three Christian symbols of Father, Son,
and Holy Spirit had been welded together with the aid of
Aristotelian and Stoic concepts into a metaphysical unity.
But before this could happen the role of Jesus had to undergo transformation. From being to his first disciples a won-
der-working prophet of God, he became successively a son
of God in superlative degree; the God-anointed (Messianic)
eschatological deliverer of the Jews; Paul's pre-existent
heavenly creator and world-savior who was yet less than
God; the Johannine Logos, mystically one with God yet inferior to the Father, and inviting his disciples to share his
divine nature and prerogatives; the Son eclipsing the Father
as the functional God of the early Christians;[33] and finally,
in the third and fourth century creeds, identical with God
and equal to the Father in power and glory.

The historical scope of God's absolute-relative polarity
is universal. But though the absoluteness and ineffability of
God had been stressed by neo-Platonizing theologians such
as Clement of Alexandria, who inherited the concept from
neo-Pythagoreanism and Philo, it was bypassed in the
Athanasian formula. But today, neo-orthodoxy's disillusion-
ment with man and his philosophizing about God has re-
juvenated it in the concepts of "The Wholly Other" (Otto),
who is nevertheless revealed, says Barth, in Christ, and the
"God beyond the God of theism" (Tillich), who is mythologically conceived as a person. But this distinction between

God as absolute and God as related is not a novelty as we have already pointed out with reference to Greek and Patristic thought; and it is a fundamental teaching of the great Asian faiths. Sankara and classic Vedantism generally distinguish between Brahman, the ineffable, absolute ground of existence, and its personal modes of relatedness to the world and the religious apprehensions of men as Ishvara, who is then particularized in the figures of Brahma, Vishnu, Shiva, Kali, *et al.* Buddhist schools posit a polarity between the ineffable reality of Sunyata or Nirvana on the one hand, and Samsara or the world of appearances on the other; between the absolute Dharmakaya and its Sambhogakaya personalizations as Buddhas and Bodhisattvas.

In the matter of the relative ranking of God as absolute and God as related, Christian thought is as divided as non-Christian. Making them equals are such men as Richardson, who speaks for neo-orthodoxy; and Charles Hartshorne, who speaks for process philosophy in insisting upon the relative absoluteness of God. For instance, Hartshorne argues that in his ontological status as unbegun and unending, God is absolute; while in his love for his creatures he is supremely related. Standing with them is the metaphysics of the Bhagavadgita, which theoretically equates Brahman and Vishnu, by making Brahman merely the ineffable dimension of the divine Lord; though for popular devotion, as in the case of neo-orthodox Christianity, it gives the edge to the theistic mode of the ultimate. In the Tantrayana version of the Buddhist Trikaya, the Dharmakaya and the Sambhogakaya-Nirmanakaya are reverse sides of the same coin of reality. On the other hand, giving the advantage to the Absolute over the Related are Hinayana Buddhism, Sankara Vedantism, neo-Pythagoreanism, Gnosticism, neo-Platonism (whether Christian or pagan), Averrhoes, Aquinas *qua* philosopher, Kant, Vaihinger, Spencer, Bradley, *et al.*

But the foregoing reappraisals of the Trinity support

the Copernican Christology. They do so by reducing the biblical Trinity to a philosophical duality, thus making the theistic, personal God (Logos, Word, Christ, Son) the center of the universe and history rather than the God-man, Jesus Christ of Nazareth. For God has at least two modes: the absolute mode, as he is in himself independent of the universe and history, and the theistic mode related to the universe and history. It is obviously the latter mode which is the axiological center of space-time and the world of men; hence Jesus' monopoly of the Logos is broken as the Apostolic Fathers Justin, Clement and Origen taught in their *logos spermatikos* doctrine, and the historical expression of it in him as "the Christ" becomes just one among various expressions of God's relatedness. Moreover, the attempt at establishing the essence-ial love of God through the social analogy to the Trinity, yet avoiding tri-theism, is a reflexive action to which current thought is driven in seeking to harmonize the indispensable belief in God as love with neo-orthodoxy's emphasis on his absolute transcendence. It is thus ancillary to the duality paradox, which shifts the religious center from Jesus to a personal God.

There is finally the possibility of a universal metaphysical trinity or a quadrinity.

The new modelling of the Christian religious Trinity after the dualistic metaphysical pattern of neo-Platonism, Vedantism, and Buddhism suggests a further possible step —that toward a metaphysical trinity. For a number of Greek and Asian faiths expand the traditional religious trinity into a meaningful modal trinity by sub-dividing God-as-related. Their common pattern is (1) God as unrelated, supra-personal absolute (self-sufficient, changeless, ineffable reality) ; (2) God as transcendent particular person (related to the universe through men's anthropomorphic mode of religious apprehension of him as their external loving creator and saviour) ; 3) God as immanent person (related to the universe through his self-objectification or manifestation in phenomena by incarnation in nature and man as their internal power of creation and salvation).

In non-dualistic Vedantism these three appear as (1) Brahman; (2) Ishvara (Brahman masquerading as a personal God) ; (3) Atman (Brahman concealing himself behind the veil of every individual self which he produces). In the Bhagavadgita it is (1) Brahman, the ineffable aspect of Vishnu; (2) Vishnu, the effable, personal aspect of Brahman; (3) Krishna and other outstanding incarnations of Vishnu including, potentially, an unspecifiable number of finite selves. In Mahayana Buddhism's Trikaya it is (1) Dharmakaya (Buddhahood: Sunyata, the Void; or Tathata, Suchness) ; (2) Sambhogakaya (a plurality of supernormal Buddha saviors, personalized apprehensions of Buddhahood) ; (3) Nirmanakaya (Buddhahood incarnate in such earthly buddhas as Gotama and Maitreya, buddhas born in other universes, and also in every being whatsoever as its immanent buddha nature). In neo-Pythagorean and neo-Platonic thought it is (1) the ineffable One: (2) the conscious-rational Reason; (3) the appreciative-emotive self-incarnating World Soul.

The Christian Trinity, if it is to parallel the foregoing philosophical pattern at each point, would look something like the following (discounting the inappropriateness of the traditional personal symbols) : (1) the ineffable Absolute, symbolized by the Father (Clement of Alexandria's and Eriugena's "Father," Plotinus' One, St. Thomas' "aseity," Kant's noumenal, divine *Ding an sich*, Otto's "wholly other," Tillich's "God beyond the God of theism"), who is the ontological ground of all things; (2) the personal God of theism through whom the absolute is religiously apprehended and who, *ab extra*, creates and sustains the universe and lovingly saves his creatures, symbolized by the Son (Judaism's "Yahweh," Jesus' "Father in Heaven," Eriugena's "Son," the first person of the biblical Trinity) ; (3) this personal God immanent in his creation, who from within evolves, saves, empowers, guides, and perfects it, symbolized by the Holy Spirit, which represents the functions of both the second and third persons of the biblical Trinity.

Yet, however sacrosanct, there is, as Richardson insists, no necessary or only threeness in God. There is a multiplicity of the Divine aspects. In his unrelated nature one can still conceptually distinguish his unbegunness, his unendingness, his simplicity, his oneness, etc. And in his related nature one can distinguish his creativity, his wisdom, his love, his judgment, his providence, his presence in each order of terrestrial and celestial nature—inorganic, organic, human. Any one or all of them could theoretically be given separate status as constituents of the Godhead, or even personified, as in the Zoroastrian *spentas,* or turned into a polytheism of nature forces, as in the early Babylonian, Chinese, Hindu, and other systems. We fail to see why any one number is a priori more sacred than another; why 7, 12, 40 or 70 are necessarily more holy than 6, 32 or 89. We fail to see why the modes or manifestations of the divine being must be restricted to 3. But if one preferred to keep intact the devotional values of the biblical symbols of Father, Son, and Holy Spirit, one could simply add, as a fourth dimension, the absolute, suprapersonal nature of God, and thus have a quadrinity. Below the Absolute, then, the Father would stand for the theistic God as transcendent Creator; the Son, for God as manifest in "singular incarnations for (this and) other unique worlds"—for extra-terrestrial Logoi or Christs in the flesh, as well as Jesus, the terrestrial Logos or Christ; the Holy Spirit, for God as immanent sustainer and perfecter of all nature and all creatures.

SUMMARY

If one adopts the interfaith trinity of ineffable Father, creator-redeemer person-Son, and incarnate immanent Holy Spirit, the coming Copernican Christology will be one in which the Logos or Creator-Redeemer mode of God replaces Jesus of Nazareth as the absolute religious center of the universe, as is adumbrated by Tillich's "Other singular incarnations for other unique worlds," and reflected in recent trinitarian discussion. It is reflected in the failure to overcome God's absolute-relative paradox through the reappraisal of the social analogy to the Trinity. It is reflected in the successful incorporation of the biblical Trinity within the framework of metaphysical duality common to great non-Christian systems and, by analogical extension, to a paralleling of their trinities. These attempts undermine the orthodox Christian doctrine of God's self-incarnation in Jesus alone, that cornerstone of Christian absolutism, break Jesus' monopoly of saving revelation, and suggest that Jesus as the Christ is not even the soteriological center of this world and human history, but is rather only one (though most Christians believe the greatest) among other mediators in other religious cultures reconciling men to God and lighting their way to their divine destiny.

The new Christology, if and when it becomes dominant, should transform the intolerant provincialism of Christianity into a new humility and a new insight into the universality of Divine grace.

FOOTNOTES FOR CHAPTER ONE

[1] Andrew Kalitinsky and other leading space travel theorists have predicted that men will visit Mars in the late 1970s. Cf. Thornton and L. W. Page, ed., *The Origin of the Solar System* (New York: The Macmillan Company, 1966), pp. 286-292. This is an anthology by outstanding contemporary scientists.

[2] Matt. 5:34-35; 11:25; 25:32. (Biblical quotations in this study will be taken from The Revised Standard Version unless otherwise indicated.)

[3] 2 Pet. 3:9.

[4] Andrew D. White, *A History of the Warfare of Science with Theology in Christendom,* (New York: D. Appleton & Co., 1913), Vol. 1, p. 139.

[5] Paul Tillich, *Systematic Theology* (Chicago: Univ. of Chicago Press, 1951) Vol. 1, p. 132.

[6] *Ibid.,* p. 133.

[7] *Ibid,* p. 136.

[8] Paul Tillich, *Systematic Theology* (Chicago: Univ. of Chicago Press, 1957), Vol. 2, p. 96.

[9] *Ibid.,* p. 163.

[10] Paul Tillich, "A Reinterpretation of the Doctrine of the Incarnation," *Church Quarterly Review,* Vol. 147, No. 294, January-March 1949.

[11] Paul Tillich, *Symtematic Theology,* Vol. 2, p. 96.

[12] *Ibid.,* p. 101.

[13] Alastair G. W. Cameron, ed., *Interstellar Communication,* (New York: W. A. Benjamin Co., 1963). This book is an anthology of articles by nineteen prominent scientists committed to research in this field, men such as Melvin Calvin, Philip Morrison, Giuseppe Cocconi, Edward Purcell and Su-Shu Huang.

[14] Thornton and L. W. Page, ed., *op. cit.*

[15] Walter Sullivan, *We are not Alone* (New York, McGraw Hill, 1964).

[16] Su-Shu Huang, quoted in Thornton and L. W. Page, *op cit.,* p. 307.

[17] *Ibid.,* p. 31-32.

[18] Quoted in Jeremy Bernstein, "Life in Universe," *The New Yorker,* May 28, 1966, p. 167.

[19] Alastair G. W. Cameron, *op. cit.,* p. 1.

[20] W. N. Clarke, *An Outline of Christian Theology* (New York: Charles Scribner's Sons, 1927), p. 304.

[21] Sullivan, *op. cit.,* pp. 283-284.

[22] Cf., especially the *Saddharma Pundarika Sutra,* where Sakyamuni, sitting on the Vulture Peak, addresses millions of buddhas and bodhisattvas from other worlds and universes.

[23] Cf. *Bhagavadgita,* Chap. IV, Verses 7, 8. See also *Bhagavata Purana, passim.*

[24] Cf. Paramhansa Yogananda, *Autobiography of a Yogi* (Los Angeles: Self-Realization Fellowship, 1959), Chap. 43.

[25] Alice Meynell, "Christ in the Universe" in Edward Wagenknecht,

The Story of Jesus in the World's Literature (New York: Creative Age Press, Inc., 1946), p. 473.

26 Paul Tillich, *The Courage to Be* (New Haven: Yale University Press, 1954), pp. 182-190 *passim*.

27 In this discussion we are deeply indebted to Cyril O. Richardson's careful study, *The Doctrine of the Trinity* (New York: Abingdon Press, 1958).

28 Claude Welch, *The Doctrine of the Trinity in Contemporary Theology* (New York: Scribners, 1952).

29 Richardson, *op. cit.*, p. 148.

30 *Ibid.*, p. 149.

31 *Ibid.*, p. 54.

32 Cf. *Ibid.*, p. 59.

33 This is A. C. McGiffert's thesis in *The God of the Early Christians* (New York: Charles Scribners Sons, 1924) which, in Lectures II and III he epitomizes by saying, "There are certain circumstances . . . together forming strong evidence of a form of primitive gentile Christianity whose God was Jesus Christ alone, and to which the God of the Jews, the creator and ruler of the world meant nothing." (p. 52.) He quotes Hyppolytus' reference (early third century) to the Modalists thus: "Cleomenes and his followers say that he [Christ] is the God and Father of the Universe." (p 78.)

PART TWO

Evidence of a Plurality of Divine Incarnations within Human History: A Biblical-Theological Approach in the Light of Comparative Religions.

Chapter II

JESUS AND THE CRITERIA FOR AN INCARNATION

IN CHAPTER ONE of this study we have attempted to show that a Copernican revolution in Christology is approaching wherein the Divine Logos or Creator-Redeemer will replace Jesus of Nazareth as the absolute religious center of the universe. Our approach was metaphysical-rational. We showed how the new Christology is adumbrated by Tillich's granting of "other singular incarnations for other unique worlds"[1] and reflected in current trinitarian discussion. It is reflected in the failure to overcome the absolute-relative paradox concerning God through a reappraisal of the social analogy to the Trinity that would preserve God's essence-ial or non-contingent love, yet escape tri-theism. It is reflected in the attempt to reduce the biblical Trinity to the metaphysical duality common to great non-Christian systems and, by analogical extension, to their trinities. All such theorizing is undermining orthodox trinitarianism, that cornerstone of Christian theology, tending to break down its monopoly of saving revelation, and to suggest that "Jesus as the Christ" may not be the soteriological center of even this world, but rather only one (Christians believe, the supreme one) among many mediators reconciling man to God.

3. TILLICH'S CRITERIA FOR AN INCARNATION

As we have noted, Tillich has qualified his earlier assertion that "the incarnation occurs only once in time and space"[2] by allowing "other singular incarnations for other unique worlds."[3] We wish in this section to offer evidence of multiple divine incarnations in this world as well. But to do so will require establishing a criterion for incarnation, and applying it to the biblical and Christian picture of Jesus.

Tillich makes essentially a metaphysical-rational approach to the concept of incarnation. He states first what the incarnation is not.[4] It is not metamorphosis. It is not that God, the Ground of all Being, became Jesus, thus ceasing to be God as some "God is dead" theologians would have it. Nor by inference is it change of residence: that God entered the body of Jesus of Nazareth, thus absenting himself from the rest of space-time and the realm of his transcendence over space-time; for in this act also he would cease to be the omnipresent Ground. It is not that an individual, preexistent, divine being, the second person of the Christian Trinity, became fused with Jesus thus producing a synthesis of two metaphysical substances, or changed his residence from heaven to the flesh of Mary's son; such notions being polytheistic.

It is, rather, the actualization in human history of an essential element in the divine life. It is the appearance in one personal life, under the conditions of existential estrangement,[5] of the "eternal unity of God and man" hitherto existing "within the divine life" in "a state of pure essentiality or potentiality".[6] It is, then, an historical manifestation of an aspect of the ineffable Ground of Being. It is the concretization of an ideal relationship—the perfect union of God and man. This particular concretization destroys, at its particular point in space-time, the existential estrangement of God and man, yet without destroying man's finitude or freedom. The incarnation, then, is dynamic, not static. It is not God metamorphosed into the human or swallowing up the human. It is not actually God at all.

It is the achievement in a single person in human history
of a perfectly harmonious God-man relationship.

The German New Testament scholar, Pannenberg,
echoes Tillich's view by rejecting the view of the incarnation
as of a hypostatical union of a preexistent Logos with a
human being for Jesus' progressive achievement of a perfect filial relationship to God, ". . . . a process continuing
through Jesus' entire life and leading to ever closer unifi-
cation with God,"[7] and culminating in his resurrection.[8]

> In dedication (Hingabe) to the Father Jesus lived
> his personal life as Son. . . . Jesus' divinity is not a
> second substance in the man Jesus in addition to his
> humanity. . . . Precisely as this man, Jesus is the Son
> of God and thus himself God. . . . He is not a synthesis
> of the divine and the human. Nor is the humanity
> absorbed in the divinity so that it disappears. Pre-
> cisely *in* his particular humanity Jesus is the son of
> God.[9]

The basic notion of religious incarnation—that the
Divine can express itself through the human, the Creator
in the creature, the Eternal in the transient—is universal
among the world's faiths. It is present in animism, spiritism, and theriomorphism as well as in anthropomorphic
polytheism and in the theophanies and mystical experiences
of theism and pantheism; in the Greek Olympian deities,
the Mahayana Buddhas and Bodhisattvas, the Shinto Kami,
the Hindu avataras, and the Bahai revelators or "Manifestations of God," as well as in the Christian Logos who
"became flesh."

Orthodox theology, however, insists that the biblical
doctrine of incarnation is radically, that is, totally different,
from all others. Tillich's unrevised statement, already referred to, that it "occurs only once in time and space" is
enlarged upon by Perry:

The ten avataras of Lord Vishnu in the Hindu religion are something altogether other than the word become flesh (incarnation) in Jesus Christ. Vishnu's avataras are not incarnations in any degree, for Vishnu does not become a real human or a real boar, but makes occasional descents into some temporary disguise to be thrown off at any moment. Hence it is a misrepresentation of Hindu avatara as well as a distortion of Christian incarnation to identify or compare the two.[10]

The issue here turns, of course, on the meaning of a phrase. What does it mean for God to "become flesh"? Disregarding the fact that Perry accepts a meaning that Tillich rejects, his analysis is further inaccurate. To say that "avataras are not incarnations *in any degree*" (italics ours) because they are temporary, whereas the biblical incarnation was permanent, is to deny that "temporary" is a degree of "permanent." As a matter of fact, there is no historical record that Vishnu disincarnated himself from either Krishna or the Buddha. And to say that "Vishnu does not become a *real* "human" (italics ours) is to deny that the Buddha was an historical personage.

The metaphysical and psychological paradoxes perceived in the relation between the divine and the human in Jesus have not been analyzed as precisely for any Greek, Hindu or Buddhist example of incarnation; it is generally enough for them that the presence of the divine is felt in the presence of the human. Existentially considered, isn't this all one can affirm about Jesus—that men felt God's presence in *his* presence? Nevertheless other views of incarnation have been held and should be examined.

In its essence, incarnation is the indwelling of the Divine, whether permanently or temporarily, in men, animals or things. But those who are not content with the simple, existential awareness of it, attempt to explain it in mythical, psychological and/or metaphysical categories. They include the following.

Christian orthodoxy alone among the religions of the world regards *incarnation as total and monopolistic:* viz., that God in his fullness permanently indwells Jesus of Nazareth, and no one or nothing else. The single exception to this claim is the possibility acknowledged by Tillich, Clarke, *et al.,* of extra-terrestrial incarnations as noted elsewhere in this study." This orthodox view will be treated later.

Other faiths, however, see *incarnation as total but selectively pluralistic,* i.e., occurring in specially chosen individuals. Vaishnavism teaches that the God Vishnu, incarnate generally throughout the universe, which is his body, also incarnates himself in selected individuals (avataras) whenever the plight of man needs superhuman succor. Though such avataras are theoretically countless, some ten, including animals, are given prime emphasis, among whom Krishna, Rama and Buddha are outstanding. The interrelationship of the two natures, divine and creaturely, is, however, not subjected to the kind of meticulous, logical scrutiny employed in the prolonged trinitarian and Christological controversies. It is, rather, accepted as fact presenting no problem or, in the case of animal avatara, as frankly mythological. And it is assumed uncritically that neither nature is, as in Christian orthodoxy, compromised or limited by the union. At the same time, the incarnated individual tends to be worshipped as Vishnu himself, just as in Christianity Jesus became the God of the early Christians, eclipsing the Father in heaven.

In Bahaism nine incarnations are listed, with others still to appear, and are variously termed Manifestations, Revelators, High Prophets. The nine include Krishna, Buddha, Zoroaster, Moses, Christ, Mohammed and Baha'u'llah. Ontologically they are identical; historically they are distinct as to human personality, limitations and message.[12]

Were any of the all-embracing Manifestations of God to declare "I am God," he verily speaketh the truth[13]

. . . for . . . these illuminated souls . . . have, each and every one of them . . . been endowed with all the attributes of God.[14]

Here also the interrelationship of the two natures is not a problem for psychological analysis.

Incarnation as total and universal is taught in Sankara's Advaita Vedantism. The view here is as different from the Christian view as pantheism is different from theism. Brahman, the absolute deity, is supra-personal, the only unambiguous reality. The whole phenomenal universe is, then, only an appearance of Brahman. Thus the human self and Brahman are fundamentally identical. Yet Brahman may be considered incarnate in every man in the sense that an entity is incarnate in all its appearances. And he could be considered only potentially incarnate in a particular man in the psychological sense that until a man realizes his identity he knows himself only as a man.

Mahayana Buddhism exhibits a comparable picture of incarnation. As opposite number to Brahman, who is incarnate in all his appearances, there is the triple Body of Buddha composed first of the unmanifest Body of the Law, Dharmakaya, which is absolute reality, formless and beyond all distinctions and relations, yet the essential hidden nature of all beings and things, and the goal of all their seeking. But secondly, this Body becomes manifest in the subtle Body of Enjoyment, the Sambhogakaya, which is the individualized and personalized expression of the former, and comparable to Sankara's Ishvara. It is the mode of existence of all Buddhas who have attained enlightenment and entered Nirvana, of all Bodhisattvas who are mercifully, yet incognito, engaged in helping others toward Nirvana, and, by extension to other faiths, all personal, savior deities whatsoever. The third Body is the empirical Body of Transformations, the Nirmanakaya, which is composed of all historical persons and sentient creatures who are en route to Nirvana. Thus, in Mahayana Buddhism, by appealing to some metaphysical distinctions, all beings whatever have a triple Buddha mind or nature incarnate in them.

Yet again, in neo-Platonic thought, we find the ineffable Absolute (God) of Plotinus—The One—emanating, overflowing, becoming incarnate in successively more discriminable modes: first Reason, then World Soul, then individual souls or persons embodied in matter; who at last, beset by evil, are able to escape it through return to their divine ultimate source.

Panpsychistic (certainly panentheistic) metaphysics, ancient and contemporary, holds that the whole of nature, which is in God, is the body of God in which he is incarnate. Ramanuja's Visishtadvaita Vedantism set forth this system in the eleventh century. Its most vigorous contemporary proponent is Charles Hartshorne, who finds its best metaphysical analysis in the thought of A. N. Whitehead. In non-technical language Whitehead summarizes his view thus:

> God is *in* the world, or nowhere, creating continually in us and around us. This creative principle is everywhere, in animate and so-called inanimate matter, in the ether, water, earth, human hearts. But this creation is a continuing process, and "the process itself is the actuality" since no sooner do you arrive than you start on a fresh journey. Insofar as man partakes of this creative process does he partake of the divine, of God.[15]

But since Whitehead does not use the word "incarnation," and since his treatment of the subject is in non-theological language and not systematic, attempts have been made to systematize and sumarize his thoughts on the subject. Without attempting in this passage to describe the nature and interrelations of the primordial and consequent aspects of God, Hartshorne writes:

> The body is simply that much of the world with which the mind, or personal society, has effective immediate

interactions of mutual inheritance, and over which its influence is dominant. Such is God's relation to all of the world, and therefore all of it is his body . . . . God is the personality of the cosmic body, the totality of societies inferior to that personal order society which is the mind and life of God.[16]

Is this not another way of saying that God is incarnate in all of the world? John Cobb summarizes Whitehead's view in slightly different fashion:

God is literally present in the region which is also our standpoint. Further, we are not to think of this as meaning only that some small part of God is there present. Thus God and not just part of God is literally present with me and *in me* [italics ours] . . . . This unique relationship of the absolute co-presence of ontologically discrete entities may be understood as productive in part of the utter mysteriousness of the experience of God.[17]

Surprisingly there is even biblical evidence that suggests the belief that God can be totally incarnate in every Christian. Why else would Jesus say, "You . . . must be perfect as your heavenly Father is perfect"?[18] Consider the following passages: "For in him [Jesus] all the fullness of God was pleased to dwell;[19] ". . . that you [Christians] being rooted and grounded in love, . . . may be filled with all the fullness of God,"[20] "until we all attain . . . to the measure of the stature of the fullness of Christ."[21] Thus, to be incarnate with all the fullness of God seems to be possible for Jesus' disciples. Whatever the phrase may connote, it is not restricted to Jesus himself.

The incarnation of God in Jesus, described as a descent of God into man, whether at his conception or baptism, and described as the self-emptying of the divine to be born in the likeness of men is,[22] in the passages just noted (as also in Tillich and Pannenberg), described as an ascent of man by spiritual maturation of what is present only in em-

bryo into the very fullness of God. This fact would seem to
justify Athanasius' assertion that "The Christ was made
man that we might be made divine."[23]

Incarnation considered as partial, whether permanent
or temporary, and potentially universal, is evident in the
Quaker theme song, "There is that of God in every man;"
and in Stoicism, as in such assertions as Epictetus' "You
are a distinct portion of the essence of God and contain a
certain part of himself in yourself."[24] Within Christianity
the doctrine is apparent in such teachings as man's being
made in the image of God, of being a child of God. It was
potentially true of the Old Testament Prophets when the
Spirit of God came upon them, and also of all Christians
who are filled with the Holy Spirit or who "become par-
takers of the divine nature" through God's promises,[25] or
who through the practice of love or confession of Jesus as
the Son of God find God abiding in them,[26] or who, just because they are believers, have one God "who is above all
and through all and in all."[27]

Brief, temporary incarnations (theophanies) are recorded widely in religious literature, almost any object being
a potential medium for a theophany. Thus God appeared to
Moses as a burning bush and as fire and thunder on Mount
Sinai. In Greek mythology, Zeus, Apollo and Poseidon appeared on occasion as human beings or even animals.

The doctrine of incarnation is both a conviction and an
enigma for all religious persons East and West. It should
be accepted as a mystery. To attempt to define it too precisely is to miss its power for religious living. Each seeker
in the quest for its meaning should listen to the interpretations of the others. The Western mind seeks to reduce it to
rational categories. Descartes treated metaphysics as though
it were geometry and Spinoza did the same for ethics.

From the Socratic insistence on the concept, to Russell's
mathematical logic, the history of Western thought has

been a supreme illustration of the primacy of the logical. Rationalism is deep in our bones and we feel secure about scientific knowledge and skeptical about religious faith.[28]

The East, contrariwise, tried to understand it by intuitive apprehension. "Intuition," writes Radhakrishnan, "is the extension of perception to regions beyond sense,"[29] and he might have added "beyond logic." It is not analytical but synthetical; not clear and distinct ideas but richly felt quality that defies description. Yet such an emphasis alone leaves the mind unsatisfied. It leaves us in a fog of emotion through which man in times past has stumbled into superstition.

But theological Christianity on the other hand, in spite of the Chalcedonian formula of two natures and one will in Jesus, has not satisfactorily reconciled the paradox of the hypostatical union of true God and true man, the infinite and the finite, in a single mortal. It was not because man's discursive reason, making use of Greek metaphysical and the best current psychological concepts, could not plumb man's being, let alone the mystery of God's being. Man is not the measure of all things. The rational metaphysics of Buddhism is no better than the Greek—it leads us into a depersonalized void. And the Vedantist pantheistic categories lead us beyond the ethical. Is it possible to catch the ocean of divine mystery in the tiny net of human categories?

We need some balance or via media between amorphous mysticism and categorical syllogisms, some Kantian recognition of the inviolability of the noumenal world, of the ultimate thing in itself transcendant over the reach of sensation and reason. We need a more pragmatic base for our religious living, a foundation that is personal and ethical. As D. C. Macintosh put it somewhere, "I have a right to believe as I must in order to live as I ought." We need an empirical criterion for the recognition of divine incarnation in human beings. And do we not find it in those persons who have supernormal powers and goodness, the ability to humble, inspire, and bless us; who can make us aware of our ultimate concern, of the supreme values for all human living, and who can lead us toward them? And will not the degree to which they possess these abilities be the degree to which we believe God is incarnate in them? Is it not pure epistemological a priorism or purely subjective faith to assert that God cannot incarnate himself more than once or in any degree less than totally and permanently? Who are we that we should instruct God how he can or cannot appear to us? Obviously the Christian and Hindu views differ widely, their difference being due to cultural, psychological and mythological conditioning. But just as certainly the two are comparable experientially. There is a common essence else no analogy would be noted by devout men of different faiths.

Having reviewed various conceptions of incarnation other than Tillich's, we turn to an examination of Tillich's criterion for an incarnation, which is also what he understands by "final revelation." The personal life involved in the God-man unity can exhibit it only through "uninterrupted unity with the ground of his being and the continuous sacrifice of himself"[30] to it so that "he becomes completely transparent to the mystery he reveals."[31] This means that everything human and finite in him, "his life, . . . his finite power and knowledge and perfection"[32] and "everything he could have gained for himself from this unity"[33] must be sacrificed to the God being revealed in him. But would not such a sacrifice be a virtual denial of his real humanity after the monophysite pattern?

However, according to Tillich, Jesus as the Christ met this requirement perfectly; he is the incarnation, the final revelation of God. By "final," he means "the last genuine . . . the decisive, fulfilling, unsurpassable revelation . . . the criterion of all the others"[34] which "as its central event . . . creates the meaning of human history."[35]

But we must ask in what sense God's self-revelation through a "transparent" Jesus makes it the "final" revelation. We agree it would be final in the sense of being undistorted. If one cannot improve upon absolute transparency as a revealing medium, then the God thus revealed would be revealed flawlessly, undistorted; that is, to perfection. And since nothing can be added to what is perfect, such a revelation in Jesus as the Christ would be final.

Yet such finality would be only a qualified or relative finality. Tillich himself makes it plain that it would not be final in the sense of being the concluding experience of revelation. There will be further revelation, but it will be dependent upon a further unfolding of the original one in Jesus as the Christ. Such reasoning is typical of all religions laying claim to universalism. It is asserted that what was earlier, contained the present preferred position, what comes later will be a maturation of the earlier, and what seems quite foreign is but a variation of the common essence. Thus the early Church found the whole Gospel embedded in the Old Testament, and Christian apologists argue that because the Logos in Jesus is universal—"the real light which enlightens every man"[36]—if men are saved through other faiths, they are saved by the Christian Logos. This agent of salvation, what Niebuhr calls the "hidden Christ," reflects the *logos spermatikos* doctrine first taught by Justin:

> Whatsoever has been uttered aright by men in any place belongs to us Christians; for next to God we worship and love the reason (logos) . . . and those who live according to reason are Christians even though they are accounted atheists.[37]

Origen, following Justin, reinforces his view:

> When God sent Jesus to the human race, it was not as though he had just awakened from a long sleep. Jesus has at all times been doing good to the human race. No noble deed amongst men has ever been done

without the Divine Word visiting the souls of those who, even for a brief space, were able to receive its operations.[38]

A spiritually perceptive contemporary, Simone Weil, echoing both men, finds the Christ among the ancient Greeks:

> The kinship between the perfectly righteous one, Prometheus, and Dionysus, the Soul of the World on one side, and on the other, Love, makes apparent beneath all these names, a single and same personage, who is the only Son of God.[39]

And Professor Panikkar writes:

> The good and *bona fide* Hindu is saved by Christ and not by Hinduism, but it is through the sacraments of Hinduism, through the message of morality and good life, through the Mysterion that comes down to him through Hinduism, that Christ saves the Hindu normally. This amounts to saying that Hinduism has also a place in the universal saving providence of God.[40]

Outside of Christendom, Hinduism's Advaita Vendantism insists that the heterogeneous pluralism of all things, physical and social as well as spiritual, are but transient appearances of the one ultimate Brahman. The classic example of this doctrine in Hindu theism is Krishna's assertion, "Even those who worship other deities, and sacrifice to them with faith in their hearts, are really worshipping me.[41] Similarly Buddhism, when it came to Japan, claimed that the indigenous Shinto gods were bona fide buddhas and bodhisattvas in disguise and that whoever is saved is saved by the Buddha nature germinal in all mankind.

Moreover it would seem that the revelation in Christ could not be final in the sense of being unrepeatable. The fact that a particular pane of glass is absolutely transparent does not preclude the existence of other panes equally transparent. Why, then, should Jesus' transparency preclude that of other men? Several such panes installed successively in the same window frame would equally perfectly exhibit the outside scene. In this situation, the scene would be "finally" revealed by the first pane, no matter how many similar panes replaced it afterwards. But this sort of finality allows for repeatability. Hence, a plurality of incarnations is theoretically possible, and would be as useful as a plurality of doctors or lawyers.

Again it would not be final in the sense of being exhaustive. The fact that two camera lenses are equally transparent does not mean that they will take identical pictures. The factor of magnification is decisive. The greater the power of the lens, the greater will be the detail in the photograph. I could take a perfect, that is, undistorted picture of the world from my back porch; but it would not reveal the whole of the world—what lies over the hill, across the ocean, or at the earth's molten core. So with revelation of God. Looking through Jesus as the Christ we see God's love for sinners. But Jesus did not reveal God's abysmal depth, his ontological structure; the purpose, manner and extent of his creation; his relation to evil; his detailed provision for man's post mortem existence. Of two men equally committed and transparent to God one might, because of greater sensitivity, intelligence, knowledge of the world, or experience of life reveal God's character and activity more fully than the other. Thus, in spite of Tillich, a final revelation could be surpassable in the sense of being augmentable. Granted their equal transparency, the Upanishadic seers, Gotama Buddha and Bah'u'llah, might reveal features of the deity not caught by the focal length of Jesus' lens.

We repeat Tillich's criteria for an incarnation or bearer of the final revelation: the personal life exhibiting or, more accurately, participating in it must be selflessly centered in the Divine Center and transparent to his nature and will, so that in him God is flawlessly and unsurpassably revealed to mankind. In enquiring whether Jesus as the Christ met these criteria, two basic questions must be answered. First, was Jesus absolutely centered in and transparent to God? Second, is the "final" revelation he mediated absolutely unique in the sense that it contains basic truths and values completely absent from all other revelations; or that it cannot be duplicated, augmented, or surpassed by any non-Christian revelator? But before answering these questions we need a closer look at Tillich's concept of revelation.

4. TILLICH'S CONCEPT OF REVELATION

Tillich acknowledges that his conviction that Jesus as the Christ is the sole bearer of the final revelation is a matter of faith, not knowledge: "The affirmation that Jesus is the Christ is an act of faith and consequently of daring courage."[42] If this were the only ground for believing it, then it is beyond public verification and has no privileged position against the equally daring and courageous faith that Krishna is an incarnation of Vishnu, that Atman is Brahman, that the humblest follower of the Buddhist path is an individual, historic expression of the absolute buddhahood. If psychological certainty is the decisive test of truth, then there is no appeal beyond confessionalism, and all the world's faiths have equal truth, however different or even contradictory to others they may seem.

But by appealing to the historical records of Jesus, Tillich goes beyond mere faith. His definition of an incarnation sets up empirical tests, and he tries to show by the recorded words and deeds of Jesus that those tests have been met. Hence, we too, must appeal to the biblical evidence if we would challenge his view. According to Tillich, revelation is man's awareness of God, and "almost every type of reality has become a medium of revelation somewhere."[43] And "every religion is the receptive answer to revelatory experience."[44] Yet only in Jesus as the Christ has the final revelation occurred. By "God," Tillich understands "Man's ultimate concern," which must be not any particular being among others but "Being Itself."[45] And this, seen negatively, is the "abyss" or "depth" of being, its "ineffable," "inexhaustible," "pre-rational" aspect, beyond the subject-object dualism, and carrying within it the threat of non-being to all finite beings.[46] Seen positively, it is the "ground" or "power" of being which resists and overcomes the threat of non-being.[47]

In such a notion of God one recognizes the ontological absolute of neo-Platonism's "One," Vedantism's "Brahman," Taoism's "Tao," Buddhism's "Sunyata" and "Bhutatathata," Kant's "Noumenal World," and Otto's "Wholly Other"—from which all finite things emerge and by which all are sustained. God as ground and abyss of being is made meaningful to us through the Logos of being; that is, the unmanifest deity, its *Ding an sich* dimension becomes manifest, self-objectified, structured, and communicable. This it does characteristically in the guise of the personal God of theistic faith, the Ishvara mode of Shankara's Brahman.

But whereas God as "Being itself" is absolute, and the immediate intuition of him is infallible, God as "Logos" or meaningfully related is cognitively at the mercy of metaphor and myth. For the latter, because of the ambiguity of language and the limitation of all finite analogies, distort all verbally expressed revelation.

> The words of Jesus and the apostles point to this new Being (the Jesus-Logos unity) ; they make it visible through stories, legends, symbols, paradoxical descriptions, and theological interpretations. But none of these expressions of the experience of the final revelation is final and absolute in itself. They are all conditioned, relative, open to change and additions.[48]

In addition to this even the finite vehicle, the historical Jesus of Nazareth, is only a fallible example, medium, or norm of the final revelation. And to worship him, that is to elevate him "to the dignity of the revelation itself" is "idolatry."[49] Thus Tillich, quite properly, "condemns a Jesus-centered religion and theology,"[50] writes finis to "Jesusology,"[51] and readily accepts liberalism's contention that "Christianity as Christianity (i.e. as a system of verbal propositions and cultic practices) is neither final nor universal."[52]

The problem is baffling. Here is the faith that Jesus as the Christ is the full and final revelation. Here also is the insuperable obstacle to that revelation: that every expression of it is incomplete and unfinal due to the distortions of the human Jesus and the ambiguities and cultural relativities of language. How valid is the truth claim of an absolute revelation if its reception and communication relativizes it? The faith in an absolute revelation seems of a piece with the fundamantalist faith that the original manuscripts of the New Testament are verbally inspired and infallible even though the Church does not and never will possess them or read them, but must rely upon Roman Catholic and Protestant translations of copies of a New Testament which have contained possibly "50,000 errors."[53]

Nevertheless, because Tillich rests his case upon it in spite of its unreliability, we must examine the New Testament evidence for the faith that Jesus was the bearer of the final revelation.

5. BIBLICAL EVIDENCE THAT JESUS DOES NOT MEET TILLICH'S CRITERIA FOR AN INCARNATION

THE PROBLEM OF HISTORICITY

The first premise of the following appeal to the text of the New Testament is that historic Christianity knows no other Jesus than the Jesus described therein. Yet modern scholarship agrees that this Jesus is not the actual historical Jesus whose words and deeds are recorded unchanged for us. Rather, it is the Jesus of history overlaid by the Christ of faith. What we have is the early disciples' memory and interpretation of his sayings and doings, what they believed he must or might have said and done, an evaluation of his meaning for them. However diversely interpreted by later Christian sects or modified by historical, textual, form and demythologizing criticism; whether it has been Judaized and legalized by Matthew, dramatized by Mark, humanitarianized by Luke, Hellenized and Essenized and spiritualized, even Gnosticized by John, or embellished by other alien thought forms—the New Testament picture of him, with all of its ambiguities and inconsistencies, is the foundation of the Christian faith. And it is this Jesus, not a problematic Jesus of history, that we must analyze to determine whether he is the only divine incarnation, the full and final revelation of God and the world's only savior.

In any hermeneutical approach to the teachings of Jesus, the attempt to interpret them must first deal with this critical problem of authenticity. So, without attempting an exhaustive examination and weighing of the evidence pro and con, a task beyond the scope of this writing and the competence of this writer, two positions will be taken here as a rationale for the use to be made of the teachings.

The first position is that the problem has not been solved and probably is incapable of solution. The second is that the solution of the problem is not essential to the argument of this book. With regard to the first position Norman Perrin proposes as criteria for determining authenticity: dissimilarity from both Jewish and early Christian emphasis, and coherence with already established authentic sayings. But he acknowledges that these criteria may well exclude sayings in which Jesus agrees with Jewish sayings

and the early Church agrees with Jesus. Nevertheless, he
concludes, "in all honesty we must assume that any given
saying has been produced by the early community unless
the opposite can be proved. 'If it could have come from the
early Church it probably did.' "[54] Such criteria would seem
to deny to Jesus all Christological and soteriological affir-
mations, and Bornkamm agrees:

> There is in fact not one single certain proof of Jesus'
> claiming for himself one of the messianic titles which
> tradition has ascribed to him. . . . In recognizing this
> we must not allow ourselves to be misled by the fact
> that the gospels themselves contain many passages
> which are clearly messianic. These should be regarded
> first of all as the credo of the believers, and as the the-
> ology of the early church. . . . We cannot even except
> from this discussion . . . the messianic titles—Messiah,
> Son of God, Son of David, Son of Man.[55]

However, Bornkamm continues, "the messianic character of
his being is contained *in* his words and deeds and in the un-
mediatedness of his historic appearance."[56] It was only
afterward, then, by virtue of his death and resurrection
that the early Church recognized his deservedness of the
messianic titles and read them back into descriptions of him
and into his references to himself.

But Kummel challenges Perrin's evidence for the in-
authenticity of Jesus' messianic utterances:

> The disputing of the future Son of Man sayings as a
> component part of the oldest Jesus tradition is there-
> fore in no way convincingly grounded by Perrin . . .
> [and in his reference to] the sayings concerning the
> Son of Man *in the present* [as being] "outside the scope
> of our present inquiry" (p. 164) . . . he may well be
> simply presupposing *that* the sayings cannot be au-
> thentic.[57] E. Schweizer's contrary thesis is mentioned
> on page 260, but not discussed.

Reginald Fuller's contribution to this discussion stems from form and redactionist criticism. He sees Christological development in three phases following Jesus' own self-understanding. According to Fuller, when we reject as inauthentic Jesus' sayings containing explicit Christology or soteriology, we find a Jesus who saw his mission as that of an eschatological prophet proclaiming the nearness of God and God's kingdom, the divine call to repentance as qualifying for membership in it, and heralding the coming of a Son of Man from heaven who would consummate it. The first phase of Church interpretation of his mission is seen in the Kerygma of the earliest Palestinian mission, which identified Jesus himself with the future coming Son of Man; and who, though exercising charismatic power in his earthly life, would reach the zenith of his lordship at the Parousia. The second phase, the Hellenistic Jewish mission, revealed an adoptionist Christology which emphasized Jesus' sovereign rule from heaven following the resurrection and mediated through the Holy Spirit. And the Christology of the third phase, the Hellenistic Gentile mission, proclaimed him the preexistent divine incarnation of God.[58]

So in spite of the inability of scholarship to determine how much of the teaching of Jesus is his own words and how much is the Church's interpretation, particularly with respect to the coming Son of Man sayings in the Synoptics, "some such overall picture of the beginnings of Christology," says Perrin, "must be accepted."[59] The developing Christology and soteriology is there, but it is primarily if not entirely the work of the early Church.

We must now defend the second position to be taken here, regarding the relation between the authenticity of Jesus' sayings and our use of them. It is, simply, that it is not the original words and deeds of Jesus, even if we could identify them, but the biblical rendering of them which is the basis of the Christian faith and life. D. M. Smith quotes

Tillich as saying "the result of the new (and the very old) questing is not a picture of the so-called historical Jesus but the insight that there is no picture behind the biblical one which could be made scientifically probable."[60]

Tillich agrees with Kahler that the description of Christ in the New Testament is the only one we have. An historically purified figure, purified of all embellishment and interpretation, would not be the Christ of historic Christianity. To strain out from the biblical picture those parts which contain interpretation would not be helpful, for it is the Christ of faith who through the centuries challenges men's lives and makes a "new being" of them. There'd be no Christ of faith if there had been no Jesus of history. But although we may be unable to recover the latter, in the last analysis we need not. His existence is presupposed in the Church's maturing understanding of him, as any man's childhood is presupposed by his adulthood.

We do not have to delineate step by historical step the continuity of the Jesus of history with the Christ of faith; the Synoptics are explicit evidence of this continuity. However else their Christological views may differ, Tillich and Bultmann agree in regarding the quest of the historical Jesus as both futile and needless. They do not devaluate the historical Jesus as Paul and John seem to do, yet they hold that Bible-based faith is not at the mercy of historical research since the former is a divinely given fuller revelation of whatever historical research can uncover. Just as physics, astronomy and biology are what they are today and not what they were for Aristotle, so the Christian faith is what it is today, not what it was for Jesus and his twelve disciples. Progressive revelation must be allowed its role in history.

The issue here is the same as that regarding Zoroaster, Laotzu, Buddha, Krishna, *et al.* So far as this writer knows, the historical facticity of their lives has never been sought by means of the kind of textual, form, demythologizing and redactionist criticism to which Jesus has been subjected. So we shall compare not the teachings of the historical Jesus with those of the historical Buddha and the historical Krishna; but rather those of the Christ of faith as portrayed in the Bible with those of the Buddha of faith as set forth in the Tripitaka, the Mahayana Sutras and the Trikaya, and with those of the Krishna of faith as described in the Bhagavata Purana and Bhagavadgita. We shall not attempt to separate in each one the wheat of history from the chaff of hero worship, legend, myth, pious imagination, progressive revelation and apotheosis; but will consider the entire documentary record of each savior as determinative of the salvation experience made possible by him. It is the whole grain of each that has produced the Christian Church, the great Vaishnava sect of Hinduism, and the Mahayana branch of Buddhism. It was the Buddha of faith who became "The Light of Asia" and the Christ of Faith who is called, "The Light of the World."

But the problem of historicity also requires that we examine Christianity's claim to be the only true religion because its divine savior alone is rooted in history—a God-Man; whereas all other saviors are merely men, or mythological or imaginary beings. But the facts do not justify this sweeping claim; at best it is a half truth. To show this we shall look at three kinds of figures determinative of religious faith.

In the first place, all founders and shapers of religious faiths have been human beings; hence, rooted in history. In Judaism, for example, we find Abraham, Moses, the prophets and the priesthood; in Christianity, Jesus, Paul, John and Augustine; in Hinduism, the Rishis, who wrote the Vedas, and Sankara, Ramanuja and Madhva; in Buddhism, Gotama, Asvaghosha, Nagarjuna and Asanga. In this respect *all* religions are historical religions.

Their founders and shapers are historical because their

existence is empirically verifiable according to the Positivist criterion set forth by such thinkers as Comte, Vaihinger and A. J. Ayer. But what is "empirical"? The physical sciences have preempted the word and restricted its connotation to what is observable by the physical sense organs. Accordingly all supernatural religious figures are non-historical—all gods, godlings, angels and demons; and they are mythologically conceived, as Tillich affirms in his well-known statement that "all theology is mythology." Hence ruled out are the members of the Christian Trinity and the angels Gabriel and Michael. Also Yaweh, Ahura Mazda, Allah, Shangti, Ishvara, Brahma, Vishnu, Shiva, Kali, Sat Nam, Amaterasu Omikami, Amida Buddha of the Shin sect, and the celestial buddhas, bodhisattvas and Naga Kings enumerated in the Lotus Sutra. Also Angra Mainyu, Satan, Mara, and St. Paul's "spiritual hosts of wickedness in the Heavenly places."

Collectively the foregoing are referred to variously as symbols of human values or disvalues (Santayana); as Maya or illusion-ridden apprehensions of the Absolute Brahman (Sankara); as anthropomorphizations of the ineffable Tao, Plotinus' One, the Madhyamikan Sunyata or Tillich's "Being Itself" and "Non being"; as "regulative ideas of pure reason" or moral postulates (Kant); as "useful fictions" (Vaihinger); as implications of our religious need (Pascal) and of "our passion for the Infinite" (Kierkegaard); as pragmatically warrantable by our "will to believe" (William James). In a word, all of the foregoing religious figures are objects of faith, not of knowledge—they are non-historical. A contemporary scholar of Buddhism, Professor Hashimoto, puts the matter thus:

> To those who say that Amida is too mythological to be an object of religious consciousness which requires a concrete and tangible historical person, Suzuki gave the Shin Buddhist's answer. "As long as we are on the

time plane of relativity, we may distinguish between
metaphysical and historical, between abstract ideas and
concrete events; but in genuine religious faith once
realized, there is no such discrimination to be made,
for faith is attained only when there is the going-beyond
of a world of contrasts, which is leaping over the gap
of dualism."[61]

Whatever one may think of Suzuki's metaphysics, it would
seem that though their functions are radically different,
Amida's ontological status is on a par with those of the
angel Gabriel and Satan. All three are integral to their re-
spective faiths, but they are alike mythological.

In the third place, some religious figures are alleged
to be both historical and supra-historical; that is, incarnations of the Divine. Such were Jesus; Rama and Krishna,
whose historical antecedents in India's culture are identifi-
able though much less clearly than is the case with Jesus,
but both known as incarnations of the god Vishnu; Gotama
Buddha who, according to Vaishnavism, was also an incarnation of Vishnu; and Baha'u'llah, an incarnation of the
divine Christ.

But the concept of incarnation is contradictory to the
concept of history. Since Divine, supernatural realities are,
themselves, by definition, non-observable, their presence in
men cannot be historical data. According to Karl Barth,
"the Word of God" incarnate in Jesus is not apparent to the
historian or psychologist but revealed only to faith, which is
itself supernaturally bestowed. Consequently, *strictly as incarnations*, neither Jesus nor Rama, Krishna, Gotama Buddha or Baha'u'llah are rooted in history, and faith in them
is not historically grounded.

To establish the historicity of gods and incarnations
one would have to change the epistemological ground rules.
He would have to widen the connotation of "empirical" to
include other data beside those of the physical senses. He
would have to appeal to other indubitable experiences beside

sensory ones as evidential of the existence and nature of the
Divine: to extra-sensory perception; to man's rational
sense; his moral sense; his esthetic sense; his religious and
mystical sense. He would argue that since man is a sample
of reality, these additional kinds of experience are also in-
dicative of the nature of fundamental reality and are, as a
matter of fact, the only evidence for theism.

Or, on the other hand, he could narrow the connotation
of the word "god" by restricting it to some natural event in
the space-time continuum as strict empirical theists have
done. Notably H. N. Wieman, in such definitions as "creative
interaction," "the process of progressive integration," "creativity" or, at the level of human inter-relations, "love."

In quite another sense Christianity claims to be *more*
historical than its rivals. Albert Schweitzer's distinction
between world-and-life-affirming and world-and-life-denying
religions is appealed to. Judeo-Christianity is declared to
exemplify the former, whereas Hinduism and Buddhism represent the latter. While it is true that the biblical doctrine
of the Kingdom of God entails stress on the transformation
of history, whereas the Asian faiths' doctrine of salvation
idealizes an escape from history, both types of faith acknowledge that the ultimate goal of man lies beyond history
—whether in Heaven, Nirvana or by absorption into Brahman. The distinction between them is not an absolute dichotomy. For much Christian thought and practice is fire-
escape religion, a passive waiting for eschatological, supernatural rescue. And, on the other hand for example, Hinduism's Ramakrishna-Vivekenanda Mission with its motto of
Siva, Seva (God and Service) and Zen Buddhism's enjoyment of and creative participation in culture reveal this-
worldly concerns.

Now to summarize Christianity's claim to be the only
historically grounded religion because only in Jesus did
God enter history to save mankind. All religions are histor-

ical in the sense that historical persons founded, structured and propagated them. Also, most religions lay claim to be rooted in the supra-historical by virtue of supernatural revelation, incarnation or mystical intuition. Thus they are a synthesis of historical persons and events, a faith which apprehends the supra-historical, and a mythology which seeks to understand the supernatural by means of analogies and metaphors drawn from human experience in the social process. In any case it would seem that Christianity has no valid claim to absolute uniqueness on the ground of its historical rootage.

But to return to our inquiry into the religious and ethical teachings of Jesus; here and in chapters III and IV we must necessarily depend upon proof texts, fully aware of the danger of taking them out of context. But this risk is unavoidable since in so many instances the chapter and verse context of a pericope or saying is itself an editorial interpretation varying according to each particular gospel writer's sense of relevancy. There is no infallible identification of original context.

WAS JESUS ABSOLUTELY CENTERED IN AND TRANSPARENT TO GOD?

What then is the biblical evidence that Jesus was absolutely centered in and transparent to God, the ground and abyss of being, by virtue of sacrificing himself as Jesus to himself as Christ?

Alleged absence of evidence of his estrangement from God: Tillich replies with an argument from silence. There are in the New Testament no traces in Jesus of the three aspects of human estrangement: unbelief in God, that is, "removal of his personal center from the Divine center;"[62] hubris or pride, that is, "self-elevation in spite of his awareness of his Messianic vocation;"[63] concupiscence, that is, "the desire for the exploitation of everything through power and pleasure."[64] Finding no verbal descriptions of such estrangement in the records, he infers the total absence of it from Jesus' experience.

But the records are not complete nor completely trustworthy. Literary and form criticism have made it quite clear that we can never know that Jesus said and did exactly what the New Testament discloses. Moreover, that picture is most certainly an idealization by devout admirers. Still further, the picture shows only a fragment of the total conscious life of Jesus. Goodspeed thinks the total time covered by the Gospels' narrative couldn't have been more than six months. Six months out of thirty years—one sixtieth of his life. Is one warranted in concluding that, because he finds no evidence of ethical or ontological distance between Jesus and God in a 2% sampling of his life, there could have been none in the unrecorded 98% of it?

Such silence involves a still further question—"Was Jesus a perfect boy?" Does not the ascription of incarnation, unless it occurred at his baptism, require that his infancy, childhood, and adolescence reveal perfect ethical and religious behavior? But the record states that he "increased . . . in favor with God and man."[65] If he had to increase in their favor, win their approval, must he not initially have been in *less* favor with both? What would a perfect child be like? Would he not have to be free from toy snatching and temper tantrums, and always devout and obedient to his parents? Would it not require that he never stole fruit, pulled a cat's tail, teased his sisters, or quarreled with his playmates? Though the Church's rejection of the apocryphal stories of Jesus' mischievousness and misdeeds would seem to deny such behavior, the mere silence of the Gospels does not warrant the denial. And its rejection of their accounts of Jesus' pre-cognition and boyhood miracles would seem to undermine the logic of incarnation at conception.

Alleged irrelevance of the question of Jesus' sinlessness: Tillich's argument then seems to presuppose an untenable doctrine of the historical adequacy and finality of the Scriptural accounts and/or to rest upon the question-begging presupposition of Jesus' sinlessness and deity.[66]

But there is evidence that even the records we *do* have do not support Tillich's contention. He formally sets aside the question of Jesus' sinlessness as "a negative term" and "a rationalization,"[67] but he does not face the issue it presents. We cannot agree with him that the term "is used in the New Testament merely to show his victory over the Messianic temptation."[68] For if Jesus "in every respect has been tempted as we are,"[69] he had other temptations than to exploit his Messiahship; and we must know whether he resisted all of these also. One passage lists guile, retaliatory threatening and reviling as temptations he resisted.[70] His challenge "which of you convicts me of sin?"[71] is to be understood from the context as referring to the particular sin of falsehood. Other passages seem, in the absence of any reference to the Messiahship, to refer to his lack of general sinfulness.[72] If he felt the characteristic human temptations, he was tempted to covet, deceive, hate and look with desire upon a woman not his wife, as well as to extract personal glory from his messianic vocation.

Hence we cannot ignore the question of moral and spiritual perfection. If Jesus did "always . . . what is pleasing to him [God]"[73] he must have been sinless; otherwise he could not have been absolutely centered in and transparent to God. But in spite of this sweeping claim in John's Gospel, the record does not establish his sinlessness as we understand the term. If to sin is to transgress or fail to conform to the will of God, then the record seems to show that Jesus sinned. He enjoined men to be perfect as God himself is perfect,[74] but seems to have fallen short of that perfection himself.

Barth, while insisting on the sinlessless of Jesus, also insists contradictorily, that in the incarnation Christ assumed fallen human nature.[75] Could he do this without slipping at times himself? Barth further declares that this human Jesus "is so apt to impress us as a little commonplace alongside more than one founder of a religion and even alongside many later representatives of his own religion."[76]

Jesus' lack of perfection is seen in his presumptive repentance of sin at his baptism[77] as described by Mark and Luke but glossed over in the Matthean and Johannine accounts. The ingenuity devoted to escaping such an implication[78] seems to argue not from the record but from messianic, possibly trinitarian presuppositions, and makes Jesus guilty of deceiving the public by going through a purification rite which had no relevance for him personally.

It has been argued that Jesus' baptism signified for him not repentance of sin and divine forgiveness preparatory to membership in the coming messianic kingdom, as it did for the multitudes with whom he shared the rite, but solely a symbolic act by which he committed himself to an active role in the messianic movement being heralded by John. But since John, as the first leader of the movement, submitted to no such initiatory rite, as intimated by Matthew,[79] why should Jesus? And if no sense of sin were involved in his baptism, how can we avoid the implication that he began his ministry by bearing false witness before the multitudes?

His lack of perfection is seen again in his reluctance, embedded firmly in all three Synoptics, at being called "good," "for no one is good but God alone."[80]

Just as Matthew was reluctant to copy Mark's implication that Jesus was baptized in Jordan confessing his sins[81] and so had the Baptizer protest the rite, so here, lest he derogate the messianic status of Jesus, he softens the confession of inferiority by rendering Jesus' remark as "Why do you ask me about what is good? One there is who

is good," thus referring his questioner to the giver of the
moral law for an answer to a purely moralistic question. But
that Mark's and Luke's rendering of Jesus' remark is the
more accurate is supported by Jesus' pointing to the Father
rather than to himself as the absolute moral norm.[82]

But Jesus describes God not only as "perfect" but also
as "holy." And man's apprehension of "the holy," as Rudolf
Otto has insisted, involves his apprehension of his own moral
imperfection, sin, and guilt. Thus when Jesus addressed God
as "Holy Father,"[83] did he not reflect his own inner sense of
ethical deficiency?

To make Jesus' disclaimer of goodness mean "You can
call me good only if you recognize me as God," seems a desperate attempt by some apologists to force the record to
conform to the dogma of the Trinity, and is comparable to
the attempts by Matthew and John to gloss over his penitence at his baptism. This disclaimer of goodness in the
Synoptics is more impressive than the single Johannine
statement of his always pleasing God, since the latter is
avowedly apologetic and far more interpretive than repor-
torial in intent.

His disclaimer of moral perfection is implied also in
the prayer he taught his disciples, "Forgive us our debts,"
provided of course that *he also* prayed that prayer. That the
"debts" referred to here are not merely services owed to
God but positive acts of wrongdoing is apparent from the
context provided by Matthew where they are equated with
"trespasses,"[84] and are bracketed connotatively elsewhere
with "sins."[85] We have no explicit evidence that he did or
did not pray the prayer. But since he could quite properly pray all the other clauses, why except this one? And
in the fact (to be expanded later) that he announced a
sharing of the main features of his divine sonship on equal
terms with his disciples, save only his particular messianic
vocation, is there not, conversely, the implicit probability

that he would also share with them the features of their
mortal human nature—its moral as well as its physical and
mental limitations?

The disclaimer is supported by Jesus' scathing name-
calling of certain Pharisees,[86] unqualified by any note of
compassion or forgiveness "because they know not what
they do." Though practiced without restraint by such men
as Luther and Billy Sunday, such "indulging in personalities" is generally condemned by Christians today as it was
by Paul,[87] and even by Jesus himself in other circumstances.[88]

It is also evidenced by Jesus' overt anger at the Pharisees when he healed on the Sabbath,[89] and his implied anger
at the temple cleansing.[90] Such outbursts are commonly justified as righteous indignation, but is there any instance of
anger which isn't construable by the angry person as a morally justifiable protest against unjust conduct or treatment?
Is there any anger which is not a temporary loss of patience
and self-control if not of forgiving love? Too, contrast Jesus'
indulgence in anger with Paul's condemnation of it[91] and
with Jesus' own condemnation of it on another occasion.[92]

It is the fashion in some quarters today to equate lack
of anger at wrongdoers with cowardice or moral indifference
or both. To cultivate anger is urged as a neglected virtue,
and violent quarrels are recommended by some psychothera-
pists in the interest of truth and psychic health. Sublimation
of such violent emotion is deemed an impossible alternative
to the acknowledged evils of suppression. Those who share
this view have forgotten what great saints of all faiths have
demonstrated, that "a soft answer turns away wrath,"[93]
that "gentleness" and "self-control" are the fruit of the
Holy Spirit,[94] that love is, as Gregg has shown,[95] a more
powerful energizer than hatred, and better able, because it
is more reflective and objective than anger, to find creative
solutions to conflict; that it acts as a shock-absorber to the

aggressions and hostilities of men, and that forgiveness
can deal with evil without sacrifice of principle, courage or
truth.

Then there is what reads like Jesus' thoughtless incon-
siderateness of his mother's feelings when he was a boy,[96]
and apparently his unkind response to a suffering woman's
pleas for help.[97] Consider also his deep discouragement and
fear of suffering and death in Gethsemane,[98] and his loss
of the sense of God's presence in the Eli cry on the cross;[99]
for are not discouragement, fear, and sense of separation
from God a lack of faith? Could one who was absolutely
centered in God, who was one with God through enjoying
"uninterrupted unity with the ground of his being," feel
abandoned by God even temporarily, and so lack faith? And
is not that sinful which "does not proceed from faith?"[100]
Certainly such experiences can't be classified as doing what
is pleasing to God, but only as a want of conformity to God's
will.

Is it not seen, moreover, in the very fact of temptation,
resisted temptation? Orthodoxy has always denied this; but,
then, our whole enquiry is a challenge to the infallibility of
orthodoxy. After all, what is temptation? Is it not, in its
simplest terms, to find evil attractive? Of course, if a thing
were not in some sense good, it would not attract us. But
temptation is to desire something in itself good which, yet,
seen in its total configuration of relations and effects, and
measured by one's moral-spiritual yardstick of values, is
relatively more evil than good. Hence it is to desire what
one believes to be preponderately bad. But Jesus condemned
such desiring. For he made it quite clear that hatred and
extra-marital sexual desire, which are respectively temptations to murder and adultery, are sinful, as are the overt
acts in which they may issue.[101] How long may a temptation
be consciously entertained before it becomes a sin? The
conventional answer is "so long as it is at the same time

mentally resisted." But according to the insight appealed
to here, the instant of desiring what is felt at the same time
to be against conscience or the known will of God is an
instant of sinning, an instant of psychical rebellion against
one's highest and holiest nature. Temptation, then, is desiring evil. But if God is not tempted and does not find evil
attractive, as the New Testament writer insists,[102] neither
should one who is centered in, united with, transparent and
obedient to him. Is it not true that to morally sensitive
persons the very fact of being tempted brings a sense of
guilt or spiritual alienation from God? According to this
analysis, then, temptation is a kind of sin—mental sin. So
if Jesus was tempted as all men are, he sinned in thought
and desire as other men do. Finally, who can possibly prove
from the records that Jesus committed no sins of omission,
howsoever free he might have been from sins of commission?

If God is perfectly loving and good, then a man's perfect union with him should endow him with those perfec-
tions and should overcome all his unfaith, fear, and discouragement. And if this conclusion be valid, then the foregoing citations from the records of Jesus' life, and infer-
ences drawn from them, portray a man who did not maintain "uninterrupted unity with the ground of his being,"
but removed "his personal center from the Divine center,"
and was infected with the existential estrangement of the
human race. Tillich is at pains to point out the limitations
of Jesus' finitude:[103] his faulty cosmology and reading of
men's characters, his mistaken eschatology, his physical
weakness, human loneliness, and mental insecurity. But his
uncertainty about his messianic vocation, his fear of suffering and death, and his doubt of God's sustaining presence
(which, according to Tillich, express only normal finitude)
seem far more culpable. Are they not expressions of a finite
being, feeling temporarily unsupported by the Infinite Being, temporarily off the beam of faith? And if so, is not

Jesus as the Christ less than the full, final, and unsurpass-able revelation or incarnation of the Divine?

Is not the sinlessness of the man Jesus a myth along with his literal human preexistence, creation of the universe, ommiscience, virgin birth, substitutionary atonement, physical resurrection and expected physical return? Are not these attributes better understood as symbols of his power to reveal God to men, to reconcile them as sinners to God's holiness and to each other? Are they not tributes paid him by human gratitude and hero-worship as in the case of the apotheosizing of founders of other faiths? Is not Jesus' sinlessness in a class with that attributed to the Buddha, Mahavira and Mohammed? Is not his incarnation, with sinlessness implied, in a class with the incarnations attributed to Krishna, Rama, the Buddha, Nanak and Ramakrishna, Baha'u'llah, and the Imperial Dynasty of Japan?

But, in the last analysis, is not literal sinlessness the foe of true religion? How could a sinless Jesus be fully a man? Would he not be God, our despair as a moral example rather than our comfort and hope? Would he not be, has he not at certain times and in some quarters actually become, a god, eclipsing the ground and abyss of all being as well as the invisible theistic God of creation as McGiffert argues,[104] and as Professor Altizer has asserted in saying God is no more since he became Jesus.[105] Would he not then justify the Jesusology Tillich himself deplores?

But not only does the record fail to show that Jesus was uninterruptedly centered in God and perfectly obedient to the divine will; it also lacks evidence that he was transparent to "Being Itself." If, by definition, Being Itself is invisible, ineffable, pre-rational, and beyond the subject-object dualism, how can it be revealed—even though Jesus were a transparent medium? No, one does not perceive the ground and abyss of all being in Jesus; rather one encounters its logos or manifestation as a personal God, appre-

hended through the distorting metaphor "Father." Neither
Jesus nor any of the apostles claimed that he revealed more
than this.

We conclude that since Jesus lacked full and flawless
transparency to and uninterrupted centeredness in God, he
does not in these respects meet Tillich's criterion of an incarnation. But if Jesus, as such a revelation of God, is at
best inaccurate and incomplete, on what grounds does Tillich insist on the finality of this revelation? Apparently he
does so on the ground of mystical faith. But if so, the belief
in Jesus as God's only incarnation is a confessional, not
a controversial matter, and not subject to empirical or even
biblical verification.

FOOTNOTES FOR CHAPTER TWO

[1] Tillich, *Systematic Theology*, Vol. 2, p. 96.
[2] Cf. footnote 9, chapter one.
[3] Tillich, *Systematic Theology*, Vol. 2, p. 96.
[4] Cf. *Ibid.*, p. 94.
[5] Cf. *Ibid.*, p. 112.
[6] *Ibid.*, p. 148.
[7] Wolfhart Pannenberg, *Jesus: God and Man*, trans. L. L. Wilkins
and D. A. Priebe (Philadelphia: The Westminster Press, 1968),
p. 304.
[8] Cf. *Ibid.*, pp. 136-137; 321-322.
[9] *Ibid.*, p. 342.
[10] Edmund Perry, *The Gospel in Dispute* (Garden City, N. Y.:
Doubleday and Co. Inc., 1958), p. 97.
[11] See pp. 15-16, chapter one.
[12] Cf. Baha'u'llah, *Bahai World Faith* (Wilmette, Illinois: Bahai
Publishing Co., 1943), pp. 22-23.
[13] *Ibid.*, p. 22.
[14] *Ibid.*, p. 20.
[15] A. N. Whitehead, *Dialogues of Alfred North Whitehead*, ed.
Lucien Price (Boston: Little, Brown and Co., 1954), p. 370.
[16] Charles Hartshorne, "Whitehead's Idea of God," in *The Philosophy
of Alfred North Whitehead*, ed. Paul Schilpp, Library of Living
Philosophers (Evanston and Chicago: Northwestern University
Press, 1941), Vol. 3, pp. 449-450.
[17] John B. Cobb, Jr., *A Christian Natural Theology* (Philadelphia:
The Westminster Press, 1965), pp. 243-244.

[18] Matt. 5:48.

[19] Col. 1:19.

[20] Eph. 3:19.

[21] Eph. 4:13.

[22] Phil. 2:6-7.

[23] Athanasius, *Incarnation.* 54:3.

[24] Epictetus, *Moral Discourses, Enchiridion and Fragments,* Everyman's Library Edition (New York: E. P. Dutton and Co., 1910), p. 81.

[25] 2 Pet. 1:4.

[26] I John 4:15-16.

[27] Eph. 4:6.

[28] S. Radhakrishnan, *An Idealist View of Life,* 2nd ed. (London: George Allen and Unwin, Ltd., 1932), p. 133.

[29] *Ibid.,* p. 143.

[30] Tillich, *Systematic Theology,* Vol. 1, p. 137.

[31] *Ibid.,* p. 133.

[32] *Ibid.*

[33] *Ibid.,* p. 135.

[34] *Ibid.,* p. 133.

[35] Tillich, *Systematic Theology,* Vol. 2, p. 96.

[36] John 1:9 *(New English Bible).*

[37] *Apology,* I, xivi, 1-4.

[38] Origen, *Contra Celsum,* VI, 78.

[39] Simone Weil, *Intimations of Christianity Among the Ancient Greeks* (London: Routledge and Kegan Paul, 1957), p. 11.

[40] Raymond Panikkar, *The Unknown Christ of Hinduism* (London: Darton, Longman and Todd, Ltd., 1964), p. 54.

[41] *The Song of God: Bhagavadgita,* trans. S. Prabhavananda and C. Isherwood, Mentor Edition (New York: The New American Library of World Literature, Inc., 1954), IX. 23.

[42] Tillich, *Systematic Theology,* Vol. 2, p. 116.

[43] Tillich, *Systematic Theology,* Vol. 1, p. 118.

[44] Tillich, *Systematic Theology,* Vol. 3, (Chicago: Univ. of Chicago Press, 1963), p. 99.

[45] Tillich, *Systematic Theology,* Vol. 1, pp. 235-252 *passim.*

[46] *Ibid.,* p. 110.

[47] *Ibid.*

[48] Tillich, *Systematic Theology,* Vol. 2, p. 151.

[49] Tillich, *Systematic Theology,* Vol. 1, p. 133.

[50] *Ibid.,* p. 134.

[51] *Ibid.,* p. 136.

[52] *Ibid.,* p. 131.

[53] Hartzell Spence, "Truth About the Bible," *Look Magazine,* February 26, 1952.

[54] Norman Perrin in *The Criterion,* Vol. 1, No. 1 (Chicago: The University of Chicago Divinity School, Winter 1967), p. 42.

[55] Gunther Bornkamm, *Jesus of Nazareth* (New York: Harper and Row, Pubs., 1956), pp. 172-73.

[56] *Ibid.,* p. 178.

57 Werner Georg Kummel "Norman Perrin's 'Rediscovery of the Teaching of Jesus' ", *The Journal of Religion* (Chicago: University of Chicago Press, Jan. 1969), Vol. 49, No. 1, pp. 64-65. Title in single quotes is Perrin's book (London: S.C.M. Press, 1967).

58 Cf. Reginald H. Fuller, *The Foundations of New Testament Christology* (New York: Charles Scribner's Sons, 1965), as reviewed by Norman Perrin, "New Beginnings in Christology: A Review Article," *The Journal of Religion* (Chicago: Univ. of Chicago Press, August 1966), Vol. 46, No. 4, pp. 491-496.

59 Norman Perrin, "New Beginnings in Christology: A Review Article," *The Journal of Religion* (Chicago: Univ. of Chicago Press, August 1966), Vol. 46, No. 4, p. 494.

60 D. Moody Smith, Jr., "The Historical Jesus in Paul Tillich's Christology," *The Journal of Religion* (Chicago: Univ. of Chicago Press, Jan. 1966), Vol. 46, No. 1, part 2, p. 135.

61 Hideo Hashimoto, *The Grace of Eko in Jodo Shin Buddhism: A Study of Grace, Sin, Salvation and Compassion in Jodo Shin Buddhism from a Christian Theological Perspective*, page 19 of a paper read Feb. 17, 1967, before the Midwest Section of the American Academy of Religion. The quote is from D. T. Suzuki, *A Miscellany of the Shin Teaching of Buddhism* (Kyoto: Shinshu Otaniha Shumushu, 1949), p. 39.

62 Tillich, *Systematic Theology*, Vol. 2, p. 126.

63 *Ibid.*

64 *Ibid.*, p. 128.

65 Luke 2:52.

66 Tillich, *Systematic Theology*, Vol. 2, p. 126.

67 *Ibid.*, pp. 126-127.

68 *Ibid.*, p. 126.

69 Heb. 4:15.

70 1 Pet. 2:22-23.

71 John 8:46.

72 1 John 3:5; 2 Cor. 5:21.

73 John 8:29.

74 Matt. 5:48.

75 Cf. Karl Barth, *Kirchliche Dogmatik* I, ii, p. 167 f.

76 Karl Barth, *The Doctrine of the Word of God* (G. T. Thompson's translation of the first half-volume of the *Kirchliche Dogmatik*), p. 188, but slightly altered in the translation of D. M. Baillie, as acknowledged in his *God was in Christ* (New York: Scribners, 1948), p. 17.

77 Mark 1: 4-9 and Luke 3:3, 7, 21.

78 Another theologically consistent way of escape has been to view the baptism as the logical implication of the sacrificial lamb theory of the atonement. Just as the sins of guilty men were transferred to an innocent animal, so here, it is alleged, the innocent Jesus took upon himself the sins of men and repented of them vicariously in the baptismal rite.

79 Matt. 3:14.

80 Mark 10:18, Matt. 19:17, Luke 18:19.

81 Mark 1:4, 5, 9.
82 Matt. 5:45, 48.
83 John 17:11.
84 Matt. 6:12-15; Eph. 2:1.
85 Luke 11:4.
86 Matt. 23:15-33; John 6:44.
87 Eph. 4:31; Col. 3:8.
88 Note the contradiction between his preaching and his practice in Matt. 5:22 and Matt. 23:17.
89 Mark 3:5.
90 Mark 11:15-17; Matt. 21:12-13; Luke 19:45-46; John 2:15.
91 1 Cor. 13:5, Eph. 4:31; Col. 3:8.
92 Matt. 5:22.
93 Prov. 15:1.
94 Gal. 5:23.
95 Richard B. Gregg, *The Power of Non-violence* (Philadelphia: J. B. Lippincott, 1934), chapters 3, 4, 5.
96 Luke 6:48-49.
97 Matt. 15:21-28.
98 Matt. 26:37-39.
99 Matt. 27:46.
100 Rom. 14:23.
101 Matt. 5:21-22, 27-28.
102 James 1:13.
103 Tillich, *Systematic Theology*, Vol. 2, p. 131-f.
104 See note 31, chapter one.
105 "God himself has ceased to exist in his original mode as transcendent or discarnate Spirit: God is (now) Jesus." Thomas J. J. Altizer, *The Gospel of Christian Atheism* (Philadelphia: The Westminster Press, 1966), p. 69.

Chapter III

THE UNIQUENESS OF JESUS' REVELATION OF GOD

But since we are concerned with meaningful and communicable revelation, we shall appeal to the New Testament's verbal and historical evidence to determine whether Jesus was the normative and final revealer of God, mythological and partial though that revelation be. And we shall address ourselves to the second basic question referred to earlier.

CAN HIS REVELATION BE DUPLICATED, AUGMENTED, OR SURPASSED?

What is the evidence that the "final" revelation mediated by Jesus as the Christ is absolutely unique in the sense that it cannot be duplicated, augmented, or surpassed by any non-Christian revelator, and hence that Jesus must be the only incarnation of God in human history?

In approaching this question we come to grips with the orthodox conviction that in no other faith than the Christian faith can one come by a "saving knowledge of God." In Tillich's terms, it is the conviction that in no other human being is the God-man unity actualized or incarnate, and through no other man can men participate fully in the New Being he introduced into the world. What then *did* Jesus reveal about God and God-man fellowship?

If Jesus Christ is the word of God incarnate—the way, the truth, the life—what did this "word" say about God that is not said elsewhere by any other mortal? Contemporary theological thinking is dominated by the strange convention that the Christian faith should rest primarily not upon what Jesus said about God, but what others have said about Jesus. True enough Jesus' deeds say something about God, but not independently of his words; rather as their implementation. His words are primary, his deeds are derivative and secondary. In his deeds he practices what he preaches, but his deeds cannot convey the full import of his message. For his teachings embrace many truths which he did not act out, such as: the general resurrection of the dead, the last judgment, the consummation of the Kingdom of God, the final destiny of the saved and unsaved, the nature of heaven and of our mode of existence there, what God is in himself (*Ding an sich*) behind the metaphor "Father," Jesus' own preexistence, the coming and work of the Holy Spirit, his own second coming. As he himself said of the distinction between his words and his physical person, "It is the spirit that gives life, the flesh is of no avail; the words that I have spoken to you are spirit and life."[1]

We cannot subscribe to today's theological fashion of downgrading Jesus' ethical and religious teaching—what he said about God, himself, man, sin and salvation—and of making the Christian faith consist in men's interpretation of his death and resurrection. It is to his teaching, then, or what has been recorded as his teaching, that we turn as the primary source of the Christian religion; and we shall conduct our inquiry by asking and answering a succession of specific questions posed by orthodox theology.

His general ethical and religious teaching: Didn't Jesus alone reveal God's will for men in the field of moral behavior, so that his ethical teachings are unique or at least vastly superior to those of all other faiths? And aren't his general religious teachings without parallel?

No. Knowledgeable scholars are in general agreement that almost all of Jesus' moral and many of his religious teachings can be found in the religious literature of the non-Christian faiths.[2] With regard to Jewish literature for example, Klausner writes:

> With Geiger and Graetz, we can aver, without laying ourselves open to the charge of subjectivity and without any desire to argue in defense of Judaism, that *through-out the Gospels there is not one item of ethical teaching which cannot be paralleled either in the Old Testament, the Apocrypha, or in the Talmudic and Midrashic literature of the period near to the time of Jesus.*[3]

Montefiore supports this judgment by agreeing with the conclusion of Gerhard Kittel, the German Lutheran scholar of Tubingen:

> If you take, he says, each ethical utterance of Jesus separately, there is hardly one to which you cannot find a Jewish or Rabbinic analogue, or of which you can say that such an analogue it would be impossible for unadulterated Judaism to have produced.[4]

As for Jesus' religious teachings, Klausner points out with regard to the Lord's Prayer, "Every single clause in it is . . . to be found in Jewish prayers and sayings in the Talmud."[5]

Dr. Hurst lists more than 500 New Testament verses or passages that borrow ideas or actual phrases from the Apocrypha and Pseudepigapha, at least 150 of them being the words of Jesus himself. Finally, with regard to Christian eschatological teaching, he lists nearly one hundred passages containing exactly similar clauses or phrases to those found in the single Jewish apocalypse of First Enoch.[6]

With regard to Jesus' ethical principles, we find throughout the faiths of mankind such basic teachings as the golden rule,[7] forgiving and loving one's enemies and overcoming their evil with good,[8] humility,[9] non-attachment to the world,[10] selflessness,[11] the primacy of inward attitude over outward conduct.[12] In the Taoist classic, the *Tao Teh*

King alone, J. Hesse found 265 verses of teaching paralleling verses of the Bible, mostly in the New Testament. No, God has revealed his will for ethical human behavior in the great non-Christian faiths as well as through Jesus.

His teaching on survival of death: Didn't Jesus alone reveal that God's power will conquer death for every man; that all men, good and bad, will survive it as individuals? And isn't Jesus' resurrection the only empirical validation of that faith?

No. Individual survival has been foundational to most of the world's faiths, certainly to all theistic faiths, and it has been believed by all men, civilized or primitive, save for a minority of materialists, monists and sophisticated rationalists, whether inside or outside the Christian tradition. The distinction made in orthodox circles between Christian resurrection and Greek immortality of the soul is superficial and negligible unless by "resurrection" one means resuscitation of the psychophysical organism. Only the most naive and materialistic would prefer resurrection with such a meaning. And if immortality means eternal psychic pre-existence as well as post-existence, it would be rejected by all except reincarnationists. But there is common ground for all varieties of faith in survival, whether it be conditional or not: the expectation that the individual subject will experience unending consciousness after death, however one may construe the meaning of "body" or the mode of one's individuality.

That Jesus' resurrection by the power of God has not offered the only empirical proof of survival is evidenced by the reappearance after his death of Samuel, through the mediumship of the Witch of Endor, of Moses and Elijah at the Transfiguration, of pious Jews at the time of Jesus' resurrection,[14] of the Virgin Mary to devout Roman Catholics. Moreover, spiritualistic practices through the ages have amassed great quantities of data on the palpable sur-

vival of the deceased.[15] Paramhansa Yogananda testified to
the resurrection of his guru, Sri Yukteswar,[16] and it is reported of Apollonius of Tyana that after his death, he was
seen by and talked to one of his disciples.[17] And there are
reincarnationist saints within Hinduism, Buddhism and
Theosophy who profess to remember previous earth experience, in support of expectation of further post mortem
experience.

It is of course widely argued that the foregoing instances of witnessed survival are purely subjective—dreams,
fantasies or hallucinations; that in the nature of the case,
that is by definition, all deviations from known natural,
(that is, physical) law, is non-empirical; and therefore
miracles are unhistorical. The same grounds are urged for
disbelief in Christ's resurrection appearances: to the disciples, to Stephen, to St. Paul, to St. Thomas at the assumption of the Blessed Virgin, to Allied soldiers on Flanders
battlefields in World War I, to Pope Pius XII. While the
validity of each appearance ought to be considered on its
own merits, and while the original appearances of Jesus are
supported by impressive testimony and by far-reaching, indubitable, historical results, all appearances of survival are
in the same category, and doubt of any one invites doubt of
all. The stream of doubt has flowed down through the centuries beginning with Matthew's statement about the original disciples' incredulity: "And when they saw him they
worshipped him, but some doubted."[18] The tendency to psy-
chologize the resurrection gained momentum from such
thinkers as Strauss, Hamann, William Adams Brown,
and Schweitzer and has received its most recent impetus
from the demythologizers who, following Bultmann's analysis, think that it was only the disciple's *belief* in the resurrection that is historical. Must an external event be registered on the optic or auditory nerve or caught on camera
film in order to have happened? What then shall we say

about clairvoyance, mental telepathy and other extra-sensory phenomena? If we allow mechanistic materialism to set the ground rules for authentic experience, to tell us before we search what alone they will permit us to find, will we not have to rule out such events, as well as religious visions? And will we not, along with Hume, De la Mettrie, Hugh Elliott *et al.*, have to deny the irreducible reality of thought and the conscious self? May there not be real objective experiences which are neither empirical nor historical in the narrow naturalistic sense because they are beyond the focal length of both? Are there not objective realities validating "the conviction of things not seen"?[19] If not, then the resurrection appearances are only hopeful imaginings, and the Christian faith in Jesus' triumph over death has no more "scientific" support and certitude than non-Christian faith in survival. But if there *are* such invisible realities, may not the pagans apprehend them as well as Christians, and their testimony to survival rest on equally valid ground?

On the basis of St. Paul's "Christ mysticism," that he was in Christ and Christ was in him, and the interchangeableness in the Fourth Gospel and Paul's writings of such terms as "Spirit," "Holy Spirit," "Spirit of God," "Spirit of Christ," "Christ," "The Lord," it has been argued that the appearances of the risen Jesus transcended naturalistic and historical categories: they were non-sensory yet not merely subjective, not explainable in sensory terms yet describable only in such terms, identical with God yet of a recognizable individual distinguishable from God. Such a view of Jesus' resurrection is still evidence of his survival and, as such, justifies the early Church's belief that their own resurrection would be in a mode similar to his.[20] Such a view is not unique to Christianity but is only the Christian variety of the hope cherished by most of mankind: a hope that ranges from the orthodox everlasting distinguishableness from God

to the pantheistic timeless identity with him, with some
paradoxical combination of the two as in Buddhist nirvana,
Hinduism's savikalpa and the utterances of Eckhart and
other mystics.

The quality of post mortem life is also generally agreed
upon: for the righteous or saved, blissful; for the wicked
or lost, painful; only a few conceive it as a colorless or unconscious existence. Our conclusion: Jesus' revelation added
nothing basic to the world-wide faith in man's survival of
death. His chief contribution was the peculiar vividness of
his own afterdeath appearances. Yet even these rest, for
their ultimate validity, not on the testimony of the separate
witnesses, but on the prior faith of all Jews except the Sadducees. For, argues Paul, "if there is no resurrection of the
dead, then Christ was not raised."[21]

His teaching that God is a person: Didn't Jesus alone
reveal that God, the Divine being, is a person?

No. This is taught by all theisms and idealisms: Zoroastrianism, Judaism, Islam, Sikhism, Bahaism, the Hinduism of Ramamuja and Madhva and the Bhagavadgita, Shingon and Amidist and Tantric Buddhism, Shintoism, the
faith of Motse and Confucius,[22] and practically all primitives;"[23] and by all idealisms which posit will, mind, reason,
consciousness, or idea as the ontological ultimate; and the
gamut runs from Xenophanes to Plato, to Stoicism, to Berkeley, to Hegel, to Royce, to Whitehead. No, belief in a personal God is practically universal among the ethnic faiths:
Jesus' revelation is not distinctive here.

His teaching of God's loving fatherhood: Didn't Jesus
alone reveal that the personal God is a Father?

No. This was taught by Plato,[24] Epictetus,[25] and six
living religions beside Christianity: Judaism,[26] Zoroastrianism,[27] Bahaism,[28] Hinduism,[55] Sikhism,[30] Amida Buddhism.[31]
Save in matriarchal or fratriarchal cultures, the metaphor
"Father" is universal as the most spontaneous and mean-

ingful metaphor for the personal God. Jesus' chief contribution here was not in the use of the term, but in the universality and tender compassion with which he invested the Father and in the extraordinary intimacy and total commitment of the relationship he sustained to him.

His teaching that God suffered in the sacrificial death of his son: Didn't Jesus alone reveal that the Father God so loves men that he suffers with and for them to the extent of sacrificing his only son in their behalf? Is not such a divine love the distinctive feature of the Christian Gospel and found only therein?

This question is so crucial to our thesis that we must treat it at some length. We begin by laying down a principle for fair comparison of religions. Simone Weil has expressed it thus:

> Among the different forms of religion there are, as it were, partial compensations for the visible differences, certain hidden equivalents which can only be caught sight of by the most penetrating discernment. Each religion is an original combination of explicit and implicit truths; what is explicit in one is implicit in another. The implicit adherence to a truth can in some places be worth as much as the explicit adherence, sometimes even a great deal more.[32]

Explicitly considered, the answer to the foregoing question is Yes: only in Christianity is the Father God described as sacrificing his only son out of love for men, and by means of that most agonizing death—Roman crucifixion. But immediately we must qualify the uniqueness of such a love. For, by implication, such love is present wherever God is conceived as Father; viz., in most of the world's living religions. For any father worthy of the name sacrifices himself for his children, even to the extent, if need be, of giving up one child in order to save the rest—a not infrequent occurrence in famine-stricken China when one child is sold into slavery to buy food to keep the others alive. And such love might well have been expressed explicitly in other religions if their theology, like the orthodox Christian teaching, had allowed only one son to the Father; and if the accidents of history had placed that son in a religious culture practicing blood sacrifice, and had pitted him as a compassionate, reforming prophet against the vested interests of a self-righteous ecclesiastical oligarchy, as was the case under first century imperial Rome. Would not the martyrdom of such a son have followed and been interpreted as a divinely offered atonement for sin?

A primitive pre-Christian parallel to the Christian divine self-sacrifice is noted by Toynbee even in cults which do not use the Father metaphor. He refers to "the vision of a vegetable God, a God of grain, a Tammuz or Adonis or Osiris who sacrifices himself in order to give man the bread of life."[33] That pagan primitives know the love of God is attested by a Roman Catholic scholar and traveler:

> Many non-Christians know . . . the one, true, and actual God . . . . nor is God's love unknown . . . even the pygmies of the equatorial forest cherish the thought of a higher being whom they can trust and love. . . . We can and must accept the possibility of supernatural love to God outside the church.[34]

If suffering is implicit in love, then African primitives believe in a God who suffers out of love for men.

But a further qualification of Christianity's self-sacrifice of the Father should be noted. Trinitarian theology has paradoxically refused to admit that the Father himself suffers in Christ's crucifixion, as the patripassionist heretics affirmed. And under Hellenistic influence, it came to remove the Father beyond even the possibility of suffering. For the Father came to symbolize the absolute or unrelated mode of God's being; only in his mode of relatedness, symbolized by the Son, did he become vulnerable to the pains of love. Christian teaching on the suffering love of the Father is thus ambiguous. As personal and anthropomorphic, he does suffer; as supra-personal and ineffable, he does not. Jesus himself saw the Father in purely personal terms. Yet, though he thought of him as suffering because of mankind's sin and suffering, he did not speak of himself as God's only son being sacrificed by his father, Isaac-wise, out of love of mankind. This conventionalized evangelistic portrait is the Church's interpretation of Jesus' death. As a matter of fact, even on the Church's terms the Father's sacrifice was not unsurpassably great. The Son was not annihilated; neither did he go to hell to suffer everlastingly instead of sinful men. He merely interrupted his blessed eternal life with the Father for a few years of painful human experience. True, the Father suffered in his son's earthly suffering; but not incommensurably more than in the humiliation and agonizing death of many another of his children. Jesus does not seem to claim, with respect to his disciples, a preferential love by his Father.[35] If the Father suffered more in Jesus than in the Christian martyrs, may it not have been because of the greater degree of Jesus' innocence and intimacy with him?

But the ambiguity of the Christian doctrine of God's suffering love is paralleled by Buddhist and Hindu theology. In Vedantism, Brahman (God in the absolute mode) neither loves nor suffers. But as Ishvara, Vishnu, Shiva, etc. (God in the theistic, father mode) he does both. A myth of Shiva portrays him drinking poison to save other gods, and today the Shaivite devotee gazes in awe at sculptured representations of his blackened throat.[36]

It is difficult for the Hindu religious consciousness to appreciate the suffering of God, so ingrained in it is the belief that ultimate reality, Brahman, is beyond human categories of thought. Even Ramanuja, the champion of theism, writes, "The one immanent Self of all things is not

touched by the sorrow of the world, for he is outside it.[37]
Yet Radhakrishnan, doubtless thinking of Brahman in his
Ishvara dimension, offers a summarizing evaluation of the
problem in his comment on the Bhagavadgita:

> He (God) shares in the life of finite creatures. He
> bears in them and with them the whole burden of their
> finitude. A God who is indifferent to the fate of the
> world cannot be the God of love. There can be no love
> without sorrow and suffering. Either the love of God
> is a fiction or the sorrow of God is a reality. Through
> the conception of Avatara, or descent of the Divine
> into the world, Hindu thought brings out how the
> Divine through suffering voluntarily accepted and en-
> dured brings the goal nearer.[38]

In the Gita, Brahman as Vishnu is described as "the offering," "the oblation," "the sacrificial fire."[39] And moved
by men's suffering Vishnu declares, "Whenever there is a
decline of *dharma*, O Arjuna, and an outbreak of lawless-
ness, I incarnate myself. For the protection of the good, for
the destruction of the wicked and for the establishment of
dharma, I am born from age to age."[40] Ten such incarnations (several of them animals) out of an indefinite number
are popularly reverenced, outstanding among them being
Rama, Krishna and Buddha. The role of these incarnations
is comparable to that of the succession of prophets sent by
Yahweh to denounce Israel's wickedness and proclaim the
divine forgiveness for all who would repent. It is analogous
to the God who so loved the world that he sent his only son
to save men from spiritual death. And such self-sacrificing
love becomes the ideal for interpersonal behavior. As Lord
Krishna expresses it:

> He who regards with an eye that is equal friends and
> comrades, the foe and the kinsman, the vile, the wicked,
> the men who judge him, and more who belong to neither
> faction: He is the greatest . . . . Who burns with the

bliss and suffers the sorrow of every creature within his own heart, making his own each bliss and each sorrow: him I hold highest of the Yogis.[41]

In Buddhism's trinity, Dharmakaya-Sunyata-Tathata (God in the absolute mode), God neither loves nor suffers; but as Sambhogakaya (the collective name for the theistic personalizations of the Absolute, the Buddhas and Bodhisattvas) he does both. In the Bodhisattva concept the suffering love of a personal savior, albeit polytheistically conceived, is made explicit. Here the Buddhist savior renounces the bliss of nirvana in a sort of Buddhist kenosis and comes to earth to share and alleviate the sufferings of men. The Jataka tales describe the sacrificial lives of Gotama in previous incarnations, and Gotama is reported as instructing Ananda to practice love toward quarreling monks and to offer to take on himself their guilt.[42] Finally, Santi Deva's "Prayer of the Bodhisattva" contains an ideal of self-sacrifice for the good of others, and self-identifying with their sufferings, which is not surpassed by any Christian teaching about forsaking all, taking up one's cross and losing one's life for the Kingdom of Heaven's sake.

Based on the Buddha's earlier admonition, "As a mother, even at the risk of her own life, protects her son, her only son, so let him cultivate love without measure toward all beings. Let him cultivate towards the whole world . . . a heart of love . . ."[43] Santi Deva exclaims eloquently:

I would fain become a soother of all the sorrows of all creatures. May I be a balm to the sick, their healer and servitor, until sickness come never again; may I quench with rains of food and drink the anguish of hunger and thirst; . . . May I become an unfailing store for the poor, and serve them with manifold things for their need. My own being and my pleasures, all my righteousness in the past, present, and future, I surrender indifferently, that all creatures may win through to their

end. . . . I yield myself to all living things; . . . they
may smite or revile me forever, . . . but may never mis-
hap befall any of them by reason of me. . . . This
thought . . . has arisen within me I know not how; . . .
it is a tree under which may rest all creatures wearied
with wandering over life's paths, a bridge open to all
wayfarers for passing over hard ways, a moon of
thought, arising to cool the fever of the world's sin.[44]

We conclude: Divine suffering love is not a monopoly of
the Christian faith; it is implicit in every faith that calls
God "Father" or "Mother," or regards him as caring for
his creatures. It is absent only when, in any faith, the divine
as personal is exchanged for the Divine as suprapersonal
and ineffable.

His teaching that salvation depends on his own death:
Didn't Jesus alone reveal that God saves men through the
death of his son, and only thus?

The answer is no. Others have taught this about Jesus,
not he himself. Jesus began his ministry by pointing to the
keeping of the Commandments (the Mosaic ten and the
summarizing two), and to penitent faith in God's forgiveness as the way to the kingdom of God. Then, according to
the records, he revealed a sense of his messianic mission
with a supernatural role for himself involving eschatological
judgment and rule. And in conjunction with this role, he
proclaimed himself and his teachings to be "the way, the
truth, and the life" of the New Age and called upon men
to believe in and follow him. Then, at the prospect of his
rejection by Israel, he came to believe that his morally
unavoidable death would be no obstacle to but rather a pre-
requisite for the coming of that kingdom. It would, somehow, in the pattern of Isaiah's suffering servant "bring
righteousness to many."[45] In terms of the metaphors he
himself, according to the Fourth Gospel, used to evaluate
his prospective death, it would, like Moses' lifted bronze

serpent, "draw all men to myself"[46] so "that whoever believes . . . may have eternal life;"[47] it would be "a ransom for many;"[48] it would, like a planted grain, bear "much fruit;"[49] it would like a good shepherd's heroic death, save his sheep from attacking wolves.[50] But the death, far from being his sole power to save, as the doctrine of atonement later represented it, was only one link in the chain of saving events. For he would subsequently conquer death for every man and return personally to usher in the eschatological kingdom.

In addition to Jesus' own interpretive comparisons, other theories of the atonement (analogies descriptive of the spiritually transforming power of his death) have been proposed from time to time by the Church; the Jewish sacrificial lamb; the ransom God paid to the Devil for the release of captive mankind; the voluntary vicarious death of the innocent divine Son to satisfy divine justice (the injured honor of the sovereign Father), thus securing pardon for guilty humanity; the moral influence upon the wicked of the spectacle of the righteous one suffering at their hands and on their behalf. Finally, in Eastern Orthodox theology, one sees salvation from sin as depending more on the incarnation, the divinizing of humanity in the historical life of Jesus, than on any forensic theory of propitiatory sacrifice. The appeal here is to St. John rather than to St. Paul: to salvation by mystic union with Christ;[51] by union with the Father through Christ;[52] by knowing the true God through Jesus, his messenger;[53] by union with God through love.[54]

The writer of First John asserts that since God is love, whoever loves demonstrates his mystical union with God. But it is held by some scholarship that the "God is love" expression is not the assertion of the general truth that God loves all men everywhere, always, and unconditionally; but that since "loved" in the phrase "God so loved the world,"[55] and elsewhere generally in the New Testament, is found in the Greek aorist tense, it is a single, completed past act and restricted to "his intention and action in Christ."[56] Such an interpretation, while exegetically sound for selected passages does not agree with other descriptions of the loving character of God, but seems to comport better with the Calvinist doctrine that Christ died only for the elect, that only Christians may address God as "Father," and that God's love is not great enough to embrace those who die as non-Christians. Such an interpretation seems to make God parochial, discriminatory and, in Leslie Weatherhead's phrase, "too small." For it seems to belie the character of the God who "sends his rain on the just and on the unjust,"[57] "is kind to the ungrateful and selfish,"[58] "is the *savior of all men* (italics ours) especially of those who believe,"[59] "not wishing that any should perish but that all should reach repentence."[60]

Although Jesus never taught that men's conscious appropriation of the merit of his death was the only ticket into the kingdom, he certainly taught that his death would have transforming effect.

The mere physical dying of a man has no redemptive effect upon others. Its power depends upon the character of the man who dies—his integrity, his love for others, the spiritual values for which he has lived and is willing to die. So Jesus' death, as part of his life, has transformed men ever since. By contrast, there is no record that a Buddha, Bodhisattva, Hindu avatara, Muslim or any other non-Christian prophet or saint or savior has been crucified and thereby helped to save men. But why should we think that crucifixion is the only valid expression and guarantee of redemptive love? Was not the manner of Jesus' death a cultural accident? And would he not still have revealed God's saving grace though he had died of illness or accident before his arrest in Gethsemane? In fact, was it not his very teaching of God's saving love for sinning Jews and wicked Romans, as well as his denunciation of hypocrisy, that occasioned his execution? Thousands of saints of all faiths whose selfless, suffering love is unimpeachable and whose influence has been redemptive have not been killed for their testimony. Is not the determinative thing the crucifixion of the ego rather than that of the body?

Suzuki compares the love of God as expressed in Christ's crucifixion with Amida Buddha's compassion for mankind in his vow to forego nirvana until he can bring all men there with him.

> In Christianity God's will or love for humanity, I may say, is expressed in the crucifixion of this only Son, i.e. as a concrete event in the history of Karma-bound beings; whereas in Shin Buddhism Amida's will takes the form of intense determination and its solemn declaration. The latter may seem insipid, inane and evaporating compared to the Christian realism. But in point of fact the Shin together with its parental Jodo has been the most irresistingly-inspiring power in the history of Far Eastern Buddhism, and this power has been exercised without ever shedding blood, without committing cruelties, without persecuting heresies.[61]

And Professor Saunders points out the universality of "the Cross":

> The cross is not an isolated act; there is a cosmic significance in self-sacrifice as the Buddhist world has more and more fully realized. . . . To both (Christianity and Buddhism) God is a loving God, and each finds in its God-man the divine quality of sacrificial love. . . . Buddhism, having no historic cross has had to invent one (viz: in the *Bodhisattva* doctrine).[62]

There is no literal cross outside of Christianity but there is the doctrine of the merit of the shed blood of the savior. A Jataka tale of the fifth century A.D. says of Gotama in previous incarnations, "More than the ocean has he shed of his blood; more than the stars has he given of his eyes."[63]

But if Buddhism and Hinduism have produced loving and self-sacrificing saviors analogous to Jesus, why is there no literal cross or heroic martyrdom in either? Toynbee answers, "Yes, it is true that the Indian religions are less heroic, but they have also been less atrocious."[64] Heroism and atrocity are correlatives: the hero can emerge only in an intolerant medium. The Zoroastrian-Judaic-Christian-Muslim tradition has exhibited outstanding arrogance, fanatic cruelty and persecution toward dissent. And similar intolerance has been practiced by Taoism and Confucianism. The Turkish historian Minhazad records that the Muslim invaders of India persecuted the Buddhist Sangha because of its alleged idolatry and beheaded or burned alive thousands of monks.[65] And the spread of Buddhism in China underwent alternate encouragement and persecution for hundreds of years at the hands of Taoist and Confucianist governments. For example, in the fifth century the Taoist emperor Tai-Wu decreed that the Buddhist religion "was to be wiped out, that not one monk, not one scriptural text, not one image was to remain in existence."[66] Later, in the ninth century, the Taoist emperor Wu-Tsung, in an attempt to reduce the power of Buddhism, deconsecrated more than 41,000 Buddhist temples and returned 260,500 monks and nuns to lay life.[67]

Of all religions, however, Christianity, which boasts that it alone knows and teaches the true love of God and true reverence for personality, seems to have been the most arrogant and bloodily intolerant and has, throughout its history, goaded Christians to butcher fellow Christians as well as non-Christians in the name of Christ and for the glory of God. A harvest of heroic martyrdoms, including the crucifixion of Jesus, was inevitable.

By contrast consider the role of Buddhism as a peacemaker:

> Buddhism is an ethico-philosophical way of life. . . . Its message of peace is so effective that in the 2,500 years of its long history not a single drop of blood has been shed in its name.[68]

The foregoing categorical statement by the British monk Mahathira has been challenged by some who can point to records of violence and bloodshed perpetrated by Buddhist monks against non-Buddhists and even fellow-Buddhists in Japan. The records are there, but they require interpretation. And the interpretation, according to trustworthy scholarship, would seem to invalidate the charge. The issue is whether the violent deed done by a religious man was motivated by loyalty to and defense of a religious belief or defense of economic or political values. According to two historians, the violence attributed to Japanese Buddhists should be understood in terms of non-theological motivation. According to Nakamura "An attitude of tolerance determined the all-inclusive and conciliatory nature of Japanese Buddhism."[69]

> Thanks to the spirit of tolerance, a massacre of heathens never took place in Japan. In this respect the situation differs vastly in Japan from that of the West. . . . Some apparently exceptional cases have occurred [persecution of Christians, local Jodo-Shin believers and the Nichiren sect]. These, however, were far from being religious persecutions in the Western sense of the word. . . . A mere difference of religious faith was generally a matter of no consequence for the Japanese unless it was considered to be damaging to the established order of the social nexus, whereas in the West a religious difference in itself would give rise to a conflict between opposing parties.[70]

Admittedly the record shows that

> after the Heian period, various large temples, which owned large estates, supported priest-soldiers, whose force was utilized to achieve the temple's demands.

There were also armed conflicts between temples and shrines. . . . According to the reports of Christian missionaries in Japan, the monasteries at Negoro always supported a host of priest-soldiers . . . Once a great bell was rung, it was said, thirty thousand soldiers could be summoned in just three or four hours.[71]

The record also shows that by the end of the tenth century ecclesiastical disagreement existed between Buddhist monasteries and Shinto shrines, and between rival Tendai monasteries which even dispatched armies to burn and loot each other. Also, the great Tendai monasteries dispatched armies to coerce the government to grant their demands. These latter confrontations however, according to Sansom, "had no religious character whatever beyond the name of the contending parties. . . . Their motive was greed for power and property."[72]

Certainly there has been little in their history of the cruel bigotry that stains our Western chronicles, and nothing to correspond to the great wars of religion, notably between Christian and heathen, but between Christian and Christian as well.[73]

To summarize, while it is true that religious and sociopolitical-economic motivations can be found mixed in bloody strife occurring between groups holding different faiths, there is nothing in the history of Buddhism to correspond to the Israelitish massacre of idolatrous Canaanites at the command of Yaweh; to the Moslem slaughter of Christian unbelievers, and the bloody Christian crusades against the infidel Saracens for their control of the Church's holy places; to the Christian Inquisition's torturing and burning of Jews, heretics and witches for their theological heterodoxy; and all for the glory of God and to maintain the purity of the Gospel. Buddhists have not tortured or killed non-Buddhists or other Buddhists in obedience to Gotama and for the spread of the Dharma.

Those Christians who denounce as sinful the faiths of monistic Hinduism, Buddhism and Taoism because they conceive of the Divine as "impersonal" (supra-personal) and/or of man as lacking an ultimately independent self should meditate on the fact that it is precisely these religions which have practiced gentleness, reverence for personality and peace throughout their history. Exception should be made as already noted of attempts to destroy Buddhism in China by debased and purely politically minded Taoist emperors. Whereas Judaism, Christianity and Islam, which insist on the sovereign independence of the personal ego and on whole-souled devotion to a personal God, have excelled in violence and drenched the world in showers of blood—their own as well as their neighbors'. In other words, the faiths that maximize personal relations have historically been chiefly responsible for inquisitions and wars of religion, while those that minimize them have set the example of interfaith harmony.

Why have so few Buddhist and Hindu saints been martyred? Because the Asian cultures shaped by these faiths are tolerant of dissent; because they successfully inculcate gentleness and harmlessness; because they believe right living is more important than orthodox believing; because they practice the principle that there are various theological paths to a common religious goal; because their seers and saints have sought to persuade more than to denounce and coerce men. The crucifixion of Jesus was the logical outcome of the conflict between his Hebrew prophetic denunciation of unrighteousness in high places and the opposing Jewish sense of divine favoritism and holier-than-thouism in certain Pharisees and Sadducees. In other cultures God's love has been mediated through quite other cultural accidents. In Hinduism it has been through the mystic sense of the Divine immanence undergoing in Maya the limitations and transience of finite things; through the sense of divine com-

passion for seekers of all faiths, no matter how groping and
imperfect their understanding might be. Not the bloody
crucifixion, but the gracious and irenic lives of the Rishis,
Patanjali, Kabir, Tukaran, Ramakrishna and Tagore, with
their realization of the divinity in all men, has been the
logical outcome.

In the Hinayana Buddhist culture it has been the ethic
of reverence for all life and the path of transcendance (crucifixion) of every man's pain-fraught ego into personal desirelessness with its attendant peace that has demonstrated
the concern of Ultimate Reality for life caught in the toils
of Samsara.

Its most recent expression has been the self-immolation
of monks and nuns in South Vietnam, first to secure justice
for the whole of Buddhist society from a corrupt Roman
Catholic dominated government, and then as protest against
the seizure of civil government by the military. "Greater
love hath no man than this, that a man lay down his life
for his friends." And were not these deaths, like that of
Christ's, atoning deaths by which the martyrs through their
voluntary suffering sought to bring repentance and righteousness to many? In Mahayana Buddhism, the dominant
influence has been the Bodhisattva doctrine and practice of
renunciation of divine prerogatives out of devotion to human
need; and the gentleness, absence of will-to-power, and
spiritual serenity of countless Buddhists has been the logical
outcome.

The cross of Christ and its redemptive interpretation
is therefore not the whole sum of the saving truth of God's
suffering love. It is rather one particular cultural pattern
among others whereby that love has been apprehended.

Suffering love is purifying and healing. This is the
essence of the Christian doctrine of the atonement; but
Christ's death did not exhaust the reservoirs of that love.
Anyone in any culture, to the degree he practices such *agape*

love, also makes atonement for human sin—that is, makes men contrite and good. Of all the world's saviors only Jesus was crucified; hence his death seems, by contrast to the others, to have unique redemptive power. But its uniqueness is not absolute; it consists in the extraordinary degree of its tragic quality—the dramatic contrast between his selfless love and his enemies' supreme egoism and hatred. But the spiritual catharsis produced by the tragedy of Christ's cross differs not in kind but only in degree from the catharsis of other tragic, God-inspired and God-sustained martyrdoms: Socrates drinking the hemlock, Polycarp being torn by wild beasts in the arena, Telemachus stoned to death for protesting gladiatorial combats, Joan of Arc and Hus being burned at the stake. The Bab going down before a firing squad, Baha'u'llah and Abdul Baha living their lives out in prison, Joseph Smith being lynched by a mob, Lincoln, Gandhi and Martin Luther King falling before fanatics' bullets, and the torturing and killing of prophets, reformers, and missionaries unnumbered; or, quite undramatically, obscure, humble Christians, sadhus and bodhisattvas quietly renouncing ego goals for the joy of serving their fellows.

The Buddha and the Christ at the same age, committing themselves to the Highest, spent their lives in selfless devotion to mankind. One died young, killed by his enemies; the other died old and peacefully among friends. But who can deny that each life has been spiritually uplifting and morally transforming to men? In each, the God who is love was revealed, even though Gotama was professedly an atheist; in each, the God who is the Ultimate Reality has been reconciling the world to himself and every man to his neighbor. We conclude: the blood of Christ is not the only redemptive power in the world. It is the demonstration of one historic person's identification with and love for God and man, and it has become a particular culture's symbol for the grace of God which is universal.

His teaching that men are saved only by God's grace:
Didn't Jesus alone teach by word and action that God pardons sinners freely by his grace without any requirement of good works or merit, and accepts them in spite of their unacceptability?[74]

No, Justification by faith alone, according to St. Paul, is taught in prophetic (not "normative") Judaism: "And he [Abraham] believed the Lord, and he reckoned it to him as righteousness;"[75] "So also David pronounces a blessing upon the man to whom God reckons righteousness apart from works;..."[76] It is taught in Hinduism's Bhagavadgita, where Krishna, the incarnation of the God Vishnu speaks:

> Even the most sinful man, if he worships Me with unswerving devotion, must be regarded as righteous; for he has formed the right resolution.[77]

> Abandon all *dharmas* [works or action] and come to me alone for shelter, I will deliver you from all sins; do not grieve.[78]

And he speaks again in the Bhagavata Purana:

> He who knowing my injunctions and prohibitions in the performance of one's own *dharma* or duties of life, even gives them all up for my sake is the best of all Sadhu-s.[79]

> Therefore, O Uddhava, care not for Sruti-s [teachings of the Vedas] or Smrti-s [religious practices and laws] for biddings and for forbiddings. Have recourse to me the *Atman* of all beings, with all devotion, and thou shalt have no fear from any quarter.[80]

And it is taught by all Bhakti sects inspired by such men as Ramanuja, Madhva, Vallabha,[81] Gosvami,[82] etc.; e.g. Saivite, Vaisnavite and Shakti sects. It is taught in the Pure Land sects of Mahayana Buddhism[83] and, most unconditionally, by the Shin sect, which "thinks that the only practice required is the calling of the Name and Title based on faith in the Amida Buddha, and all other practices are to be abandoned."[84] Mikogami summarizes the idea of salvation solely by the grace of Amida Buddha (the Tathagata) :

> In Shin Sect the confrontation between the Tathagata and I is understood as the relationship between the savior and the saved . . . . The Tathagata is the Absolute Power and I am absolutely powerless. . . . Thus since Tathagata and I are absolutely "other" beings, I can never build the bridge to the world of the Tathagata. The only way is the Tariki-eko (transference by Other Power). Through the Power of the Name of Tariki-eko, the bridge between the Tathagata and me is constructed. Herein exists the way for sinful me to be saved. There is absolutely no other way;[85]

It is taught in Islam;[86] in Sikhism: "Salvation is obtained by bearing love to God".[87] and in Taoism:

> Tao is the sanctuary where all things find refuge. . . . All things depend on it for life, and it rejects them not. . . . It loves and nourishes all things. . . . Why is it that the men of old esteemed this Tao so highly? Is it not because it may be daily sought and found and can remit the sins of the guilty? Hence it is the most precious thing under heaven.[88]

These faiths make it plain that man can do nothing to merit or purchase divine love; that it is the free gift of the sovereign Creator or Savior, which requires only to be humbly and lovingly accepted in order to be enjoyed. Simply calling in faith upon the name of Amitabha or Vishnu or Shiva or Allah is enough, as in Christianity, "everyone who calls upon the name of the Lord will be saved."[89]

Justification by faith alone is present even in non-theistic systems. The essence of it is to feel accepted just as you are, not repudiated, by ultimate reality. Thus the supra-theistic monist, the naturalist and the humanist have no sense of having to win the favor of the universe in order to be supported and blessed by it. Margaret Fuller "accepted the universe"; non-theists don't question the fact that *it* accepts *them*. There are laws that must be obeyed—Karma, the Tao, natural law—if one is to minimize suffering. But these are guides provided by nature, of which all creatures are part, for their growth and development. Just as every child who has normal, loving parents is loved and accepted by them no matter how often he does wrong or how often he is disciplined, so the religious humanist rests in the confidence (akin to Santyana's "animal faith") that in spite of his finiteness, ignorance, egocentricity and proneness to evil, he does not have to buy, merit or work for acceptance by the Cosmic Reality which brought him into being.

Such in non-theistic terms is the operation of the grace of God. Whatever is given to us, unmerited, is divine grace, and this grace is enormous: our life itself, our habitable planet, our ancestry and progeny, our inherited culture and traditions, our minds and bodies, our upward reach toward transcendant value. What is there that man hasn't received? What is there that isn't grace—except the evil men do in prostituting its gifts?

The fundamental doctrine, deriving from St. Paul and St. Anselm, that God couldn't pardon sinners until Jesus had been punished in their stead as a blood sacrifice to satisfy divine justice, was not taught by Jesus and has been repudiated as immoral by a number of modern evangelicals as well as by Abelard, the Unitarians, and other liberals. Certainly it is not found in any of the living non-Christian theisms. It seems to be a vestigial organ of the primitive religion which required human sacrifice to appease God's hatred of sinners. Most certainly in Christianity it is restricted to the juridical analogy (myth) which depicts man's attainment of fellowship with God through the anthropomorphic pattern: crime—prisoner—prosecution—judge—sentence—proxy victim—pardon; and perpetuated realistically in the transubstantiation doctrine of the Roman Catholic Mass.

Such human sacrifice was outgrown by Judaism, which replaced it first by animal sacrifice, as reflected in the story of Abraham's decision not to burn his son Isaac; and then repeatedly down-graded by prophetic voices in favor of the spiritual sacrifice of "a broken and a contrite heart"[90]—a sacrifice enjoined by Paul in the words, "present your bodies a living sacrifice, holy, acceptable to God, which is your spiritual worship;"[91] and practiced by Quakers in lieu of the sacrament of the Lord's Supper.

In the light of this development and of the variations in the concept of atonement, Otto's dichotomy between the Christian and Hindu bhakti doctrine of salvation is unrealistic. "India" he wrote, "knows of a savior, [Krishna], but not of an atoner [Christ]."[92] There is a difference here, but it is not an essential one. It is analogous to the difference between saying, "I have transportation to New York" and "But I have no car." The essential thing is getting there; how I get there depends on local conditions. If a Hindu is actually "saved" by Krishna, an "atoner" in addition would not seem to be needed. Thus while it is essential that I obtain salvation, the particular theological explanation of how I get it is of secondary importance. The intrinsic value in salvation is religious peace, being reconciled to or accepted by or united with the power that determines our ultimate destiny. The method of obtaining such peace is relative to cultural and psychological differences. In Christianity there are the methods of blood sacrifice, repentence and mystic union. In Hinduism there are the paths of jnana, karma, and bhakti marga. In Buddhism we find enlightenment, the noble eight-fold path, the grace of Amitabha, and satori.

Legalism, though rejected by Jesus and the early Church, has a way of creeping back into Christian attitudes as it does into all other faiths. But the revelation of God's unconditional acceptance and forgiveness of sinful man is certainly not a monopoly of the Christian Gospel.

FOOTNOTES FOR CHAPTER THREE

1 John 6:63.

2 References to non-Christian literatures will not include all the faiths, nor will they be necessarily the clearest statements in any particular faith: they constitute a general sampling.

3 Joseph Klausner, *Jesus of Nazareth* (New York: The Macmillan Co., 1946), p. 384.

4 Claude G. Montefiore, "The Originality of Jesus," The Hibbert Journal, XXVIII, October 1929, p. 98.

5 Klausner, *op cit.*, p. 387.

6 Cf. George L. Hurst, *The Literary Background of The New Testament* (New York: The Macmillan Co., 1928), *passim.*

7 Taught by Motse: Lin Yutang, ed., *The Wisdom of China and India*, "Universal Love" (New York: Random House, 1942), Vol. 2, Chap. 15, pp. 794-795; and six living religions besides Christianity: Judaism (Leviticus 19:18; Tobit 4:15; Letter of Aristeas, p. 207); Hinduism (Mahabharata 13:115:22 and five other passages); Buddhism (Sigalovada Sutta 31); Taoism (Suzuki and Carus, trans., Tai-Shang Kan-Ying Pien, etc.) (Chicago: Open Court, 1906), pp. 17, 19, 53, characters 196-228; Confucianism (The Analects 15:23); Islam, (R. O. Ballou, ed., *World Bible*, "The 42 Traditions of the An-Nawawi," The Viking Portable Library, p. 476, paragraph 8.).

8 Taught by Plato (Republic 335 B-E; Crito 49 B-E; Gorgias 472 D-475 E) and nine living religions besides Christianity: Judaism (Proverbs 15:1; 25:21-22; Jeremiah 29:7); Islam (Koran 13:22; 23:98); Sikhism (Bhai Gur Das' Analysis, War 28; *The Sikh Religion*, 6 vols., trans. M. A. Macauliffe) (Oxford: Clarendon Press, 1909) Vol. 4, p. 261; Bahaism (Abdul Baha in J. E. Esslemont, *The New Era*, pp. 189-90); Hinduism (Laws of Manu 6:48; Mahabharata 5.39:73-74); Jainism (Dasaveyaliya 8:37-39); Buddhism (Dhammapada 1:5; 17:3); Taoism (Tao Teh King LXIII and XLIX, Lin Yutang's translation); Confucianism (Shu King 4.2.3; Mencius 4.2.28.4-5, 6; in James Legge, trans., *The Chinese Classics, A Translation*, (New York: Alden 1885 Vol. II, p. 18).

9 Taught by six living religions besides Christianity: Islam (Koran 17:29); Sikhism (*Hymns of Guru Arjan*, Sukhmani, Ashtopadi 3.6: Macauliffe, *op. cit.* 3.206; cf. Trumpp, Adi Granth, 383); Buddhism (Santi Deva, "The Prayer of the Bodhisattva," *The Path of Light*, trans. L. D. Barnett (New York: E. P. Dutton, 1909) pp. 45 and 88-89; Taoism, Tao Teh King, *passim*); Confucianism (Li Ki 1.1.1.25); Hinduism (Bhagavadgita 13:7; 16:2-3, 13-18; 18:53).

10 A cardinal teaching throughout Hinduism, Buddhism, Jainism, Taoism.

11 Buddhism (Santi Deva, "The Prayer of the Bodhisattva," *op. cit.*); Hinduism (Bhagavadgita 2:71; 6:6; 12:13-14); Taoism (Tao Teh King VII, Lin Yutang's translation).

12 Buddhism's doctrine that it is the inner states of mind which produce good or evil acts; Confucianism's doctrine that the cultivation of the inner self is the first step to transforming the conduct of the

world; Hinduism's great emphasis that mind control through metaphysical realization is the only guarantee of good conduct.

[13] J. Hesse, *Lao Tzu: A Pre-Christian Witness to Truth* (Basel: Missions Buchhandlung, 1914), *passim.* The German edition is listed as follows: J. Hesse. *Lao-tsze ein Vorchristlicher Wahrheitszeuge.* Basel, 1914, Verlag de Basler Missionsbuchhandlung. (Basler Missions-Studien, heft 44.)

[14] Matt. 27.52.

[15] In addition to findings recorded by the British and American Societies for Psychical Research, and such early classics on the subject as those by F. W. H. Myers, Charles Richet, Hamlin Garland, William Crookes and Oliver Lodge, one should consult recent books such as: Marcus Bach, *They Have Found a Faith* (Indianapolis: Bobbs Merrill, 1946), the relevant chapter; George S. Eddy, *You Will Survive After Death* (New York: Rinehard, 1950); Rayner C. Johnson, *The Imprisoned Splendor* (New York: Harper & Bros., 1953); S. Ralph Harlow, *A Life after Death* (New York: Doubleday & Co., Inc., 1961); Stuart E. White, *The Unobstructed Universe* (New York, E. P. Dutton, 1959); and half a dozen other books by the latter and his wife Betty.

[16] Paramhansa Yogananda, *Autobiography of a Yogi* (New York: Philosophical Library, Inc., 1946), Chapter 43.

[17] Philostratus, *The Life of Appolonius of Tyana*, Vol. 2, rev., trans. F. C. Conybeare, *The Loeb Classical Library* (Cambridge, Mass.: Harvard University Press, 1950) p. 405, BK. VIII, C. 31.

[18] Matt. 28:17.

[19] Heb. 11:1.

[20] Phil. 3:21.

[21] 1 Cor. 15:13-16 (Goodspeed translation).

[22] According to John C. H. Wu, the great Chinese jurist, scholar, and Confucianist turned Roman Catholic, in *Beyond East and West* (New York: Sheed & Ward, 1951), pp. 61, 153. See also Lin Yutang, *The Importance of Living* (New York: John Day Co., 1937), p. 409.

[23] Paul Radin, *Monotheism Among Primitive Peoples* (Special Publication of the Bollingen Foundation, No. 4; also by the Ethnographical Museum, Basel, Switzerland, 1954).

[24] *Timaeus* 37C-38A.

[25] *Discourses*, Book III, Chap. 24.

[26] "Father" is used of God twenty-eight times in the Old Testament alone.

[27] Yasna 45:4, in D. J. Iram, *Divine Songs of Zarathustra* 56 (London: Allen & Unwin, 1924); Zendavesta, in R. O. Ballou, *World Bible*, Viking Portable Library (New York: Viking Press, 1944), p. 186.

[28] 'Abdu'l Baha in J. E. Esslemont, *op. cit.*, pp. 119, 122.

[29] Six times in the Rig Veda; Yajur Veda 37:20; Bhagavadgita 9:17; 11:44.

[30] *Hymns of Guru Arjan*, Todi; Macauliffe, *op. cit.*, 3. 383 or Majh, *ibid.*, 3.112.

31 "Hymn of Shinran" in K. J. Saunders, *Epochs in Buddhist History* (Chicago: Univ. of Chicago Press, 1924), p. 178.

32 Simone Weil, *Waiting for God*, trans. Emma Crawfurd (New York: G. P. Putnam's Sons, 1951), pp. 184-185.

33 A. Toynbee, *Christianity Among the Religions of the World* (New York: Scribners, 1957), p. 101.

34 Father Thomas Ohm in Sidney Cave's review of his "The Love of God in the Non-Christian Religions," *The International Review of Missions*, Vol. 40, No. 159, p. 346.

35 John 16:26-27; 17:23, 26; 3:16.

36 Cf. Kenneth J. Saunders, *The Gospel for Asia* (New York: Macmillan, 1928), p. 146.

37 Katha Upanishad 5:11.

38 P. A. Schilpp. ed., *The Philosophy of Sarvepalli Radhakrishnan*, in *The Library of Living Philosophers* (New York: Tudor Publishing Co., 1952), p. 798.

39 Bhagavadgita 4:24; Cf. also 9:16 (Paramananda's translation).

40 Bhagavadgita 4:7-8 (Prof. D. S. Sarna's translation).

41 Bhagavadgita, trans. S. Prabhavananda and C. Isherwood, *op .cit.*, pp. 64, 67.

42 Cf. *Majjhima-Nikaya*, C. IV.

43 Sacred Books of the East, Vol. 10, Part 2, *The Sutta Nipata*, trans. V. Fausböll (Oxford: Clarendon Press, 1881) p. 25.

44 Santi Deva, "The Prayer of the Bodhisattva," *op. cit.*, p. 37 ff.

45 Isa. 53:11 (Goodspeed).

46 John 12:32.

47 John 3:15.

48 Mark 10:45.

49 John 12:24.

50 Cf. John 10:14-15.

51 John 15:1-7.

52 John 17:21-23.

53 John 17:3.

54 1 John 4:7, 12, 15, 16.

55 John 3:16.

56 Prof. Clinton Morrison in a letter to the writer.

57 Matt. 5:45.

58 Luke 6:35.

59 2 Pet. 3:9.

60 1 Tim. 4:10.

61 D. T. Suzuki, *A Miscellany on the Shin Teachings of Buddhism* (Kyoto: Shinshu Otaniha Shumshu, 1949) p. 56.

62 Kenneth J. Saunders, *The Gospel for Asia*, pp. 205-206.

63 *Ibid.*, p. 205.

64 A. Toynbee, *op. cit.*, p. 109.

65 Cf. J. Kashyap, "Origin and Expansion of Buddhism," *The Path of the Buddha*, ed., K. Morgan (New York: The Ronald Press Co., 1956) p. 49.

66 Zenryu Tsukamoto, "Buddhism in China and Korea," *op. cit.*, p. 219.

67 Cf. *Ibid.*, p. 221.

68 The Venerable Mirisse Gunasiri Mahathera, Monk-in-charge of the Buddhist Vihara, Knightsbridge, London, England, writing in a report to its members by the Church Peace Union.

69 Hajima Nakamura, *Ways of Thinking of Eastern Peoples*, trans. Philip P. Wiener (Honolulu: East West Center Press, 1964), p. 388.

70 *Op. cit.*, pp. 392-3.

71 *Op. cit.*, p. 493.

72 George Sansom, *A History of Japan to 1334* (Stanford, California: Stanford University Press, 1958), Vol. 1, p. 223.

73 *Op. cit.*, p. 222.

74 Matt. 5:45; Mark 2:15-17; Luke 5:20, 6:35-36, 7:47-50, 19:10; John 3:15, 36.

75 Gen. 15:6.

76 Rom. 4:1-12 (specifically 6).

77 *The Bhagavadgita* trans. Swami Nikhilananda (New York: Ramakrisha-Vivekenanda Center, 1944), p. 232.

78 *Ibid.* p. 368.

79 P. N. Sinha, *A Study of the Bhagavata Purana*, 2nd ed. (Adgar, Madras, India: The Theosophical Publishing House, 1950), p. 600.

80 *Ibid.*, p. 602.

81 Cf. Das Gupta, *A History of Indian Philosophy* (Cambridge, England, Oxford University Press, 1955), Vol. 4, pp. 58, 89, and 346-359.

82 Cf. Das Gupta, *Ibid.*, pp. 415-428.

83 Mitsuyuki Ishida, "Shin and Jodo Buddhism," *The Path of the Buddha*, ed. K. W. Morgan (New York: The Ronald Press Co., 1956), pp. 331-339.

84 *Ibid.*, p. 335.

85 Mikogami, *Kyogyoshinsho Gaikan*, pp. 38, 39; quoted by Hideo Hashimoto, *op cit.*, p. 13.

86 Koran, Sura XLII, 25, and stressed particularly by the Murjites "who believed that faith alone is sufficient for man's salvation." See A. E. Affifi in K. W. Morgan, ed., *Islam, The Straight Path* (New York: The Ronald Press Co., 1958), p. 147.

87 *Hymns of Guru Nanak*, Asa Ashtapadi: M. A. Macauliffe, *The Sikh Religion, etc.*, 6 Vols., (Oxford: Clarendon Press, 1909), 1.316; precise location not obtainable. Also cf. *Hymns of Guru Arjan*, Sukhmani, Ashtapadi 17:2; Macauliffe, *op cit.*, 3.249; cf. Trumpp, *Adi Granth*, p. 409.

88 Lionel Giles, trans., *The Sayings of Lao Tsu*, Wisdom of the East Series (London: John Murray, 1905), pp. 21, 28.

89 Rom. 10:13.

90 Ps. 51:17.

91 Rom. 12:1.

92 Rudolf Otto, *Christianity and the Indian Religion of Grace* (Madras, India: The Christian Literature Society of India, 1929), p. 59.

Chapter IV

DID JESUS CLAIM TO BE GOD, AND MANS' ONLY SAVIOR?

HIS ALLEGED TEACHING THAT HE REVEALS GOD BECAUSE HE HIMSELF IS GOD

Is THERE ANY record that he ever said he was God, God's only son, God's only incarnation, or God's only savior for mankind, or that he laid claim to such attributes as "creator of the universe," "omniscience," "virgin birth," and "sinlessness."

DID HE CLAIM IDENTITY WITH OR SUBORDINATION TO GOD?

Instead of saying he himself was God, he subordinated himself to God, his father, in every reference he made to their relationship except those asserting mystical oneness: "The Father is greater than I;"[1] "But of that day or that hour no one knows, not even the angels in Heaven, nor the Son, but only the Father;"[2] "Why do you call me good? No one is good but God alone;"[3] "The Son can do nothing of his own accord, but what he sees the Father doing;"[4] "For as the Father has life, in himself, so he has granted the Son also to have life in himself,"[5] "that they may know Thee, the only true God, and Jesus Christ whom Thou has sent;"[6] "I am ascending to my Father, and your Father, to my God and your God."[7] In the last two quotations Jesus clearly distinguishes his father, as the only true God, from himself as God's messenger; then he asserts that he acknowledges the same God and has the same father as his disciples. This dependence on God is evidenced in his prayer life, in which he habitually prayed for strength and guidance, and in his torment, when in Gethsemane he felt he must yield his personal will to God's will that he die, and when on the cross he felt that God had deserted him.[8]

Neither is the flat identification of Jesus Christ with God taught by any other New Testament writer or character. (Alleged exceptions to this statement will be treated later.) Instead, a clear distinction is made between Jesus Christ as Lord on the one hand, and the Father as God on the other. The usual formula is "God our Father and the Lord Jesus Christ,"[9] which is repeated with only a few slight variations at least thirty-six times and found in every book in the New Testament except the Gospels and Third John. Jesus is never called "God the Son" to parallel "God the Father," which would be necessary if full deity were attributed to him. It is only the Father who is called "God"; Jesus bears only the less exalted title, "Lord."

IS HIS TITLE "LORD" A DEIFIC TITLE?

Much has been written to make "Lord" a deific title for Jesus. But the evidence does not support the claim. It is true that Yahweh, the God of Israel, is called "Lord" (*adonai* in the Hebrew Old Testament and *kurios* in the Septuagint); and the title gradually came to have this significance for Jesus as his apotheosis developed. But "Lord," as it is used throughout the Bible, even by Jesus himself in referring to characters in his parables, is also widely used as a simple term of respect, like "Sir," to address any individual who exercises special authority, religious or secular: Canaanite and mystery cult Gods, self-deified Roman Emperors, kings, princes, tyrants, nobles, prophets, patriarchs, military leaders, angels, notably worthy person-

age, slave owners, even husbands. Mediaeval and contemporary usage with this broad significance is apparent in the
feudal distinction between lords and their serfs, and in the
titles of British nobility.

It was inevitable that the disciples should use it for
Jesus, though the rest of the evidence in the New Testament seems clearly to restrict its significance to a non-deific
category. If they had been convinced of Jesus' deity and
needed a distinctively divine title for him, would they have
been content with the extremely ambiguous "Lord"?

Not only do the New Testament writers clearly distinguish between the Father who is God, and the Son who is
Lord, but they subordinate Jesus the Son to God the Father.
In the first preaching of the *Kerygma* in Acts, the preachers
Peter and Stephen never refer to Jesus as "God" or even
"Son of God," but use non-divine titles. Peter uses "man,"
"servant," "prophet," "righteous one," "Christ," "holy one,"
"author of life," "leader," "savior." Stephen uses "righteous
one," "Son of man," and "Lord."

Moreover, there are specific statements of subordination. "You are Christ's and Christ is God's;"[10] here, Paul
teaches subordination by analogy: just as the Corinthian
Christians belong to Christ and so are dependent on him,
Christ belongs to and hence is dependent on God. "Yet for
us there is one God, the Father, from whom are all things
and for whom we exist, and one Lord Jesus Christ through
whom are all things and through whom we exist;"[11] here
Jesus as channel or instrument of creation is subordinated
to God, the sovereign, originating, creative power, reflecting
the logos doctrine of Philo and the neo-Pythagoreans. "The
head of Christ is God;"[12] again analogically as the head
rules the body, so God rules Christ; not the Father rules the
Son, but God rules Jesus Christ. "The Son himself will also
be made subordinate to God who made all things subject
to him, and thus God will be all in all;"[13] If Christ will be

subjected to God in the future, his status of identity or equality with God now is contingent, not a necessary attribute of deity. "He is the image of the invisible God."[14] He is not God, but God's likeness, as in the case of Adam. "The God of our Lord Jesus Christ, the Father of Glory."[15] Our Lord had a God whom he worshipped—he wasn't that God, he didn't worship himself. "For there is one God, and there is one mediator between God and men, the man, Christ Jesus."[16] He is not called the "God-man," but "the man" who mediates between God and his fellowmen.

EVIDENCE OF HIS ALLEGED IDENTIFICATION WITH GOD

We must now examine putative identifications of Jesus with God as made by New Testament writers and characters. How shall we interpret Paul's assertion, "For in him the whole fullness of deity dwells bodily"?[17] Obviously he can't mean that God is confined spatially and temporally within the body of Jesus. But if he means that God's total being is not diminished or restricted by entering Jesus, he contradicts his kenosis or self-emptying doctrine: "Christ Jesus who, though he was in the form of God, did not count equality with God a thing to be grasped, but emptied himself, taking the form of a servant, being born in the likeness of men."[18] If he emptied himself of the fullness of God and of his equality with God, then must he not have become less than the Chalcedonian trinitarian Son who was "very God of very God"? But if the "fullness"   be interpreted as the fullness of God's purpose of human redemption rather than of God's ontological substance, the kenosis doctrine is still contradicted. For in the incarnation Christ fulfilled rather than emptied himself of God's redemptive purpose. The assertion also contradicts all other passages by Paul in which he states Jesus' distinctness from and sub-

(πλήρωμα)

ordination to God. Paul's assertion would seem to be a mystical intuition which does not yield to logical, metaphysical analysis; and, as part of the problem of incarnation, it is treated elsewhere in this study.[19] But at least it is not the flat identification, "Jesus is Yahweh   ," but rather the incontestable "God is *in* Jesus."

In two other passages the implication of Jesus' deity is removed by alternative manuscript readings: 2. Pet. 1:1 reads, "Our God and Savior Jesus Christ," and Titus 2:13 reads, "Our Great God and Savior Jesus Christ." The alternate readings found in the Authorized Version and footnoted in the R.S.V. and New English Bible read respectively: "Our God and the Savior Jesus Christ" and "the Great God and our Savior Jesus Christ." Even if the passages are textually preferable to their alternates, they are clearly at variance with the otherwise unanimous New Testament distinction between God and the Lord Jesus. Found, as they are, in letters written in the middle or late second century, it is understandable that they might reflect the movement toward apotheosis seen in Ignatius' statement, "Our God, Jesus the Christ, was conceived by Mary,"[20] and in Polycarp's phrase, "Our Lord and God, Jesus Christ."[21]

A fourth passage is Thomas' alleged exclamation in the presence of the risen Jesus, "My Lord and my God."[22] If it is textually and grammatically unimpeachable, it is yet highly suspect because of the notably apologetic and Gnostic-Greek character of this Gospel. The writer's purpose is to prove that Jesus is the Son of God. So, if being a creature he yet participates in the nature of the Creator, as the rest of the Gospel portrays him, he merits divine sonship a fortiori more than Adam does.[23] Also if this Gospel is an interpretation of Christ for Greek minds, it is understandable that a God-man, after the pattern of the Olympian deities, would be more impressive than a Jewish Messiah—and the Greeks did speak of their God-Men as "Gods". Sociologically

(Θεός)

speaking, however, it seems unlikely that a non-Hellenized, monotheistic Jew would confuse Jesus, a carpenter-teacher from Nazareth, with Yahweh, who created the universe.

In the only other possible identification of Jesus with God, in John's prologue, Jesus is related to God the Father through the theologically ambiguous logos. If this is the Stoic logos or God, the identification would seem to hold. But if it is the logos of Philo, God's agent of creation, then "son of God" who is subordinate to God is the more appropriate designation. The latter alternative is also suggested by the phrase, "the logos was *with* God." Corroborating this exegesis (if Goodspeed's rendering is to be trusted) is John's later denial to the divine son, of the deific attribute of self-existence in the remark that "just as the Father is self-existent, he has given self-existence to the Son,"[24] thus making it derived rather than aboriginal. But if "self-existence" is rendered "life in himself" (as in the Authorized, R.S.V. and Phillips translations), or even as "life-giving power in himself" (as in the New English Version), the attribute in question is still a donation from the Father; and since it is not a part of the son's eternal essence, it violates the orthodox homo-ousion formula.

But in any case we are not justified in identifying Jesus of Nazareth with the logos. "The logos became flesh" does not bear such a literal interpretation. The logos (God) did not metamorphose into the body of a Jewish carpenter thus ceasing to be the logos. Rather, it is to be understood as "the logos entered, indwelt, became incarnate in Jesus of Nazareth." Thus Jesus contains, manifests, reveals, is united with the logos (God), but is not flatly and univocally God; otherwise the true human nature of Jesus is lost and Jesusology is unavoidable.

Finally, the flat identification of Christ, as the logos, with God would require a literal rather than a figurative or mystical understanding of "He who has seen me has seen

the Father,"[25] and "I and the Father are one."[26] And this
would then have to be rendered by the theologically impossible "I am the Father, and there is no other Father
than me." If, however, oneness be understood as "sharing
a common purpose," then could not Paul or any other committed Christian say "I and the Father are one"?

With the attribution of full deity to Jesus by such
leaders as Ignatius and Polycarp, already cited, Jesus becomes as McGiffert has shown, "the God of the early Christians," eclipsing the Father in Heaven.[27] From then on,
apotheosis moves to crystallization in the trinitarian formula
of Nicea, a formula by which the Church sought to reassure
the Gentile worshippers of Jesus, who were converted from
the dying and rising, savior-God mystery cults, that Jesus
was also a God with power to save and yet, at the same time,
to avoid tri-theism.

IS HE THE ONLY-BEGOTTEN SON OF GOD?

Jesus called himself God's son, but not God's "only"
son. For he knew Jewish religious literature well enough to
know that there were other sons of God: Israel collectively,[28]
righteous and obedient Jews,[29] Hebrew kings at the coronation ceremony,[30] certain Hebrew judges or pagan deities
who are also called "Gods"[31]—and to which ascription Jesus
appealed to justify his own divine sonship[32]—Satan and
other angelic or heavenly beings,[33] unclassified Jewish persons,[34] and indirectly all who called God "Father," including
Jesus' Pharisaic opponents even though on occasion he
accused them of acting more like children of the devil.[35]
Finally and most broadly, since Adam is called "the son of
God,"[36] being created in his image and likeness, all human
beings are the sons of God since they are Adam's offspring.

Though he is called the "only   son" five
times in the Johannine writings,[37] the phrase is not found
elsewhere and it is not Jesus' self-designation. The use of

(μονογενὴς)

the phrase is to stress the uniqueness of Jesus' sonship. He is portrayed neither as a merely created son like Adam or Israel or any other human being born of the will of the flesh; nor as merely an adopted son by virtue of spiritual rebirth; but as God's one and only Son, eternally begotten or sired by the Father out of his own being, and born of Mary.

Literally of course he is not a son of God at all, nor is God a father at all; for God is not a male, human progenitor with physical parts and passions and a wife. When used non-literally, "son of" is a metaphor, in the Hebrew idiom having the force of "like," "resembling," or "characterized by." Examples of such usage are found in the fifth chapter of Genesis where the age of each ante-diluvian is expressed in translation as "the son of x number of years." Further, David is described as a "son of death,"[38] Christians, as "sons of the resurrection,"[39] Judas, the "son of perdition,"[40] Adam, the "son of God"[41] because made in God's image.

But even in the metaphorical or non-physical sense of "begotten," Jesus is not the *only* begotten son of God. The biblical record indicates that others before him were "begotten" sons. The first was a Hebrew king at the time of his coronation when God said to him as recorded in the second psalm: "You are my son, today I have begotten you."[42] This formula may have been spoken by some celebrant at the inauguration ceremonies of succeeding kings and was still later interpreted as applying to the ideal king, the Messiah, when he should come. When the early Church became convinced that Jesus was this Messiah, they transferred the ascription to him.[43] And there is evidence that it was apparently regarded by the New Testament writers as having been spoken by God directly to Jesus at his baptism,[44] and perhaps at the transfiguration.[45] The words are only approximately the same as those spoken to the king, but the sense of divine authorization of the son's role is the same. Also, a Western text reading of Luke's version of the formula in an impressive number of manuscripts is identical with the wording of the psalm.[46] Moreover, the author of Hebrews assumes that the exact words found in the psalm were spoken to Jesus: "You are my son today I have begotten you."[47] And there is no record of comparable words being pronounced by God except at the baptism and transfiguration. We conclude that Jesus is not the *only* begotten son of God but came to share that status with Hebrew kings after the conviction of his messianic kingship developed.

NATURAL VERSUS ADOPTED SONSHIP

The pronouncement of begotten sonship seems to lend support to the adoptionist Christology, that Christ also is an adopted son of God. Whereas Paul seemed to believe that Jesus attained sonship by rising from the dead;[48] and Matthew and Luke, that he gained it at his conception;[49] John gives the impression that the descent of the Spirit upon him at the Jordan made him God's son;[50] so also Mark, that he became God's son at the baptism.[51] For if we can assume that the wording at the baptism, "Thou art my beloved Son; with thee I am well pleased,"[52] is a corruption of the wording in the psalm, Acts and Hebrews, then God must have said to Jesus at the Jordan, "You are my son; today I have begotten you"—thus transforming Jesus from a natural into an adopted, supernatural son.

Yet, while Jesus did not call himself God's *only* son or only *begotten* son, he characteristically referred to himself as "*the* son of God" or simply "the Son." Now grammatical usage of "*the* Son" does not preclude the existence of other sons. For example, "I am the son of Mr. Jones" does not imply he has no other sons; if I have brothers I am not required to say "I am *a* son of Mr. Jones."

But the use of the definite article may indicate that one has special or unique status among other sons, and this seems to be the emphasis when Jesus used the phrase. For example, "no one knows the Father except the Son and anyone to whom the Son chooses to reveal him."[53] Here *the* son is distinguished from all other sons because he alone has special knowledge of the Father. In what then does Jesus' sonship make him different from all other sons of God? John alone of the Gospel writers finds this uniqueness in Christ's eternal preexistence as agent of creation, but they all agree that it is his special commission as spiritual Messiah: to reveal God's nature more fully to men, to judge their unrighteousness, to offer them eternal life, to establish a more broadly conceived Kingdom of God, and to bequeath this role to his followers.

But we must explore the relevance to mankind in general of his distinction between natural sons by creation and spiritual sons by adoption. It is not a sharp dichotomy; for while natural sons may become spiritual or adopted sons by faith in Christ,[54] all natural sons show spiritual sonship in varying degree—the degree to which they exhibit perfect Godlike behavior.[55] The criteria for measuring the degree of spiritual sonship include: doing God's will,[56] loving,[57] loving one's enemies,[58] being a peacemaker.[59]

Spiritual sonship is thus a paradigmatic relationship which doubtless none may fully attain but all may approach. If perfection were required for adoption, none could be called true children. Jesus' Pharisaic opponents, though claiming sonship in the natural sense, were declared unqualified in the spiritual sense because they rejected Jesus' God-given teaching.[60] Whereas Cornelius, a "dog of a gentile" because he was a pagan Roman, was, according to Jesus' standard, a spiritual son of God and so recognized finally by the Apostle Peter.[61]

But adoption, with its dichotomous implication (no one can be partially adopted in the legal sense) is a Pauline teaching; Jesus does not use the word. According to Jesus, all human beings are God's children by birth and more or less spiritually filial according to their degree of Godlike behavior. But Jesus' interpreters, noting that faith in him produced such a radical spiritual transformation (Jesus called it "a new birth") wrongly made it the sole touchstone of spiritual sonship, so that no others beside Christians had the "power to become children of God."[62] And it is to this distinction, blindly adhered to, that must be attributed much of the subtle, spiritual arrogance shown by some Christians toward devout men of other faiths or of no faith. To summarize, "sonship" has several meanings. "Son of" in the loosest or colloquial sense means "like" or "characterized by," as in the description of James and John as "sons of Thunder." Metaphorically and universally all human beings are God's children because they are created through Adam in the image of God. Others are deemed God's sons by virtue of being specially chosen by God for specific purposes—such as Israel collectively, kings, judges, prophets and others exercising authority under God. Still others are sons in the distinctively New Testament sense of being "born of the Spirit," and of being "true sons" to the degree of their filialness, obedience to God, and love of their fellowmen. Uniquely Jesus is the son of God by virtue of his messianic vocation.

IS HIS SONSHIP DIFFERENT IN KIND FROM THAT OF HIS DISCIPLES?

But though by common consent of the Church Jesus exhibited God's likeness to a superlative degree, he did not call himself God's son in an exclusivistic sense with respect to his followers, for he wished them to accept that status for themselves and to share it on equal terms with himself. Their equal sonship is implied in the "Our Father" of the prayer he taught them, unless it can be proved that Jesus himself never prayed this prayer. It is also implied in his message to his disciples, "I am ascending to my father and your father, to my God and your God;"[63] for here, with respect to God the Father, Jesus' sonship and theirs are on the same footing. Since he calls his disciples,[64] and whoever else does God's will[65] or loves his enemies,[66] his spiritual brothers, are they not therefore also spiritual sons of God? Do they not share his sonship also because they share, or *may* share fully, his knowledge of God,[67] his power or even surpass his power,[68] his resurrection from the dead,[69] his experience of God's love,[70] his other-wordliness,[71] his glory,[72] according to Paul his divine inheritance,[73] his redemptive mission,[74] his preaching,[75] his cross,[76] his divine authority including that of declaring sins forgiven,[77]—and his oneness with God?[78]

In passage after passage in the Gospels, and under various figures of speech, Jesus proclaims himself man's savior from ignorance, sin and death by being a channel of divine truth, forgiveness, and the gift of eternal life; but nowhere does he explicitly declare himself God's *only* savior for mankind. But would he not have done so had he known himself to be God's *only* son and incarnation—the *only* way, truth, and life? However, since he does not seem to have known about Zoroaster, Laotze, Confucius, Buddha, Krishna, or the mystery religion saviors, he had no basis for comparison.

Looking back on Jesus' thought of himself as savior, from the vantage point of our greater knowledge of other cultures and religions, we approve his silence as against the monopolistic claims made for him by his followers. For we note, for example, how Gotama the Buddha, "the Light of Asia," has saved millions of men from the suffering caused by self-centered craving, and replaced the fear of death by the assurance of eternal bliss; and how Krishna, "the Hindu Christ," has reconciled millions more to God by offering freedom from all sins, supreme peace and the eter-

nal abode. Yet, according to Jesus, it is faith in God and
penitence toward him which saves. As revealer of God's
love, Jesus sees himself as a mediator, offers himself as an
intercessor, and declares that faith in him is indirectly faith
in God: "He who receives me receives him who sent me."[79]
But in the last analysis it is not Jesus, even as spiritual Messiah, who saves, but the Father: "The Father is greater than
I,"[80] and "The Father who dwells in me does his works."[81]
And in his last discourse he seems to relinquish even his
office of mediator and to refer men directly to God: "I do
not say to you that I shall pray the Father for you, for the
Father himself loves you."[82]

DO HIS CLAIMS TO SPIRITUAL AUTHORITY
IMPLY HIS DIETY?

But there remains the problem of certain claims made
by Jesus which, it is alleged, only deity could truthfully make.
What shall we say of Jesus' bold claims for wide spiritual
authority: "I am the light of the world,"[83] "the bread of
life,"[84] "the resurrection and the life."[85] That Jesus is not
the *only* light of the world is clear from his declaration to
his disciples, "*You* are the light of the world."[86] That Jesus
himself (his flesh and blood) is not "the bread of life"
which came down out of heaven, which men must eat if
they would live, is made plain by Jesus when he declares
that "it is the spirit that gives life, the flesh is of no avail;
the words that I have spoken to you are spirit and life."[87]
The bread of life, then, is Jesus' words, Jesus teachings.
By implication, then, by whomsoever in any religion there
are revealed truths also taught by Jesus, that person, too,
is the bread of life. And the study of comparative religions
shows that there are a number of such persons.

That Jesus is not the *only* "resurrection and the life"
is evidenced by two facts. First, taking the phrase, "the resurrection and the life" in its metaphysical sense—that it

will be Jesus' power which raises the physically dead at the last day[88]—we note the delegating of this power to him by God;[89] which makes him God's instrument of the resurrection rather than the Creator of life from the dead in his own right. Such a claim by Jesus could not be grounded in the role of the expected Jewish Messiah, for it is not he but Yahweh who will effect the general resurrection. And it was not Jesus, but God who—if we take the narrative uncritically—raised certain worthy Jews to life quite independently of Jesus.[90] Moreover it was God who raised Jesus, not Jesus himself. Hence Jesus' claim to be "the resurrection" does not make him God.

But if resurrection be taken figuratively as an arising from sin into righteousness, from estrangement to fellowship with God, as seems to be Jesus' intent in contrasting it to "the resurrection at the last day"[91] in the Fourth Gospel, which consistently spiritualizes the eschatology of the Synoptics—as seems to be Paul's intent also in identifying it with the regeneration involved in baptism and union with Christ[92]—then these facts belie Jesus' monopoly of resurrection. For not only were many Old Testament characters righteous before God and in close fellowship with him, but according to Peter, many another in other non-Christian faiths "who fear him and does what is right is acceptable to him.[93] The Christian "new being" described by Paul Tillich is not the only new being. In other cultures, too, we witness men rising from lives of sinfulness and ontological anxiety to lives of goodness and peace with the Supreme Being: loving, selfless sainthood is a spiritual fruit of Islam, Vedantism, Confucianism and Buddhism as well as of Christianity. We conclude, then, that others beside Jesus are "the resurrection and the life."

But a few explicitly exclusivistic sayings of Jesus, in which he seems to offer himself as *the only* way of salvation require attention. In the light of his equating of eternal

life with knowing the Father and himself as the Father's
emissary,[94] how shall we interpret "no one knows the Father
except the Son and anyone to whom the Son chooses to reveal him"?[95] We might explain it by saying that Jesus' finitude and lack of omniscience kept him ignorant of the fact
that pagans did actually know, had known in the past, and
in the future would know God as a loving father quite independently of his Gospel. Or one might explain it qualita-
tively by saying Jesus meant that he knew of no one who
knew the Father as profoundly and intimately as he himself
did. Certainly Jesus brought a new intimacy and universality into the concept of the divine fatherhood which shocked
his Pharisaic opponents. But in any case what objective
standard of measurement is there to determine how well
anyone knows the Father?

Did Jesus imply that no one can be saved unless he
shares *to the full* the whole wealth of Jesus' knowledge of
God? His first disciples shared it,[96] but have all Christians
done so ever since? If not, then many Christians with a sub-
Christlike apprehension of and relation to God will be lost.
On the other hand millions of non-Christians who love, do,
in their loving, know God, if Jesus' teaching about love in
the Sermon on the Mount, the Last Judgment, and the role
of love in John's first letter (unless it can be established
that John believed that only Christians can love) is taken
at face value.[97] Whichever explanation one prefers, the unqualified exclusiveness of Jesus' knowledge of the Father
disappears.

A comparable crucial passage is in John's Gospel: "I
am the way, the truth, and the life; no one comes to the
Father but by me."[98] The usual interpretation of this passage is that no one can be saved who doesn't accept Jesus'
death as the atonement for his sin. But in view of the highly
interpretive character of this Gospel it has been argued that
the saying is an original tribute to the felt uniqueness of

Jesus given by an early Christian preacher, which has been metamorphosed into an utterance from Jesus' mouth. But even if Jesus spoke the words, their soteriological exclusiveness seems exegetically unwarranted. Here again there are alternative interpretations. First, the fact that he is the way, the truth, and the life does not semantically require that he be the *only* way, truth, and life, any more than the answer to a motorist, "Yes, this is the way to New York" requires that there be no other routes. As we have noted, the history of religions attests that men of various faiths have found in varying degree the way to, the truth about, and life with the Father quite independently of Jesus.

Again, if Jesus believed he was the Messiah and had his messiahship in mind, he was justified in striking an exclusivistic note. To the Jew no more than one Messiah was conceivable; and without a Messiah there was no salvation for Israel. But since the messiahship was originally an ethnocentric role, Jesus cannot be conceived as competing with founders of other faiths; and the statement might well read "No Jew can come to the Father but by Me." If, however, Jesus had in mind the superiority of his own unique intuitions of the nature of God, then he would be justified in meaning something like this: "No one can appreciate the fatherliness of God *as I know it* unless he follows my way, accepts my truth, and shares my life with God." This could be said without excluding from heaven those who knew the fatherhood differently or less fully than Jesus did. Among those who stand in God's presence in eternity there may well be those who knew God less well on earth than some of their fellows did. Is this not an implication of the admonition to all believers "to lead a life . . . increasing in the knowledge of God?"[99] In any case by this affirmation Jesus is not damning to hell those who have never heard of him, or, having heard, do not understand the fatherhood of God in precisely Jesus' terms, or whether, having heard or not, think of God primarily as compassionate "ruler" as in Islam, as loving "mother" as Ramakrishna did, as "father-mother" as Christian Scientists do, or even as "beyond personality" as do supra-theistic Vedantism, Buddhism and Tillichian neo-orthodoxy.

The fact that the Apostle Peter, a few weeks after the resurrection experiences, declared of Jesus, "and there is salvation in no one else, for there is no other name under heaven given among men by which we must be saved"[100] does not prove Jesus to be God's only savior for mankind. Peter may have meant merely that *for Jews* there was no other soteriological option than the crucified Jesus whom God had made their Lord and Messiah. Certainly this was the view of the early Jerusalem Church and its Ebionite successors,[101] who extended the sole saviorhood of Jesus to Gentiles as well, but only on condition that they first become Jews.[102] Peter may even have meant, though this seems doubtful because of his ethnocentrism, that Jesus was also the only savior of the whole human race.

In any case the assertion is the opinion of a fallible human being (unless one accepts the Roman Catholic dogma of papal infallibility) expressed in the ambiguous language of an historically less than perfectly trustworthy literary record. For a man who was patently mistaken about the imminent return of Christ to save men could be ignorant about the scope of that salvation. Peter was an uneducated fisherman. He could scarcely have known that Zoroastrianism, Plato and Stoicism taught the loving fatherhood of God long before the birth of Jesus; or that quite independently of the Christian Gospel a religion of faith in the grace of a personal God was emerging in India as reflected by the Bhagavadgita.

Several other extraordinary claims also call for analysis. There is Jesus' claim to preexistence, which is elaborated as preexistent agent of creation by such biblical writers as the author of John's Gospel, chapter one,[103] by Paul,[104] and by the author of Hebrews.[105] Jesus' own assertions found only in John are: "Before Abraham was born, I am"[106] and "my glory which thou hast given me . . . before the foundation of the world."[107] The claim to personal pre-existence is, however, by no means unique with Jesus. It is the presupposition of Hinduism and Buddhism and taught by Plato, the Pythagoreans and the ancient Egyptians. There is a Jewish tradition of the preexistence of the Messiah found in Fourth Ezra, Ethiopic Enoch, the later Baraithas of the Talmud, the Targum on Zechariah 4:7, and in the later Midrashim[108] It has been held by such Christian thinkers as the great Origen and the English philosopher J. E. McTaggart.

Is it sufficient to counter these facts with the rejoinder, "But only Jesus' claim is valid"? To answer this question in the affirmative one must invalidate all rival claims and solve the whole problem of the historical accuracy of the Fourth Gospel—a project into which we cannot enter here. But it is relevant to inquire whether Jesus' assertions stem from his mystical experience, or are the writer's reading back into his mind and mouth—God's "word" (logos) that created the universe as recorded in Genesis; the Philonian logos-creator; or the Gnostic emanation doctrine—all of which are also reflected in Colossians and Hebrews? However one interprets Jesus' assertions, they do not make him ipso facto deity or absolutely unique among his fellowmen.

Moreover, as Son of Man he claims the authority to forgive sin.[109] Here again he could not appeal to messianic precedent, for nowhere in Jewish apocalyptic does the Messiah perform this function. So the scribes were understandably shocked when Jesus said to the paralytic, "My son your sins are forgiven,"[110] But Jesus deliberately refused to fit the anticipated messianic pattern. If he seems to have accepted the messianic title, he filled it with the new role his Father in Heaven directed him to play.

It is hazardous at our temporal and cultural distance

from him to describe his messianic consciousness much beyond his obvious rejection of the role of political-social
savior of the Jews. But certain of his attitudes toward forgiveness are revealed in his teachings. Certainly he agreed
with his critics that only God could forgive sins. But he
disagreed over who had the right to speak for God by declaring when the conditions for forgiveness had been met.
The scribes believed that only the divinely ordained priesthood could, when the legal sacrifices had been performed,
absolve the sinner in God's name.

But Jesus stood in the prophetic tradition of Amos,
Micah, Isaiah, Jeremiah, Jonah, the Testaments of the
Twelve Patriarchs, and Hillel—which proclaimed that true
penitence was enough; that the only sacrifice pleasing to
God was "a broken and a contrite heart."[111] Speaking thus
as a prophet and, in a sense, as Son of Man, a representative
of the spiritual democracy of all men, he challenged the
ecclesiastical vested interest of the Jewish priesthood. So
when he intuited faith and humility in the sick man, he declared his sins forgiven.[112]

And it is important to note that he does not say "*I*
forgive your sins;" rather, using the passive voice, he says,
"Your sins *are forgiven*;" that is, by God. God alone dis-
penses forgiveness from heaven, but as Son of Man, Jesus
claimed authority on earth to speak for God when the conditions for forgiveness had been met. Other incidents support this view. To the sinful woman who anointed his feet
at the Pharisee's dinner, he said, "Your sins are forgiven;"
but only after he had observed her faith, her penitence, and
the loving gratitude which was evidence that she had already
experienced forgiveness.[113] In the historically dubious story
of the adulteress he said when he sensed her contrition,
"Neither do I condemn you; go and do not sin again."[114]
Finally, he extended his Son of Man authority to declare
sins forgiven to Peter and to all the rest of his faithful

disciples.[115] We conclude: the authority to declare that a man's sins are forgiven by God belongs to any follower of Jesus if he sees true penitence in the sinner.

Again, Jesus claimed authority as Son of Man and Son of God to judge the living and the dead at the last day, to pass sentence on the wicked and to reward the righteous,[116] functions which orthodox Judaism had reserved to God himself, since the Messiah is no more than a man. Yet there is precedent for this function of the Messiah in the noncanonical First Enoch, particularly chapters 45, 51, 62, 69. And the derivation from it of Jesus' story of his presiding at the Last Judgment is impressive. But the authority of the Son of Man in both the biblical and pseudepigraphical accounts is the same—a delegation from God. As John put it, "the Father . . . has given him authority to execute judgment because he is the Son of Man."[117]

Moreover it is not Jesus' arbitrary, personal fiat which judges; it is his teachings which will judge at the last day.[118] And the teachings themselves are not his own but given to him by the Father.[119] To summarize and conclude: Jesus' claim that he will judge the living and the dead at the last day is not a claim to deity; nor does it give him a monopoly of judgment, as evidenced by Paul's rebuke to the Corinthians, "Do you not know that we are to judge angels?"[120] All men are judged by the light they see and the truth they hear, whether these be mediated by conscience, the Torah, Zoroaster, Laotze, Confucius, the Buddha, Krishna, or Jesus.

Yet again, could any but God declare "Heaven and earth will pass away, but my words will not pass away?"[121] It is understood of course that "heaven" refers to the physical universe and not to the eternal abode of God and his redeemed. But this sweeping declaration is also made for the Torah by orthodox Jews, and Jesus concurred when he declared," till heaven and earth pass away not an iota, not

a dot will pass from the law until all is accomplished."[122]
It is made for the Koran:

> The Quran is not a temporary wonder. . . . It is the
> truth, the truth which proves itself, and while it appeals
> to reason it transcends reason and thus shows its divine
> origin.

> It is a fact, stable and durable, which remains un-
> changed and eternally present.[123]

> It is the final revelation . . . given . . . to all men
> everywhere.[124]

It is also asserted of the Vedas:

> The source of the Vedas is only God, the divine foun-
> tainhead of all knowledge. God revealed the Vedas to
> the Primary Creator, Brahma, and through him the
> earliest sages and their pupils, the "See-ers" saw the
> eternally existing Vedas.[125]

The intent of Jesus' assertion is of course to immortal-
ize the teachings within the Aramaic words he spoke; and
in so far as they are *true* they are imperishably true. But
the truth of some of them, particularly in the areas of cosmology and eschatology, is questioned by sincerely committed Christians as well as by non-Christians. We list some
of these: that God will torture in hell forever all who do
not believe in Jesus and who die unrepentant;[126] that the
word "Satan" stands for an evil personal being, God's arch-
enemy on earth;[127] that much illness and insanity is caused
by discarnate evil spirits or demons.[128] Others are convinced
that history has proven Jesus mistaken in his declaration
that the Messianic Kingdom would be established before the
twelve disciples completed their Palestinian mission of
preaching and healing,[129] and that he would return to earth
on the clouds of heaven with his angels within the lifetime
of some who heard him speak.[130]

Biblical criticism has made many of this generation

unsure whether Jesus actually uttered such teachings; and if he did, whether he meant them literally or only figuratively, as teaching devices to establish rapport and motivate good behavior. It is argued by some liberals that in order to communicate meaningfully with his first century Jewish audience, Jesus deliberately used the prevailing cosmology, demonology, eschatology and apocalyptic although, being ahead of his time, he did not personally subscribe to them. Others, such as Schweitzer, believe him to be strictly a child of his time and culture and hence unable to transcend its thought forms. All we can say with assurance is that if he meant such "words" literally, they *have* "passed away" from contemporary Christian faith.

Finally, consider Jesus' claim justifying the world mission of his followers: "All authority in Heaven and on earth has been given to me. Go therefore and make disciples of all nations."[131] Could anyone less than God exercise "all authority in Heaven and on earth"? On earth perhaps, but hardly in Heaven. But here again Jesus is subordinate to God; his authority is only delegated. And it would seem that the rendering of "full" authority rather than "all" authority, as in the Goodspeed and New English Bibles, is preferable. "All" authority suggests that God has abdicated in favor of Jesus, while "full" authority indicates only that Jesus received *enough* authority to commission his disciples.

The use of "all" carries still another implication, that of exclusiveness viz., that no other religious leader has the right to spread his faith. Islam, Buddhism, Vedantism, Bahaism lack divine authorization to evangelize; their work is contrary to the will of God. This is the view of some Christian apologists.

For example: "There can be no reconciliation of the Gospel with other centers of faith except as those other centers abdicate and acknowledge the sovranty of God in Christ."[132] And again:

> The Catholic Church is the only organization authorized
> by God to teach religious truth and to conduct public
> religious worship. . . . Any religious organization which
> is separated from the Catholic Church . . . lacks the
> approval and authorization of God.
>
> From this it follows that . . . no one has a real right to
> accept any religion save the Catholic religion.[133]

Such views should be rejected for they deny the basic
freedom and responsibility given to man by God. Man has
the right to be wrong, to commit sin, to "go to hell" as well
as to be right, to obey God and to go to heaven.

The historic facts are that each founder of a new religion has, like Jesus, felt called, authorized and commissioned by the Highest to the task of witnessing to the truth
revealed to him and, in spite of all opposition, promulgating
it personally, and/or through his disciples. Ikhnaton, Moses,
Zoroaster, Mahavira, the Buddha, Mohammed, Nanak, Baha-
'u'llah,—each relinquished security and privilege to serve
and publish the will of God as a personal mandate to him.

Some argue that no one but Christ has been divinely
called to reconcile men to God, all other claimants to this
calling being insincere or self-deluded; certainly they are
God's enemies, as a contemporary Christian scholar has
written: "All non-biblical religions belong to one and the
same category—sin."[134] "They actually lead men away from
God and hold them captive from God."[135] Such a conception
of divine revelation can hardly be more antithetical to the
view which sees the life-transforming work of God's spirit
in every human sense of guilt, every concern for the well-
being of others, every aspiration toward self-transcendance
and hunger for cosmic meaning and peace. But the nature
and scope of revelation was treated *more fully,* earlier.[136]

DO HIS MIRACLES PROVE HIS DEITY?

The miracle-working power of Jesus is of course no
evidence of his unique divinity. For every kind of miracle

performed by Jesus had already been performed by some Old Testament character, except only the virgin birth. And Jesus' contemporaries, the Pharisees, could cast out demons.[137] Miracles are recorded among the Egyptians and Greeks. Jesus commissioned his disciples to perform miracles, including the raising of the dead,[138] and predicted that whoever believed in him would perform even greater works than Jesus' own.[139] Christian history has verified that prediction in large measure from the apostolic miracles recorded in Acts down to Roman Catholic Lourdes, Protestant Oral Roberts, and Christian Science. The founders or their associates in the twelve main living religions are credited with miracles; and six of their founders or outstanding devotees beside Jesus, with supernatural or virgin birth: viz, Zoroaster, the Buddha, Mahavira, Krishna, Laotze and Ramakrishna.

DID THE WORSHIP OF JESUS IMPLY HIS DEITY?

Do not biblical assertions that men "worshipped" Jesus indicate his deity? No, the answer is "not necessarily." The principal Greek word for "worship" in the New Testament is   , which means to "kiss (the hand or the ground) toward; . . . It is to render homage to men, angels, demons, the devil, 'the beast,' idols and to God."[140] This word is directed most often to Jesus and to God, but also to ordinary men. For example, Cornelius the Roman Centurion worshipped Peter,[141] and the king in Jesus' parable is worshipped by his servant.[142]

When it is directed to Jesus as by the man healed of congenital blindness,[143] it is rendered "worshipped" by the R.S.V., Authorized, and Phillips translations, and by the more literal "bowed before him" (New English Bible), and "fell on his knees before him" (Goodspeed translation). Parenthetically, if this grateful man regarded Jesus as the Messiah, as the passage suggests, his worship would not

προσκυνέω

have been deistic; for no Jew thought of the Messiah as a divine being. Hence the status attributed to Jesus by his disciples and various beneficiaries when they "worship" him will vary according to what each worshipper thinks of him: as incarnation of God, Son of God, Messiah, miracle worker, prophet, inspiring teacher.

To summarize Jesus' exclusivistic sayings and sweeping religious claims: He did not claim to be the world's only savior. The seeming exclusiveness of his and others' soteriological claims for him may be interpreted as referring to the Jews alone; in his role of Messiah he was *their* only hope of salvation. Or if these claims had universal reference, they may indicate that the speaker was ignorant of God's revealing and saving work outside of the Mediterranean world, and illustrate every man's propensity to regard his own conviction of a truth as valid and normative for all men. Or, however sincerely believed, they are not in fact unique, since comparable claims had been made or were to be made by others.

DO HIS ASSERTIONS OF ONENESS WITH THE FATHER PROVE HIS DEITY?

Jesus' assertion of oneness with the Father needs special extended comment. What he is asserting in such comments as "I and the Father are one," "He that hath seen me hath seen the Father," "I am in the Father and the Father in me," is neither the dogma of the trinity nor the assertion of a monopolistic incarnation. It is rather an historical demonstration of ideal God-man relationship. It is also the center and goal of mystical experience in all high religions which, at its apogee, is the bliss of union with ultimate reality and goodness. The great mystics of all faiths have made comparable assertions, and all other persons may, and ought to make them. For the goal of life is the complete actualization of human potentiality in union with

God, its source and destiny. It is an experience so transcendent that man's earth-bound consciousness participates
in cosmic consciousness; an obedience so complete that one
knows it is God in him who does his will through the human
will; a love so consuming that the finite self seems to be
swallowed up in the infinite Self.

It is a common comment on discussion of such mystic
oneness with the divine that Jesus was either asserting he
was God when he made such claims, or else he was insane;
and since his total creative impact upon the human race
could not have been the work of a lunatic, he must actually
have been "very God of very God." The inference is commonly drawn that for any other person to make similar
claims is to write himself off as demented regardless of any
spiritual uplift his life may have given to others. How
readily one forgets, if indeed it is ever realized, that comparable claims have been made by a long tradition of Christian mystics, among whom several are especially noteworthy.
Meister Eckhart wrote, paralleling the high claims of Jesus:

> When the soul achieves this [union with the uncreated],
> it loses its identity, it absorbs God and is reduced to
> nothing.[144]

> The soul imbibing God turns into God as the drop be-
> comes the ocean.[145]

> Before the creation of the world Am I.[146]

> God made all things through me, when I had my exist-
> ence in the unfathomable ground of God.[147]

> God is the same one that I am (*tat tvam asi.*)[148]

> God in the fullness of his Godhead dwells eternally in
> his image (the soul itself).[149]

Likewise Suso:

> In an ineffable manner, it happens to him as to a drunk
> man, who forgets himself, is no longer himself. He is
> quite dead to himself, and is entirely lost in God, has
> passed into Him, and has become one spirit with Him

in all respects, just as a little drop of water that is
poured into a large quantity of wine.[150]

and Walt Whitman:

Thought of the Infinite—the All, Be thou my God.[151]

Swiftly I shrivel at the thought of God,
At Nature and its wonders, Time and Space and Death,
But that I, turning, call to thee, O Soul, thou actual me.
And lo! thou gently masterest the orbs,
Thou makest Time, smilest content at Death,
and fillest, swellest full, the vastnesses of Space.[152]

What do you suppose I would intimate to you in a
      hundred ways,
but that man or woman is as good as God?
And that there is no God any more divine than yourself?
And that is what the oldest and newest myths
finally mean?[153]

Jewish mysticism may be represented by Abulafia, the
thirteenth century Kabbalistic mystic:

The man who has felt the divine touch and perceived
its nature is no longer separated from his
Master [here evidently meaning God], and behold
he is in his Master, and his Master is he, for
he is so intently united to Him that he cannot
by any means be separated from Him.[154]

And Buber, describing Hasidic mysticism, quotes several of
its Zaddicks:

Men think they pray before God, but it is not so, for
prayer itself is divinity.[155] There is a very high holiness; if one enters it, one becomes detached from all
being.[156]

In Islam the Sufi mystic Al Hallaj was crucified for declaring, "I am the truth," and "If thou seest me thou
seest Him [God], if thou seest Him, thou seest us
both."[157] The Sufi, Bayazid of Khurasan, is said to have
said " 'I' and 'God' is a denial of the Unity of God . . .
for tis God that speaks with my tongue, and I have

vanished."[158] The Bab, herald of Bahaism, was executed by a firing squad for such utterances as,"I am the Primal Point from which have been generated all created things . . . I am the countenance of God, whose splendor can never be obscured, the light of God whose radiance can never fade."[159] Bahu'a'llah, the "Manifestation of God" who founded Bahaism, wrote "There hath not been in my soul but the truth, and in myself naught could be seen but God."[160] And although God was conceived suprapersonally, or impersonally by them, analogous claims have been made by Plotinus, the Greek founder of neo-Platonism:

In this seeing we neither hold an object [external to ourselves] nor trace distinction; there is no two. The man is changed, no longer himself nor self-belonging; he is merged with the Supreme, sunken into it, one with it.[161]

. . . wrought to splendour, brimmed with intellectual light, become that very light, pure buoyant, unburdened, raised to Godhood, or, better, knowing its Godhood.[162]

And by Suzuki, the outstanding interpreter of Zen Buddhism to the West, who describes the mystic experience of satori:

In *satori* there is always what we may call a sense of the Beyond; the experience indeed is my own but I feel it to be rooted elsewhere. The individual shell in which my personality is so solidly encased explodes . . . my individuality . . . melts away into something indescribable, . . . the feeling that one has arrived finally at the destination.[163] . . . . It means an infinite expansion of the individual, . . .[164] must make one feel above all things intensely exalted.[165]

And by Chuangtze, the Taoist mystic:

Only the truly intelligent understand this principle of the identity of all things.[166]

The universe and I came into being together; and I, and everything therein are one.[167]

We are embraced in the obliterating unity of God.[168]

And by the Rishis who wrote the Upanishads; and by Rama-krishna, the outstanding Hindu mystic of modern times:

[Ramakrishna] : God alone dwells inside this body.

M [a disciple] : you tell us that you and the Mother [the goddess Kali] are one. Likewise, Christ said, "I and My Father are one."

M : I feel that Christ, Chaitanyadeva [a bhaki saint], and yourself—all three are one and the same. It is the same person that has become all these three.
[Ramakrishna] : Yes, yes! One! One! It is indeed one. Don't you see that it is He alone who dwells here in this way [pointing with his finger to his body].[169]

But still more impressive is the realization that such one-ness with the Supreme is affirmed by millions of Vedantists when they say "Brahman is Atman," thus affirming the essential divinity of man; and by millions of Buddhists when they affirm that one divine Buddha nature in them makes them one with the Ultimate Reality (whether Dharmakaya, Bhutatathata or Amitabha).

Such mysticism is the spiritual center and apogee of the great world faiths, and its practitioners are not insane unless one is willing to regard Jesus and St. Paul as demonic and mad respectively, as their detractors insisted. For Paul, who had achieved mystic oneness with Christ[170] and an ineffable, supra-terrestrial experience in the third heaven[171] shared the stoic view which describes union with God as the birthright of all men,[172] as Jesus declared it to be for his disciples.[173] Paul considered it the business of the Church to help every Christian to attain "to the measure of the stature of the fullness of Christ,"[174] and asserted that all Christians were actually undergoing that transformation progressively.[175] But would not failure to attain to Jesus' mystical relationship with God be a falling short of the

measure of the stature of Christ's fullness? The writer
of John's first letter is very specific about the reality of
such God-man inter-immanence.[176] Paul Tillich concurs in
the belief of man's essential oneness with God. He writes,
"Essential humanity includes the union of God and
man"[177] "In Jesus as the Christ the eternal unity of
God and man has become historical reality. . . . This event
could not have taken place if there had not been an eternal
unity of God and man within the Divine life."[178]

But Tillich does not go as far as Paul, for he rules out
the possibility that Christians can attain to Christ's *fullness*. By participation in the New Being through faith in
Jesus as the Christ, they may approach yet never achieve
his complete union with and absolute transparency to God.
In Vedantism, however, as in Paul, anyone may achieve full
union with the Supreme Being; though, unlike Paul, there
is presupposed for him a succession of earth lives for the
completion of the process. Such union differs also in being
commonly thought of as the absolute identification of the
finite self, or Atman, with the Absolute Self, or Brahman,
by following one of several paths: Jnana, Karma, and
Bhakti Marga. And in Buddhism any man may achieve it by
realizing and cultivating the Buddha nature within him till
all the ego with its compulsive cravings is burnt out. In
achieving his goal of desireless selfless bliss or Nirvana, he
may follow the Hinayana path of self-purification or the
Mahayana path of faith and loving service.

MYSTIC UNION AND THE PROBLEM OF THE
ONE AND THE MANY

If it be objected that for Jesus and most Christian mystics the ultimate union is a personal I-Thou, subject-object
communion, while for monistic Vedantism and Buddhism it
is a man-God fusion into an identity transcending personal
encounter and the subject-object polarity, several things

must be noted. In the first place it is clear that in Jesus' experience he was not obliterated in the Father. Other Christian mystics, especially of the neo-Platonic persuasion such as Eckhart, sometimes speak as though they had done so, as we have noted.

Yet in one place Eckhart seems to say that in the mystic experience one reaches a point of intuition where he looks both ways at once—at his own creaturely, individual experience of bliss, and at the all-inclusive Divine experience of it.

This latter conception is a bhakti or religion-of-love protest against the loss of self through absorption. It insists that there is more religious value in two selves (God and man) in creative communion, than in a situation where one self, God, absorbs the other, man, and thus fixates himself in sterile loneliness. As the poet Ramprasad expressed it, "I like eating sugar, but I have no desire to become sugar."[179] This dualistic version of the samadhi experience is designated as "savikalpa" (by contrast to the non-dualistic "nirvikalpa") and is described by Zimmer as "a fully conscious state of absorption founded on an ecstatic identification of two entities that are still felt to be distinct."[180] Radhakrishnan puts it thus: "In the moment of its highest insight, the self becomes aware not only of its own existence but of the existence of an omnipresent spirit of which it is, as it were, a focussing;"[181] and he quotes William James as saying, "In mystic states we become one with the Absolute and we become aware of our oneness."[182]

The nirvikalpa advocates criticize the mystic's enjoyment of two-in-one bliss as egocentric, a short circuiting of the "bliss" of final self-abandonment. In addition to bliss, they seem to demand their own rational explanation of it. But how do they know that the Absolute may not prefer two-in-one bliss to his own solitary bliss?

An illustration from Hartshorne's panentheistic phil-

osophy, even if only a crude analogy, may be clarifying on
this point.[183] The God-universe relationship is like the mind-
body relationship. Though I am in my instincts, organs, and
separate cells and they are in me, neither of us is flatly the
other; but there is a mutual participation in an organic
whole. Though God is in his creatures and they in him,
neither of the pair is flatly the other; but there is a mutual
participation and self-realization in the divine whole. Now
if a single one of my body cells or organs should develop
the requisite awareness, it might share a part of my mind's
experience in addition to maintaining its own private and
more limited experience. So in *satori*, enlightenment, and
samadhi, the individual subject which is "I" may share part
of the experience of the supreme, all-inclusive Subject in
addition to, and while retaining, its own self-experience as
one of the included subjects.

To prove that pantheistic mysticism is false because
failing to meet the ethical criterion, one would have to demonstrate that the mystical pantheism of the "I am God"
identity is per se incapable of generating a genuine ethic
like that of the "God and I" unity of classical theism. But
the difficulty here is that some bona fide theists are immoral
and some pantheists are saints, as well as vice versa. Again,
that some persons may move from one experience to the
other or, as noted earlier by Radhakrishnan, James and
Hartshorne, may blend the two experiences in a single
awareness.

From the standpoint of logic it is incontestable that
contradictories cannot both be true. The laws of non-contra-
diction and excluded middle hold for all human thinking.
Must we then declare either theism or pantheism to be
false? But these alleged contradictories may be merely a
verbal paradox, logically mutually exclusive, but resolvable
existentially in the actual experience of living. Why may
they not be in a class with other paradoxes: freedom vs.

determinism; mind vs. body; idealism vs. materialism; energy as wave vs. energy as particle; God as absolute vs. God as relative; Jesus as divine vs. Jesus as human? And what shall we say of St. Paul's declaration: ". . . work out your own salvation with fear and trembling; for God is at work in you both to will and to work for his good pleasure."[184] Is this a violation of logic or a valid human experience? To conclude: may not pantheism and theism be valid aspects of a higher synthesis which transcends our logical categories?

In any event the psychological problem in the nirvikalpa view seems insoluble. Gotama's doctrine of *anatta* (no soul) would seem to leave no human subject to experience nirvana, yet nirvana is emphatically a human experience. Whether there are a multiplicity of such experiencers or only one, the Absolute, or some concept-baffling combination of the two, remains the hoary unsolved metaphysical problem of the one and the many.

We conclude, then, that Jesus' assertion of oneness with God does not make him univocally God; for any union presupposes two who are united. And they do not make him the only example of incarnation, or an absolutely unique and final revelation. They seem to indicate rather that Jesus was the first great mystic in Jewish history who, in a religious culture which conceived God as external, unapproachable, and transcendent, discovered that he is immanent and intimate, "nearer to us than breathing, closer than hands and feet;" and that eternal life or heaven is a state in which we find our lives by uniting them with his life.

FOOTNOTES FOR CHAPTER FOUR

1 John 14:28.
2 Mark 13:32.
3 Mark 10:18; Luke 18:19.
4 John 5:19.
5 John 5:26.
6 John 17:3.
7 John 20:17.
8 Matt. 27:46.
9 Rom. 1:7.
10 1 Cor. 3:23.
11 1 Cor. 8:6, Cf. Col. 1:16; John 1:3, 10; Heb. 1:1-2.
12 1 Cor. 11:3.
13 1 Cor. 15:28. (New English Bible).
14 Col. 1:15; cf. 2 Cor. 4:4.
15 Eph. 1:17.
16 1 Tim. 2:5.
17 Col. 2:9; cf. 1:19.
18 Phil. 2:5-7.
19 See pp. 126-127.
20 Epistle to the Ephesians, chapter 18.
21 Epistle to the Philippians 12:2.
22 John 20:24.
23 Luke 3:38.
24 Cf. John 5:26.
25 John 14:9.
26 John 10:30.
27 McGiffert, *op. cit.*
28 Exod. 4:22; Hos. 1:1; Mal. 2:10.
29 Ps. 103:13.
30 Ps. 2:7.
31 Ps. 82:6.
32 John 10:34-36.
33 Gen. 6:2, 4; Job 1:6, Ps. 89:6-7.
34 Wisd. of Sol. 14:3; Sirach 23:1, 4; Jubilees 1:22-25.
35 John 8:41; 44.
36 Luke 3:38.
37 John 1:14, 18; 3:16, 18; 1 John 4:9.
38 1 Sam. 20:31.
39 Luke 20:36.
40 John 17:12.
41 Luke 3:38.
42 Ps. 2:7.
43 Acts 13:33; Heb. 1:5; 5:5.
44 Mark 1:11; Matt. 3:16; Luke 3:22.
45 Mark 9:7; Matt. 17:5; Luke 9:35.
46 Though the preponderance of manuscript evidence favors the present reading, the Psalm 2:7 reading *is* found in D, a, b, c, d, ff2, 1, r. It is cited by Augustine, Justin, Clement, Methodius and

Epiphanius; and it is preferred by W. Manson, Zahn, Kloster-
mann, Harnak, Moffatt and Streeter.

[47] Heb. 1:5; 5:5.
[48] Rom. 1:4.
[49] Matt. 1:18; Luke 1:35.
[50] John 1:32-34.
[51] Mark 1:11.
[52] Luke 3:22.
[53] Matt. 11:27.
[54] Gal. 3:26; 4:5; Eph. 1:5; John 1:12.
[55] Matt. 5:45-48.
[56] Mark 3:35.
[57] 1 John 4:7.
[58] Matt. 5:44-45.
[59] Matt. 5:9.
[60] John 8:43.
[61] Acts 10:2, 22, 34.
[62] John 1:12.
[63] John 20:17.
[64] John 20:17.
[65] Mark 3:35.
[66] Matt. 5:44-45.
[67] Matt. 11:27; John 15:15.
[68] John 14:12.
[69] John 5:28-29.
[70] John 16:26-27; 17:23.
[71] John 17:14, 16.
[72] John 17:22-24.
[73] Rom. 8:17.
[74] John 20:21.
[75] Matt. 10:5-14; Mark 6:7-13, 30; Luke 10:1-20; John 17:18.
[76] Mark 8:34-35; Luke 14:27; Matt. 16:24-25.
[77] Matt. 16:19; 18:18; John 20:23.
[78] John 14:23; 17:21-23; 1 John 4:12-13, 15-16, as the Johannine
letter writer understands that oneness.
[79] John 13:20.
[80] John 14:28.
[81] John 14:10.
[82] John 16:26-27.
[83] John 8:12.
[84] John 6:48.
[85] John 11:25.
[86] Matt. 5:14.
[87] John 6:63.
[88] John 5:28-29; 6:39, 40.
[89] John 5:21, 26; 6:39.
[90] See *supra*, page 71, note 14.
[91] John 11:24.
[92] Col. 2:12-13; 3:1; Eph. 2:1, 4-6.

93 Acts 10:35.
94 John 17:3.
95 Matt. 11:27.
96 See *supra*, p. 109, note 67.
97 Matt. 5:44-45, 25:34-36; 1 John 4:7-8, 12, 16.
98 John 14:6.
99 Col. 1:10.
100 Acts 4:12.
101 Acts 5:31.
102 Acts 15:1; 10:28, 34, 35.
103 John 1:1-3, 10, 15, 30.
104 Col. 1:15-17.
105 Heb. 1:2.
106 John 8:58.
107 John 17:24.
108 Cf. Joseph Klausner, *The Messianic Idea in Israel* (New York: The Macmillan Co., 1955), p. 359.
109 Mark 2:10; Matt. 9:6; Luke 5:24.
110 Mark 2:5.
111 Ps. 51:17.
112 Luke 5:20.
113 Luke 7:36-50.
114 John 8:11.
115 Matt. 16:19; 18:18; John 20:23.
116 John 5:22; 26:27, 30; Matt. 25:31-46.
117 John 5:26-27.
118 John 12:47-49.
119 John 7:16.
120 1 Cor. 6:3.
121 Matt. 24:35; Mark 13:31; Luke 21:33.
122 Matt. 5:18.
123 Mohammed Abd Allah Draz, in *Islam, The Straight Path*, ed. Kenneth W. Morgan (New York: The Ronald Press Co., 1958), p. 16.
124 Mohammed Rasjidi, *ibid.*, p. 403.
125 V. Raghavan, in *The Religion of the Hindus*, ed. Kenneth W. Morgan (New York: The Ronald Press Co., 1953), p. 265.
126 Matt. 25:41, 46; 18:8; Luke 16:26.
127 Matt. 4:10; Luke 10:18; 13:16; 23:3, 31; John 13:17.
128 Mark 1:21-37; 5:1-20; 9:14-27.
129 Matt. 10:23.
130 Matt. 26:64; Mark 8:38; 9:1.
131 Matt. 28:18-19.
132 Edmund Perry, *The Gospel in Dispute* (Garden City, New York: Doubleday and Co., Inc., 1958), p. 220.
133 Francis J. Connell, "The Catholic Position on Freedom of Worship," *Columbia*, Dec. 1943, XXIII, No. 5, p. 6.
134 Perry, *op cit.*, p. 106.
135 *Ibid.*, p. 83.

[136] See *supra*, Chapter 2, Section 4.

[137] Luke 11:19.

[138] Matt. 10:8.

[139] John 14:12.

[140] International Standard Bible Encyclopedia, p. 3110.

[141] Acts 10:25.

[142] Matt. 18:26.

[143] John 9:38.

[144] Raymond B. Blakney, trans., *Meister Eckhart*, First Torch Book Ed. (New York: Harper and Bros., 1957), p. 89.

[145] Rudolf Otto, *Mysticism East and West*, trans. B. L. Bracey and R. C. Payne, Living Age (New York: Meridian Books, Inc., 1951), p. 22.

[146] *Ibid.*, p. 203.

[147] *Ibid.*, p. 100.

[148] *Ibid.*, p. 12.

[149] *Ibid.*

[150] Henry Suso, *Little Book of Eternal Wisdom and Little Book of Truth*, trans. J. M. Clark (London: Faber and Faber, Ltd., 1953), p. 185.

[151] Walt Whitman, *Leaves of Grass:* With Autobiography (Philadelphia: David McKay, 1900), p. 439.

[152] *Ibid.*, p. 353.

[153] *Ibid.*, p. 94.

[154] G. G. Scholem, *Major Trends in Jewish Mysticism* (London, 1955). p. 140 f., quoted in Sidney Spencer, *Mysticism in World Religion* (Baltimore: Penguin Books, 1963), p. 188.

[155] Martin Buber, *The Legend of Baal Shem* (New York: Harper and Brothers, 1955), p. 27.

[156] *Ibid.*, p. 21.

[157] John B. Noss, *Man's Religions*, rev. ed. (New York: The Macmillan Co., 1956), pp. 722, 723.

[158] *Ibid.*, p. 722.

[159] George Townshend, *The Promise of All Ages* (Wilmette, Illinois: Bahai Publishing Committee, 1935), p. 135.

[160] J. E. Esslemont, *Baha'u'llah and the New Era*, rev. ed. (New York· The Bahai Publishing Committee, 1937), p. 57.

[161] Plotinus: *The Enneads*, VI 9:10, trans. S. MacKenna, rev. 2nd ed. (London: Faber and Faber, Ltd., 1956.)

[162] *Ibid.*, VI:9:9.

[163] D. T. Suzuki, *Zen Buddhism: Selected Writings* of D. T. Suzuki, ed. William Barrett. Doubleday Anchor Books (Garden City, New York: Doubleday and Co., Inc., 1956), p. 105.

[164] *Ibid.*, p. 107.

[165] *Ibid.*, p. 108.

[166] Chuangtse, in the *Viking Portable World Bible*, ed. Robert O. Ballou (New York: The Viking Press, 1944), p. 553, being selections from *Chuangtzu, Mystic, Moralist, and Social Reformer*, trans. H. A. Giles (London: Bernard Quaritch, 1889).

167 *Ibid.*, p. 554.
168 *Ibid.*, p. 556.
169 S. Nikhilananda, trans. *Ramakrishna: Prophet of New India* (New York: Harper and Brothers, Publishers, 1942), pp. 202, 204, 198 respectively.
170 Gal. 2:20.
171 2 Cor. 12:2-4.
172 Acts 17:28; Eph. 4:6.
173 John 14:20, 17:21-23.
174 Eph. 4:13.
175 2 Cor. 3:18.
176 1 John 3:24, 4:12-16.
177 Tillich, *Systematic Theology*, Vol. 2, p. 94.
178 *Ibid.*, p. 148.
179 S. Nikhilananda, trans., *The Gospel of Sri Ramakrisha* (New York: Ramakrishna Vivekenanda Center, 1942), p. 858.
180 H. Zimmer, *Philosophies of India*, ed. Jos. Campbell (New York: Pantheon Books, 1951), p. 436.
181 S. Radhakrishnan, *An Idealist View of Life*, rev. 2nd ed. (London: George Allen and Unwin Ltd., 1937), p. 103.
182 *Ibid.*, p. 105.
183 Cf. C. Hartshorne, *Man's Vision of God* (Chicago: Willett, Clark, 1941), chap. 5.
184 Phil. 2:12-13.

Chapter V

JESUS AND THE FELLOWSHIP OF FAITHS

6. AGREEMENTS AND DIFFERENCES BETWEEN THE FAITHS

WE CONCLUDE OUR answer to two basic questions: "Was the saving revelation of God in Jesus total, final and absolutely unique?" and "Was he thus the only divine incarnation?" No. The Christian or biblical faith has no monopoly of saving revelation. The basic features of Christian faith are found in the other faiths: the moral standard summarized in the absolute ethic of love; the assurance of personal survival of death; God as a loving person, a father who suffers for and with his human children and forgives, justifies, and saves them by his grace; the redemptive power of divine love demonstrated in the vicarious suffering of a human exemplar; the mystical union of God and man as the goal of life for all men rather than the monopoly of a single God-man; and the insight (grasped by some Christians though not found in Jesus' teachings) that the ultimate reality, although apprehended by man as a personal being, is also, in dimensions of his nature beyond man's apprehension, suprapersonal, beyond the subject-object polarity, and ineffable.

It makes little difference that the several faiths make varying ethical emphases; couch their theologies in different names for God, cultic symbols and myths; exhibit diverse rituals, organize and administer their faith in different structural patterns. For they each have in varying degree (justifying the principle of the analogy of being and of Leibnitz's calculus) what all have in common. One makes explicit what another holds only implicitly. They all cultivate mystical God-man fellowship and union as the *raison d'être* of human existence, and love as its ideal social expression. They all in varying degree save men from egocentric individualism, moral guilt and ontological anxiety to self-transcendance, cosmic reconciliation and religious peace.

A Buddhist scholar, Masutani, has stressed the fact that Christian salvation is salvation through trust in a person, Jesus, because of man's moral impotence. The Japanese term for such dependence is *tariki,* meaning "faith in another's power;"[1] in Hindu parlance it is the cat-hold way of salvation; whereas Buddhist salvation is salvation through right understanding and the practice of true principles taught by the Buddha, needed because of men's ignorance. This is the familiar *jiriki* or "faith in self-power,"[2] which Hinduism terms the monkey-hold way of salvation. But, having pointed out this difference, he goes on to say that the antithesis holds only with respect to Theravada Buddhism. For the Mahayana Pure Land or Amida sects, numerically far larger than Theravada Buddhism, share the Christian concept of salvation by faith in the power of another, in their case, faith in Amitabha.

However, the contrast drawn by Masutani is misleading. It is not between Theravadism and Christianity as such, but between Theravadism and one branch of Christianity —the main line, orthodox, largest branch spearheaded in the modern world by the Reformed churches. For them, salvation is by faith alone. But down the historic stream of Judeo-Christianity flows a smaller current of do-it-yourself salvation. Rising in Judaism's salvation by obedience to Torah, it emerges in the New Testament letter of James and later in Pelagianism. Throughout the following centuries it is evident in the Roman Catholic soteriology of penances and indulgences and, since the Enlightenment, has flowered and spread in religious humanism. This small current within the main stream of Christian thought is the Christian variety of Theravada *jiriki,* faith in self-power.

These two ways of salvation also divide the faith of Hinduism; on the one hand into salvation by intellectual effort as in the Jnana Marga of Advaita Vedantism, or by psychophysical self-discipline as in the regimen of Raja Yoga, or by the good works or cultic practices of Karma Marga; and on the other hand into salvation by the Bhakti Marga of loving devotion to a personal God because of his forgiving and enabling grace. But it is the insight of Hinduism to recognize each way, or darsana, as effective, depending upon differences in individual temperament and psychology. The two ways seem endemic to mankind, ignoring the boundaries that separate cultures and faiths. They seem to complement each other, for faith without works is dead and works without faith are empty. It was St. Paul who nicely reconciled the extremes in his admonition, "work out your own salvation with fear and trembling; for God is at work in you, both to will and to work for his good pleasure."[3] To save a man from drowning, the degree of help given will depend on the amount of strength and will power he possesses. If he has gone down for the third time, or is unconscious and inert, he'll have to be removed bodily from the water and rescusitated by the lifeguard. If he is exhausted and desperate, but conscious and rational, he can cooperate with his rescuer by grasping the life-saver thrown to him. If he is merely weak and confused, he can respond to shouted orders and save himself by swimming in a certain direction or manner. Or, finally, if he is a good swimmer in good condition and familiar with the movements of current and tide, he'll not need help from another when the perilous rip tide threatens to engulf him; he'll merely call upon his own reserves of strength and knowledge.

So, when one is spiritually in extremis, he'll have to be saved wholly by the external power of God, as in transcendental Calvinistic theism. If he is merely in danger, he can save himself by appealing to the moral strength and spiritual wisdom with which God has endowed him, as in immanent theism or humanism. If he is in some condition midway between the two, he'll cooperate with God in effecting his salvation, as in the transcendent-immanent theism presupposed by St. Paul's reconciling words.

Another factor is temperamental. Some persons are congenitally or, by conditioning, self-reliant, activist and optimistic (William James' "healthy-minded" type), and will feel responsibility for their own self-improvement. Others are, for the same reasons, dependent, passive and pessimistic (William James' "sick soul" type), and will not feel saved unless someone else saves them. When these indiviual differentia become dominant in a group, corresponding types of sectarian salvation emerge.

Wherever maximum religious freedom operates, each particular temperamental type will be drawn to the sect providing for its temperamental needs. Without such freedom, the various types will be forced to conform to a collective type of salvation with which they may not be individually congenial. Within Protestant Christianity, for instance, one finds the extremes of humanist groups and hyper-Calvinist groups with gradations between; whereas in Roman Catholic cultures, the type of salvation pattern is rigid and religiously uncongenial both to the extreme salvation-by-election-and-grace alone type and the extreme save-yourself-humanist type.

Still, it is insisted, since Christianity alone has made God's hatred of evil and love for sinners central, it alone is the true faith and it alone can really save men. It is true that Christianity, far more than Hinduism and Buddhism, stresses the personal mode of God and the primacy of love in religion and ethics. On the other hand, the Asian faiths, far more than Christianity, stress the ineffable dimension of God and man's need to detach himself from the world and from his own tyrannical ego. True enough, Christianity, more than the Asian faiths, preaches prophetic resistance to evil, and the religious mandate to make the social structure conform to its ethical ideals and every man's thought and practice conform to its theological and liturgical pattern. But in so doing, Christianity has greatly exceeded the other faiths in the practice of arrogance, intolerance, coercion, and violence. They, on the other hand, have cultivated the philosophical acceptance of the mystery of evil and man's transcendance of it through mystical experience. Hence their world witness, contrary to the Christian witness, has been without the bloodshed of the inquisition and holy war; has been rather a Godlike tolerance of conscientious differences, a Godlike reverence for all life.

Historic Christianity has stressed man's depravity; the Asian faiths, his divinity. Christianity has stressed joy in the victorious struggle against evil; the others, serenity in detachment from it. Christianity meets sin head-on by combatting it through the will and, when this fails, by juridical atonement myths which absolve men from responsibility and penalty for it. The Asian faiths, following the Greek insight, realize that sin's power lies primarily in human ignorance and so meet it by enlarging man's knowledge of his true nature and spiritual resources. They approach sin obliquely, by a feint, by the withdrawal of frontal opposition, by shifting the ground of the struggle from the lower, moralistic to the higher, metaphysical ground; by withdrawing man's motivation for sinning through teaching that the ego goals he so compulsively grasps are as evanescent as morning dew along with the visible world and life itself, and that any enemy whom we would injure is in reality ourselves since we are all parts of the One Spirit, the One Ultimate Being.

In our day orthodox Christianity still seems to be playing a role comparable to that of Peter and the Judaizers of the first century. As they insisted that all non-Jews submit to the Jewish Torah and circumcision as a condition for admittance to the Christian fellowship, so twentieth century orthodoxy is insisting that all non-Christians submit to Christian theology and sacraments as a condition for admittance to fellowship with God. There seems little to choose between the spiritual blindness of these two provincialisms; both are strangers to Jesus' universalism. Jesus did not damn all faiths save faith in himself. Rather, he welcomed all men of faith and Godly living as his spiritual kin—"Whoever does the will of God is my brother and sister and mother."[4] And he proclaimed in principle the divine fellowship of the various ethnic faiths when he declared, "many will come from East and West and sit at table with Abraham, Isaac, and Jacob in the Kingdom of Heaven."[5] "For he that is not against us is for us."[6]

No, Christianity is not true while the other faiths are false; Christianity alone redemptive, and the others escapist or destructive. Each contains truth and error, and is subject to the prostitution and perversion of its pure essence. Each both reveals and conceals the secret of our existence. Each is life-enriching and life-denying. Each draws man toward the Divine. Each makes its contribution and plays its chord in the greatening symphony of the Cosmic Composer.

7. NON-CHRISTIAN FAITHS AS SHARERS IN THE INCARNATION

There is no quantitative, rational or documentary test for the incarnation claim made for Jesus. There is only the intuitive-pragmatic—the final test is experiential. Christians testify that through Jesus they become aware of God, feel the judgment of God yet find peace with God. Ecclesiastical and authoritarian criteria are secondary to and derivative from this. Neither history nor theology can convince men that God was in Christ; but becoming convinced of God through existential encounter with Jesus, they write theology to justify their subjective convictions on rational grounds or in mythological terms. But if this is so with regard to God in Christ, how shall we evaluate the equally experimental avowal by a non-Christian that he has found peace with the Divine through Buddha, Krishna, or Baha'u'llah, and certifies it by the empirical demonstration of what the New Testament regards as the ethical "fruit of the Spirit"[7] in his life? If an incarnation is one through whom the Divine possibilities of life are channeled to men, why should not these others also be termed incarnations?

On the basis of our anlysis of Tillich's view, there never has been an incarnation. But we believe his interpretation to be both too idealistic and too narrow. The religious life, any kind of life for that matter, as it is lived day by day moves in a maze of relativities. Tillich, who is with his fellow existentialist neo-orthodox, a chief publicist of the ambiguities of life and who is also the champion of the relativity of divine revelation, should have gone one step further to recognize the relativity of incarnation. Not only is God what he is in himself as absolute: the ineffable power, ground, and abyss of reality. He is also what he is as related and manifest to men in various cultures through successive generations. And this disclosure to and discovery by man is according to a calculus of revelation. God is known to be immanent in the world bit by bit, here partially, there more fully, but never completely or finally in a single person or event in the space-time process.

God is incarnate throughout the body of the cosmos, for he is united to it all by immanence; but he is more fully and clearly revealed in its higher than in its lower forms— the gradient from the lower to higher being the direction of lesser to greater freedom, sensitivity, rationality, moral responsibility, and creativity. In this hierarchy of the media of revelation, Jesus, say most Christians, stands at the top. But he is not isolated. He is surrounded by spiritual colleagues. revelators, sons of God, other partial incarnations of the Divine Being. He stands with Ikhnaton and Zoroaster, Moses and Jeremiah, Laotse and Motse, Plato and Plotinus, Buddha and Ramakrishna and Gandhi, revealing God's nature and grace to men. And we have reason to believe that in the millenia ahead, other fuller but still partial incarnations will take their stand upon the spiritual shoulders of these, and, in this and other universes, lift the sight and point the way of God's evolving creatures to their high destiny in him.

The view of the incarnation presented here does not distort the true manhood of Jesus; it does not downgrade his personal work or the saving power of his ministry. It does not minimize the fact that "God was in Christ reconciling the world to himself, not counting their trespasses against them and entrusting to us the message of reconciliation."[8] Rather, it widens the scope of God's concern for men by showing that he has not confined his reconciling work to only one place and one time in history, but carries it on in all places and at all times through those whom he selects and commissions to reveal himself.

Jesus did not rule out as false hopes other faiths and paths to goodness and God. An Israelite himself, he yet said of a Roman Centurion's faith, "Believe me, I have never found faith like this even in Israel."[9] Jesus was not jealous of his divine calling. He did not forbid or denounce or depreciate others beside himself who were bidding for the spiritual allegiance of men. Nor should the Church, which is his body. The spirit of the small boy who boasted to a neighbor boy, "My dad can lick your dad," is foreign to the spirit of the Christian message to the non-Christian world. The spiritual leaders of mankind are colleagues, not rivals. Loyalty to Jesus does not require that we speak disparagingly of the others. To paraphrase St. Paul: "So let no one boast invidiously of men. For they all belong to you: whether Zoroaster or Isaiah, Socrates or Confucius, the Rishis or the Buddha or Jesus. And you belong to them, and you all belong to God."[10]

So for Jesus' followers there is no place for holy war, radical displacement of rival faiths, persecution of heretics, arrogant condescension, or narrow partisanship. There is room only for a single cooperative fellowship of all men, seeking the truth about God and being sought by the God who is love, through those spiritual pioneers in whom he is progressively incarnating himself. It is a fellowship in which, because they love one another, each both gives and accepts creative criticism in the assurance that thus they will correct each others' errors and experience a growing spiritual good beyond the present limited goodness of any one.

And the Divine nature thus being incarnated is not the private property of Christianity. It is what Hinduism tries to describe in the Ishvara symbol; what Mahayana Buddhism points to in the Sambhogakaya concept; what Whitehead was describing as "The consequent nature of God." It is the universal creator-savior of all possible worlds hidden under the names: Yahweh, Amitabha, Vishnu, Shang-ti, Allah, Christianity's preexistent logos or Christ. It is the foundation of the coming Copernican Christology.

FOOTNOTES FOR CHAPTER FIVE

[1] Fumio Masutani, *A Comparative Study of Buddhism and Christianity* (Tokyo: Young, East Association, 1957), *passim*.
[2] *Ibid.*
[3] Phil. 2:12-13.
[4] Mark 3:35.
[5] Matt. 8:11.
[6] Mark 9:40.
[7] Gal. 5:22-23.
[8] 2 Cor. 5:19.
[9] Matt. 8:10. (Phillips translation).
[10] Cf. 1 Cor. 3:21-23.

PART THREE

Evidence of a Plurality of Divine Incarnations within Human History: A Psychological-Pragmatic Approach Based on Religious Experience and Moral Values

Chapter VI

SALVATION AS THE ENJOYMENT OF RELIGIOUS PEACE

"THERE IS NO salvation outside the Church," wrote Bishop Cyprian in the third century. His assertion poses our problem. Is salvation the exclusive prerogative of Christians, or is it an inclusive human experience available to all men in all cultures at all times, and mediated by all religions? If we are to answer this question, we must describe the experience of salvation and determine its scope as found among the various religions.

Every human experience, including the salvation experience, may be viewed either from within, by the experiencer himself, as a private feeling, or from without, by other human beings who observe him, as a kind of public behavior. Salvation exhibits, then, both a subjective, individual-emotional pattern and an objective, social-moral pattern. To be saved means that the saved person, as contrasted to the unsaved man, will "feel" in a distinctive way and behave toward others in a distinctive manner.[1] These twin criteria of religious salvation were identified at the turn of the century by William James:

> When we survey the whole field of religion, we find a great variety in the thoughts that have prevailed there; but the feelings on the one hand and the conduct on the other are almost always the same; for Stoic, Buddhist, and Christian saints are practically indistinguishable in their lives. The theories which religion generates being thus variable, are secondary; and if you wish to grasp her essence, you must look to the feelings and the conduct as being the more constant elements.[2]

146

It will already be apparent that the present approach to the question of salvation is not the conventional one of biblical or creedal orthodoxy. Rather than being metaphysical or merely theological, the approach is pragmatic, psychological, behaviorist. It represents an attempt to get behind such theological language as is required to describe it, to the existential reality which salvation produces in a man's life. We are concerned with the effects of the salvation event, rather than with its causes or conditions. Our stance is not unlike that of the blind man whom Jesus cured. When the Pharisees questioned him about Jesus' religious credentials, he ignored all Christological and theological issues and replied simply, "Whether he is a sinner I do not know; one thing I know, that though I was blind, now I see.[3]

In the first place, then, salvation is a kind of feeling state. We may epitomize the feeling of salvation as "religious peace," defining this as one's sense of victory over alienation from God or the supreme religious object, over guilt with its fear of divine punishment, and over that meaninglessness and fear of death which are associated with what Tillich calls "ontological anxiety."[4] In considering the possible universality of religious peace, we must ask several questions. If such peace is found outside the Christian Church, may we not conclude that Christianity has no monopoly of salvation? If the Buddhist finds bliss in enlightenment; if the Vedantist finds it in union with Brahman; if the Bhakti finds it in blessed fellowship with Shiva, Vishnu, Amitabha, or Vairocana, what right do we have to say that since such people do not find bliss in Jesus, they have not really found it♣ Is not their testimony decisive?

8. TESTIMONIES TO NON-CHRISTIAN RELIGIOUS PEACE

Rather than answering such questions a priori, we should pay attention to some testimonies to non-Christian religious peace. An Anglican clergyman reportedly seeking to convert Gandhi asked him the existential question, "Have you found peace?" When Gandhi replied that he had, the churchman concluded the conversation with the remark, "Then I have nothing more to say to you."[5] Does not this conclusion validate non-Christian salvation? Again, before being hanged in Sungamo prison, Hideki Tojo, Japan's premier during World War II, wrote a poem expressing his religious hope:

> It is goodby.
> Over the mountains I go today
> To the bosom of Buddha
> So, happy am I.

Some Christians might argue, as does E. D. Soper, that since Tojo underwent no deathbed conversion following the Christian pattern of guilt confessed and forgiveness sought, and instead saw his "war crimes" as merely the outworking of karmic law, he therefore could not have found peace.[6] But aside from the name Buddha for his saviour, how does his religious peace differ essentially from that of the dying Jew who looks forward to rest "in Abraham's bosom" or that of the Christian who sings of being "safe in the arms of Jesus"?

It is even more sobering to find non-Christians who believe that they have something better than what Christianity has to offer. Consider the note of condolence sent to the widow of Joseph L. Smith, the Egyptologist, from the Muslim watchman of an Egyptian tomb: "I went to the Mosque and asked God to overlook the fact of Mr. Smith being a Christian, and to help him to Paradise."[7] Again, unless certain modern Hindus felt that they had a quality of religious peace needed by American Christians, they would not have sent to the United States as missionaries Swami Paramhansa Yogananda and swamis of the Ramakrishna-Vivekenanda Mission. And that modern Buddhism has a gospel of salvation which it finds lacking in American Christianity is strikingly set forth in these lines from one of its hymns:

> Who are these brave youths and maidens bearing
> torches in their hands?
> These are Buddha's noble soldiers from the far-off
> eastern lands.

> Ever forward they are marching, bearing treasures
> to the West,
> Living waters to the thirsty, to the weary peace
> and rest.[8]

9. OBJECTIONS TO NON-CHRISTIAN RELIGIOUS PEACE

To all such testimonies the Christian may characteristically respond, "The quality of religious peace depends upon the character of the savior who mediates it; and I prefer to rest in the arms of Jesus rather than in those of Abraham or the Buddha or Krishna, for Jesus is the only divine savior." Yet the plain truth remains that the Jew, the Buddhist, and the Hindu have overcome ontological anxiety and found religious peace even as the Christian has. Because I love my wife supremely and find emotional peace in our marriage, I am not thereby justified in saying to another man, "Since you are not married to my wife, then no matter how happy you claim to be with your wife, you are not really happy." I am no more justified in saying to a Buddhist, "Since you have not found peace through my Jesus, then no matter how religiously at peace you claim to be in the Buddha, you have not really found peace." As there are degrees of happiness in marriage, so there may very well be degrees of blessedness for men of different faiths, who yet stand together in the presence of God. Who is to say whether the activist, moralistic Christian

or the passive, mystical Hindu has found the deeper peace—
who but God alone? There is simply no other court of appeal
here than that of sincere testimony. "In the last analysis,"
writes Hocking, "a religion has no domain other than that
of the heart's peace, and the individual heart is the sole
judge of its own peace."[9]

Hendrick Kraemer, speaking for those who distrust any
subjective norm, attempts to invalidate non-Christian religious peace. He insists that the testimony of those who
are not Christians is untrustworthy; hence, they are presumptively unsaved: "the claim that these religions lead
people often into a deep and satisfying religious experience
may be wholly justified, but yet this undeniable fact does
not guarantee that there is truth or the same truth in them.
. . . We know too well that men live mostly by fictions from
which undoubtedly they often derive deep feelings of satisfaction."[10] By contrast, according to Kraemer, the Christian experience of salvation is based on truth.

But his position is not valid. Our response to it is *tu
quoque*. Kraemer has no criterion for absolving the Christian faith from dependence upon fiction—or myth, the more
accurate designation for theological language which is only
metaphorically or analogically true, rather than literally
true. Informed students of religion and language will not
contest Tillich's statement that "all theology is mythology."
The reason is that imperceptible realities cannot be equated
univocally with perceptible ones. To call God "Father," is
to use a mythological expression, since a literal "father"
is a male human being whose spermatozoon has fertilized
the ovum of a human female, thus producing a live human
embryo. If by "fictional" is meant those features of an analogy or metaphor which are untrue to fact and thus falsify
their object, it follows that the "fatherhood of God" contains a Christian fiction as do the descriptions of Christ as
the "son of God," "lamb of God," and "bread of life." How-

ever, if Kraemer will grant that there is saving truth in
these Christian myths (fictions), he should, presumptively,
grant truth to Hindu and Buddhist myths (fictions).

Futher, Kraemer would invalidate non-Christian religious peace because he considers it the fruit of a spurious
kind of salvation. For whereas Christian Salvation saves
one from sin and guilt and gives an ethically based peace,
Buddhist salvation is a salvation from suffering; and hence
the peace it brings is merely relief from esthetic discomfort
and, lacking any moral quality, its peace is not genuinely
religious. He writes:

> Buddhism and Christianity are both . . . religions of
> salvation . . . yet however sublime these conceptions
> may be, both cannot be true. The Buddhist salvation
> means salvation from existence as such, because exis-
> tence is suffering, which is necessarily evil. In Chris-
> tianity it means salvation from sin.[11]

But let us look at these two ways of salvation in more detail.
Neither one is flatly true or false. Each is a religious experience to be judged by the quality of satisfaction it af-
fords. But it is inaccurate to say that Buddhist salvation is
"from existence as such" if this means annihilation; for no
living Buddhist sect holds this.

The emphatic and repeated denial of the existence
of the soul or individual self in Buddhism is contradicted
by the rest of the system. The problem is, of course, the
referent of the term "self." From the objective point of
view of the non-Buddhist the self is presupposed in the denial of the self—who is doing the denying if there is no
self? Is it not the self that is concerned to deny the self's
existence? It is the self which is addicted to craving; which
suffers; which needs but is ignorant of the way to enlightenment; which exercises toward others loving kindness,
compassion, sympathetic joy and equanimity; which trans-
migrates, that is, carries the karmic pattern of each pre-

ceding incarnation over into each succeeding incarnation; which, with adequate meditation and mind culture can "acquire the power of looking back into its previous lives,[12] and "which . . . has as much identity with the previous one as the adult of today has with the child that he was; nothing less and nothing more;"[13] which is responsible for all its past, present and future actions, and is free to act differently, thus transcending the lock-step of the determinism of dependent origination; which constantly seeks and finally may enjoy the bliss which is nirvana. As in Christian Science, evil is not eliminated by calling it "error," so in Buddhism the self is not eliminated by calling it "a process of continued change;" for change presupposes something which remains constant as it undergoes change. It is not eliminated by saying it may be analyzed into five component skhandas and is merely a stream of karmic energy, for something integrates the skhandas and directs the energy. The attempt to eliminate the self is no more successful than Hume's and for the same reason: the self cannot be observed for it is always the observer and can observe only the non-self. One must come round finally to a Buddhist version of Descartes' indubitable certitude, "I suffer therefore I exist." Professor Nakamura of the University of Tokyo lays to rest the popular teaching of the non-existence of the self:

> It is quite wrong to think that there is no self at all according to Buddhism. . . . He [Gotama] admitted the existence of the self as the subject of action in a practical and moral sense. In the *Digha Nikaya,* the Buddha says, "He thus abstaining lives his life void of longings, perfected, cool, in blissful enjoyment, his whole *self* ennobled."[14] (italics ours)

Whether in nirvana the countless individual experiencers of bliss will fuse into a single experience of bliss, must await confirmation beyond history and the categories of consciousness as we know them.

But with regard to the annihilation of this self in nirvana, Nakamura continues:

> One who has attained Enlightenment is far from having dissolved into non-being; it is not he who is extinct, but the life of illusion, passions, desires . . . . Nirvana is a lasting state of happiness and peace . . . . The craving etc. for extinction in the sense of annihilation or non-existence was indeed expressly repudiated by the Buddha.[15]

Moreover Kraemer's view misrepresents vast numbers of Buddhists, such as the Amida sects, who *do* believe in individual immortality. If the term *annata* (no self) means "self-denial," losing one's ego craving for this world in order to enjoy the divine nirvana life, then it does not differ ethically from Jesus' teaching about losing one's life in order to find it. But if it means simply escape from earthly life because it is painful, the definition is accurate and applies to Christianity as well as to Buddhism.

It is true enough that Buddhism's chief emphasis is on suffering rather than on sin, but this should not invalidate its salvation. The concept of "sin" is predominantly Semitic, the state of alienation from or disobedience to the will of a personal God. Hence it is also a factor in all other theistic faiths such as the Hindu bhakti and Mahayana Buddhist sects. On the other hand, in Oriental pantheistic and atheistic systems such as Sankara Vedantism, Theravada Buddhism, and Taoism, the analogous concepts of personal "evil"—ignorance, compulsive craving, self-assertion—are the obstacles to salvation. The difference between the two concepts, hence, is not one of substance but of relationship: the same act, murder, is a sin against a personal God in theism and an evil in relation to its effect on society and one's own ideal destiny in non-theistic systems.

While Christianity names sin as the chief evil, its motive for escaping it is the same as the Buddhist salvation motive—to enjoy in heaven freedom from the suffering which sin entails. Buddhism's way of salvation is stated in the four noble truths: (1) all men suffer (2) the cause of suffering is compulsive, selfish craving (3) to get rid of suffering one must get rid of such craving (4) the way to get rid of this craving and to arrive at the bliss of nirvana is to follow the eight-fold path of salvation outlined by Buddha. But in the last analysis there is little to choose between salvation from sin because of the suffering it brings of separation from and punishment by an offended God (which is the Christian view), and salvation from suffering caused by the sin of selfish desire which flouts the moral law of the universe, karma (which is the Buddhist view).

All suffering is intrinsically, hence necessarily, evil. However, in many instances it may be discovered to be instrumentally good. As such it is tolerated more readily by Christians than by Buddhists. In fact, Christians, like the Stoics before them, have tended to resign themselves to evil, to make a virtue of necessity, to say the most irrational and frightful evils are somehow good because they are the will of God. Buddhism is more realistic, less ready to say that suffering is good. But both prefer heaven-nirvana. Paul is emphatic in his preference of heavenly to earthly life: yet, like the Bodhisattva, wills to serve mankind on earth.[16]

The Buddhist reasoning is psychologically the more honest. Suffering is man's chief enemy—physical, mental, moral. To be rid of it, one must get rid of the "sinful" or evil (inordinate, compulsive, egocentric) desires and cravings—*tanha*. Just as in Christianity, Kraemer to the contrary notwithstanding, the "sin" is in the will, not the mind; hence the Buddhist seeks to destroy the egotistic will. When the ego goes, "sin" goes; and when "sin" goes, the suffering goes. The Buddhist description of "sin" as egotistic desire is not materially different from the Christian notion of *hubris*—prideful self-will which acknowledges no divine will above it.

But the Christian logic, because it derives from a theistic premise, sees moral evil as an offense against or disobedience to a personal God; whereas the Hinayana Buddhist logic, proceeding from a humanist premise, sees it rather as an infraction of the impersonal law of karma, or as alienation from one's true nature as desireless bliss. If Kraemer's criticism implies that Buddhism wishes to escape the suffering yet retain the "sinning," we confront an almost willful misunderstanding. But the watershed between the two views is not that one salvation gets rid of sin and the other doesn't; it is that one has a theistic and one a humanist conception of sin. Yet even this distinction disappears in the Tantrayana and Mahayana branches of Buddhism, where sin takes on the coloring of offense to personal deities. Shinran, the founder of Jodo-Shin Buddhism, had an intense consciousness of sin in the Semitic theological sense;[17] but his view of it, according to Hideo Hashimoto of Lewis and Clark College, was well within the Buddhist tradition. But if it be objected that the Buddhist view encourages a light view of sin, it can be retorted that the Christian view encourages a morbid view of it. In both views, however, sin is essentially self-centered living, and salvation is the religious peace enjoyed by escape from the suffering such living entails.

To sum up: salvation may be identified as the feeling state of religious peace, and this feeling is enjoyed by non-Christians.

FOOTNOTES FOR CHAPTER SIX

[1] This statement hardly needs justification. For if the experience of salvation makes no difference in a person's life, it is either an illusion or the normatively religious person is a schizophrenic.

[2] William James, *Varieties of Religious Experience*, Modern Library Edition (New York: Random House, 1902), p. 494.

[3] John 9:25.

[4] St. Paul made such peace evidential of salvation when he wrote to the Church at Rome (Rom. 5:1). The Ephesian letter expands the idea (Eph. 2:11-20).

[5] W. E. Hocking, *The Coming World Civilization* (New York: Harper & Brothers, 1956), p. 143.

[6] Cf. E. D. Soper, *The Inevitable Choice* (New York: Macmillan, 1957), p. 132.

[7] Associated Press Release, Washington, D. C., Dec. 23, 1950.

[8] Hymn 210, "Light From the East," Hymnbook of the Koyosan Temple of the Shingon Sect, Los Angeles, Cal.

[9] Hocking, *op cit.*, p. 156. The position taken in this study is that subjectivism — whether sensory, emotional, rational, cognitive, or intuitional — is, in the last analysis, the only means of validating objective reality. A person's judgment may need correction by the judgment of others or by his own later judgment; but all judgments whatever are subjective. Any allegedly objective reality is merely a subjective inference drawn from experience which is itself subjective. There is no escape from the egocentric predicament into the reality of things in themselves.

[10] Hendrick Kraemer, *Religion and the Christian Faith* (Philadelphia: Westminster Press, 1956), p. 85.

[11] Kraemer, *op cit.*, p. 85.

[12] U. Thittila, "The Fundamental Principles of Theravada Buddhism," *The Path of the Buddha*, ed. Kenneth W. Morgan (New York: The Ronald Press Co., 1956), p. 99.

[13] *Ibid.*, p. 98.

[14] Hajime Nakamura, "Unity and Diversity in Buddhism," *The Path of the Buddha*, ed. Kenneth W. Morgan (New York: The Ronald Press Co., 1956), p. 377f.

[15] *Ibid.*, p. 381f.

[16] Phil. 1:23-24.

[17] Cf. Hajima Nakamura, "Gutako Hitan to Tsumi No Ishiki" (Lamentations of Gutako and The Consciousness of Sin"), *Shinshu Zenshu*, IV, 1958, p. 165.

Chapter VII

SALVATION AS LOVING BEHAVIOR

HOWEVER, SINCE A man's profession of religious peace with God may evidence a merely egocentric esthetic enjoyment, a subjective self-indulgence without ontological reference, it is by itself incomplete evidence of salvation. It needs to be supplemented and tested by an objective principle. The mystical needs to be rounded out by the ethical, for "faith without works is dead." Love for God and love for men are two sides of the coin of salvation. Love for God is genuine only if it generates and passes over into love for one's neighbor, "for he who does not love his brother whom he has seen, cannot love God whom he has not seen."[1]

Therefore, in the second place, salvation as religious peace needs attestation by a kind of social behavior whose criterion is love. And we must know how the inner peace correlates with outer conduct. Is the allegedly saved person sincerely committed to the good of others? Is he morally a better person and easier to live with because he is less selfish than the unsaved person? The biblical answer gives an emphatic "Yes."[2]

10. IS LOVE A VALID CRITERION?

If it be objected that this may not be acceptable to other faiths as a valid criterion of salvation, the answer is that love is taught in the scriptures of practically all of the world's living religions. And many passages advocating self-sacrificing altruism are found in both Buddhism and Hinduism in ways comparable to Jesus' teaching.[3] But do non-Christian faiths agree that love is the *supreme* ethical criterion of salvation? At first glance, one might think they would not so agree. Other virtues than altruistic love seem to dominate, certainly quantitatively, their moral teachings: righteousness in Zoroastrianism, Judaism, and Islam; purity and courage in Shinto; detachment from this world in Hinduism; gentleness and patience in Buddhism; filial devotion in Confucianism; ascetic self-denial in Jainism; humility and non-assertiveness in Taoism. But the experience of C. Burnell Olds of Okayama would seem to answer the question affirmatively. He reports an interesting experience of religious fellowship involving leaders of five Buddhist sects, one Shinto sect, and three Christians. After a year of discussion the group agreed that "the essence of religion is love—love as the basis of the universe and as the root of human righteousness."[4] It seems probable that a similar conclusion would be reached by other sensitive and informed representatives of the world's faiths.

But an objection is raised here. The word "love" is highly ambiguous so that while all may agree on the word, each religion may mean something different by it. Professor King has made a careful study of this problem as it relates to Buddhist versus Christian understanding of the term.[5] He distinguishes the four aspects of love in Buddhism against the New Testament description of it. These aspects, which in his classic, *Path of Perfection,* Buddhagosha called "the four blessed dispositions" or "illimitables," are described as follows: (1) *metta,* "loving kindness," is self-sacrifice for another, even to death: (2) *karuna,* "compassion," is empathetic suffering with a sufferer; (3) *mudita* "sympathetic joy," is joy in the joy of others; (4) *upekkhà,* "equanimity," is an emotionally detached attitude toward the one to whom the other aspects of love are directed and is considered the crowning virtue of the four.

The first three are counterparts of Christian love, but the fourth seems its antithesis. Yet it has a justifying rationale. It is comparable to Aristotle's "golden mean," for it is a psychological balance wheel to protect one against emotional extremes by maintaining objectivity. It will prevent "metta" from loving unwisely, of being over-protective, of neglecting discipline. It will prevent "karuna" from dragging the lover down to the level of the sufferer's misery so that he cannot raise the sufferer. It will prevent "mudita" from becoming overly optimistic and unrealistic.

All such Buddhist love seems Christian. But Professor King points out other features of this Theravada virtue, which tend to weaken its power. The Buddhist theoretical denial of the worth of persons as enduring individual selves lessens the urgency to sacrifice for them. So also does the feeling that one must not interfere with the law of karma, which decrees that each person must suffer for his own sins committed in a previous life. Further, this four-fold love is seen as a self-benefitting meditational practice, rather than a program of remedial social action. For to the degree it is practiced, it will advance one's own spiritual development toward nirvana.

Indirectly, of course, benefits accrue to the loved one. In a sort of equivalent to Christian intercessory prayer, closer however to Christian Science "absent treatments," the one who loves, by a sort of telepathy, radiates goodwill outward to all creatures. This action helps them not only by setting them a good example of holiness, but also by surrounding them with a beneficial aura calculated to reinforce their efforts toward a more favorable incarnation.

The enlightened self-interest involved in this description is apparent not alone to Christians. It is one of the major criticisms leveled at Theravada love by Mahayanism that its nirvana seeker pursues his private path to bliss with little if any redemptive concern for his fellow-sufferers —a sort of "every man for himself and the devil take the hindmost" attitude.

Against such an attitude set the anguished love of Paul for his fellow Jews who were rejecting salvation through Christ: "For I could wish that I myself were accursed and cut off from Christ for the sake of my brothers, my kinsmen by race."[6] Mahayana Buddhism, by stressing active-redemptive Metta love, seeks to correct the merely passive sharing of suffering in Theravada's stress on Karuna type love and thus, in its Bodhisattva doctrine, approaches the spirit of St. Paul. Here the nirvana-bound traveller, having reached the portal of bliss, turns his back upon it and vows never to enter until, with his help, all creatures whatsoever can enter with him.

But let the Christian who downgrades Theravada love beware of self-righteousness. Let him only whose love is without self-interest or merit-seeking cast the first stone. Thus Mahayana love and New Testament love are the same in theory, but few human beings consistantly obey its high demand in practice. The Hinayana devotee fails to rise to the Bodhisattva practice, and the Christian who loves in word only, rather than in deed, fails to practice the love taught by Jesus and Paul. Nevertheless, to the degree that love is practiced, salvation is present:[7] this is the ethical criterion. And on the basis of this criterion the evidence seems to show that men are being saved in all faiths.

11. TESTIMONIES TO NON-CHRISTIAN LOVE

Consider the following sampling of prominent Christians, ancient and modern, who have seen in the loving or Christlike conduct of their non-Christian brothers authentic evidence of salvation. In speaking of Socrates, Heraclitus, Abraham, Elijah, et al., Justin Martyr affirms that each has "his share in a little seed of the Divine Reason (logos spermatikos)"[8] and lives according to reason; and those who live according to reason and virtue, Justin regards as really

Christians.[9] St. Augustine and Abelard agree substantially with this view. In the *Divine Comedy,* Dante admits the pagan Emperor Trajan to heaven because he seemed to be a Christian at heart. Zwingli envisions a future assembly in heaven that will include, in addition to Christ and Christians, outstanding Jewish patriarchs and such pagans as Hercules, Socrates, Aristides, and the Catos and Scipios: "In short, there has not lived a single good man . . . from the beginning of the world to the end, which you will not see there in the presence of God."[10] John Wesley and Gotthold Lessing share Zwingli's view. William Penn writes that "the humble, meek, merciful, just, pious, and devout souls are everywhere of one religion; and when death has taken off the masks, they will know one another, though the diverse liveries they wear here make them strangers."[11]

Turning to more recent thinkers, we note the widely-quoted statement by Harry Emerson Fosdick that Rabbi Stephen S. Wise was the "best Christian in New York City." Nicolas Berdyaev has affirmed that "Christians may very well recognize that the Hindu, the Buddhist, the Jew, the Muslim, the free-thinking spiritualist, if they strive after God, the spiritual life, truth, and goodness, may be much nearer to God and Christ than the outward adepts of Christianity."[12] James B. Pratt puts it strongly: "Many a Buddhist and Confucianist is a Christian in all but creed and name."[13] Joseph Haroutunian once stated publicly, "I expect to find Gautama Buddha in heaven when I get there."[14] And John C. H. Wu, brilliant Chinese jurist converted from Confucianism to Roman Catholicism, has paid this tribute to his Confucian father: "If there was ever a man possessed by the passion for goodness it was my father. . . . My father was not a Christian, but I am quite sure that Christ has said to him: "Come, blessed of my Father, take possession of the Kingdom prepared for you."[15]

If one objects that the foregoing praise of non-Christians is due to superficial observation or the bias of personal friendship, he is free to make his own investigations—to mingle among the foreign students and religious leaders now in this country and to get to know them personally. He will surely discover that many of these men and women are no whit behind many Christians when it comes to integrity, humility, moral sensitivity and unselfish concern for others. On the other hand, it will not be very difficult to find "saved" Christians who are bigoted, demanding, selfish, and hypocritical, whose hearts are not at rest in God, and who live anxious and prayerless lives.

One is reminded of the lines by Robert Burns:

There's so much good in the worst of us
And so much bad in the best of us
It hardly behooves any of us
To speak ill of the rest of us.

Is salvation as evidenced by loving behavior universal in scope? Paul Tillich affirms that it is. He argues that since God has revealed himself in some degree to every man, to the degree of his affirmative response to that revelation, every man is saved; and, further, that this response is measurable in part by the degree of love which a man manifests in his life.[16] However, no man is totally saved because no man perfectly loves, "not even those who have encountered the healing power as it appears in Jesus as the Christ."[17]

The public test of salvation is not profession. "Not everyone who says to me 'Lord, Lord,' shall enter the kingdom of Heaven, but he who does the will of my Father who is in Heaven."[18] If God is love, as the writer of First John affirms, those who love greatly are greatly like God and close to him whether they be Buddhist, Jain, Vedantist, Bahai or atheist; while those who love only a little, even if they be Christians, are only a little like God and at a distance from him.

Some neo-orthodox theologians, agreeing with Nietzsche and religious liberals, are even willing to concede that Christians are no better morally than non-Christians; for to affirm their superiority would be sinful pride or moralism, not Christianity. Yet to concede this is far from conceding that non-Christians are saved. For them, the distinguishing mark of the Christian is not outward conduct, but an inward faith—the faith that they are forgiven and accepted by God in spite of their unacceptableness. But such a faith does not necessarily make them better persons; it necessarily saves them no matter how unethically they may live. But such radical discontinuity between faith and works is quite remote from the teaching and spirit of Jesus.

12. KRAEMER'S OBJECTION TO THIS CRITERION BASED ON HIS DICHOTOMY BETWEEN RELIGION AND BIBLICAL REVELATION

Hendrick Kraemer, however, makes only minimal concessions to the possibility that God is redemptively at work among men outside of the Christian Church. He does so because he attributes to the non-Christian faiths an erroneous apprehension of God, and because he refuses to admit the presence of human distortions and relativities in the biblical revelation. To support and justify an absolute Christ, he absolutizes the Bible. Being suspicious of religious experience and all philosophizing and theologizing, he accepts "Christ alone" as the only saving revelation, and the written records of Christ as the infallible record of that revelation. He writes: "Biblical thinking . . . is a type wholly sui generis, distinct from religious thinking."[19] "The logic proper to it is so severe that the least deviation from it, or falling out of step with it, is registered by one or another kind of confusion."[20] Kraemer's fear of deviant thinking leads him to verbal purism. His reason for contrasting bib-

lical revelation to all religion is that "the Bible entirely lacks
the term 'religion'."[21] This he says in spite of the presence
of the root word   (religion) in Acts 26:5, Col. 2:18,
and three times in 1 James.[1] And the reason he disallows
general revelation in nature and history is that "such abstract . . . generalizations: Nature, History . . . are unbibli-
cal and, moreover, not true to fact . . . . They do not represent anything real."[22] He goes on:

> In its historical course the Christian faith has assim-
> ilated many naturalistic, moralistic and philosophical
> ideas and practices, which go under the name of "Chris-
> tian Religion." . . . But these assimilated elements either
> militate against or, at least, are not derivable from the
> central concept and facts of the biblical revelation.[23]

We are not surprised, then, that this nominalist purist
rejects the whole developing structure of Christian thought
unless it can be stated in the exact words of the Bible. Thus
would Kraemer freeze Christian theology in the vocabulary
of two to three thousand years ago.

He then proceeds to make a fatal admission, and yet
to deny that it contradicts his basic contention: "The finiteness and relativity of human wordings of the truth, including the truth which is in Christ and which is Christ . . . are
facts—and not at all disturbing facts—for those who live
by faith in God's righteousness in Christ, and not by theological doctrines.[24] Kraemer does not seem to recognize
that "God's righteousness in Christ" is itself a complicated
theological doctrine involving such juridical concepts as
substitution, propitiation, and imputation of innocence and
guilt, and superseding the Jewish doctrine of legal righteousness. Nor does he see that many other biblical teachings
are Jewish and Greek theological and philosophical interpretations of what Jesus Christ meant to his first and second
century followers. For example, the simple statements in

θρησκεία

John's prologue about the divine, world-creating logos who became flesh are shot through and through with the metaphysical presuppositions of neo-Pythagoreanism, Philo, Stoicism, and Gnosticism.

A root cause of Kraemer's disregard of the fallibility of biblical statements is his idea of revelation. For him, it is "God's act, independent of any experience."[25] Man is absolutely passive under the divine aggression and, like Locke's *tabula rasa*, makes no contribution to what God writes thereon—no philosophical preconceptions, no standards of value, no laws of logic, no sociological patterns for understanding religious intuitions, no structure of meanings embedded in human language. The only trouble with this view is that it denies the reality of one half of revelation. Revelation is a two-way street; it is not a unilateral action unless one regards man as a puppet. No matter how important the content of the revelation from God may be, it comes wrapped in the words and symbols provided by human culture. Without this secular container there would be no sacred content, and the former conditions the latter. Tillich is right when he says, "One can reject culture only by using it as the tool of such rejection."[26] Moreover, any new revelation would be meaningless unless it were analogous in some respect to something already known, whether by previous revelation or through purely rational-empirical investigation. It would have to contain more than the past; but unless it contained some of it, man would not even perceive it. This law of learning seems incontestable. Granting its validity, every revelation, as soon as it enters the awareness of the receiver and is categorized and verbalized by him, will become relativized and distorted by him. Because of Kraemer's neglect of this truth, he is able to absolutize the biblical revelation and claim monopoly for the salvation it mediates.

Consequently Kraemer's evaluation of the various religions—including Christianity as distinct from the biblical revelation—is that they cannot save a man. At best, they contain a certain "beauty," "richness," "truth," "sublimity," and "elevating and liberating power."[27] They provide men with varying degrees of temporal religious satisfaction, but not eternal salvation, for this is obtainable only "in Christ."[28]

13. THE WEAKNESS OF KRAEMER'S OBJECTION DUE TO HIS VAGUE CONCEPT OF SALVATION

In view of such wholesale relegation of mankind outside the biblical faith to the status of "unsaved," one wonders what is in store for these persons according to Kraemer's version of the biblical revelation. Does Kraemer expect God to torture them everlastingly? Yet, unless one regards the New Testament description of the final state of the wicked both critically and metaphorically, he must believe in a God who is a divine sadist; for such a god is implied when the descriptive words are taken literally.[29]

Of course one cannot ignore the concept of the just judgment of God—it is fundamental to any system of ethics. But just what is its nature and in what experienceable forms is it manifest? It is commonly described in the New Testament as the "anger," "wrath," or "vengeance" of God. But to take these terms literally is to contradict Jesus' basic teaching on God's love for the wicked; it is to make God less moral than millions of his human children. Certainly a Christlike God could not be guilty of personal spite, retaliation, or revenge. Whatever its value, God's judgment is at least remedial in intent, the intent to do men good. The scientifically minded will see the suffering involved in judgment as the operation of natural laws—physical, physiological, psychological, sociological. In an orderly universe each action triggers a corresponding reaction. In falling from a rooftop one cannot escape the injury dictated by the law of gravity.

Hence Jesus could say "the measure you give will be the measure you get."[30] and "all who take the sword will perish by the sword."[31] And if there be natural laws in the spiritual world, to ignore them will entail inevitable spiritual retribution, whether one sees it as the operation of impersonal karma or a Cosmic Teacher's love-motivated principle of education.

Nakamura, speaking for Buddhism, agrees:

> Even the love of God contains, on the other side, punishment for evil. However, the Buddha is the Great Compassion itself, and there is no such thing as punishing man. Punishment is that which each man invites upon himself as the natural consequence. If punishment by Bodhisattva can be conceived, it is nothing else than an expedient (hoben) to save suffering, evil men. Therefore there is no concept of eternal punishment in Buddhism. There cannot be such a thing as "the punishment of the Buddha."[32]

Furthermore, Kraemer's case against the non-Christian faiths is pointless unless he specifies what it means to be unsaved, what the alternative is to the salvation he advocates. In our generation such terms as "saved," "lost," "heaven" and "hell" have become largely emotive words used by evangelists to move men from sin to righteousness. But these terms now lack empirical reference and existential meaning and hence, for thoughtful persons, they have lost even a pragmatic function. They once stood for absolutely discontinuous states—everlasting rapture on the one hand and everlasting torture on the other—with faith in Christ as the all-determining factor between them. But since such meanings of "saved" and "lost" seem both absurd and immoral to the modern mind, they might well be described as Christian nonsense. Heaven is laughed at for connoting the boredom of idleness or, at best, interminable singing; and hell, because it turns God into a sadist. No man can be evil enough to deserve the latter fate. Calvin could approve the burning of Servetus, for he believed that its benefit to the Church far outweighed its brief cruelty to the victim. But neither Calvin nor any other Christian in whose heart is the love of Jesus could possibly enjoy listening through all eternity to the agonizing screams of a Servetus or even a Hitler or a Stalin, knowing all the while that such torture would never make them better persons, protect the Church, or do any other conceivable good to anyone—simply because it was never intended to do so. Theologians who insist that all those who are "outside" Christ are unsaved are under an obligation to state just what the condition of the unsaved is; and to state it to morally sensitive and spiritually minded Vedantists and Buddhists. Otherwise, how can they either maintain intellectual integrity or present a meaningful Christian gospel?

FOOTNOTES FOR CHAPTER SEVEN

1 John 4:20.
2 Cf. Matt. 22:34-40; 25 John 13:35; Rom. 8:1-11; 1 Cor. 13; Gal. 5:19-22; John 4:7, 16.
3 In addition to Santi Deva and the Bhagavadgita quoted *supra*, pp. 78-80, see *The Mahabharata*, trans. R. C. Dutt, The Temple Classics (London: Dent, 1898) Vol. 12, p. 237; and *Srimad Bhagavatam*, trans. S. S. Rau (Tirupati, India: Lakshmana Rao, 1928), p. 113.
4 W. E. Hocking, *Living Religions and a World Faith* (New York: Macmillan, 1940, pp. 201, 271, 274.
5 Winston L. King, *Buddhism and Christianity: Some Bridges of Understanding* (Philadelphia: The Westminster Press, 1962), Chapter III.
6 Rom. 9:2-3.
7 1 John 4:7-8.
8 Apology II, xiii.
9 Cf. *Ibid.*, I, xlvi, 3.
10 Ulrich Zwingli, in *Zwingli and Bullinger Library of Christian Classics*, (Philadelphia: Westminster Press, 1953), Vol. 24, pp. 275-76.
11 Quoted in *Faiths and Fellowship*, ed. S. D. Millard (London: Watkins, 1936), p. 79.
12 Quoted *Ibid.*, p. 79.
13 James B. Pratt, *The Pilgrimage of Buddhism* (New York: Macmillan, 1928), p. 724.
14 In an address at Park College during the week of March 16, 1952.
15 John C. H. Wu, *Beyond East and West* (New York: Sheed and Ward, 1951), pp. 20, 23.
16 Cf. Paul Tillich, *Systematic Theology* (Chicago: Univ. of Chicago Press, 1957), Vol. 2, p. 177.
17 *Ibid.*, pp. 166-167.
18 Matt. 7:21.
19 H. Kraemer, *op cit.*, p. 499.
20 *Ibid.*, p. 348.
21 *Ibid.*, p. 239.
22 *Ibid.*, p. 354.
23 *Ibid.*, p. 62.
24 *Ibid.*, p. 372.
25 *Ibid.*, p. 213.
26 Paul Tillich, *Systematic Theology* (Chicago: Univ. of Chicago Press, 1963), Vol. 3, p. 196.
27 Kraemer, *op cit.*, pp. 83, 84, 39 and *passim*.
28 *Ibid.*, pp. 30, 32 and *passim*.
29 Cf., Rev. 20:10, 14-15; 21:8; Matt. 25:41, 46.
30 Matt. 7:2.
31 Matt. 26:52.
32 Trans. Hajime Nakamura, *Jihi* (Compassion Mercy) (Kyoto: 1956), p. 181.

Chapter VIII

"SAVED" VERSUS "LOST" RE-MYTHOLOGIZED AS A SPIRITUAL CONTINUUM

IN THE THIRD place, the universality of salvation will be more convincing if the notion of "saved" vs. "lost" is re-mythologized. We propose the abolition of the myth of the absolute dichotomy between "the righteous" and "the wicked," and the spatial discontinuity between "the golden streets" and "the lake of fire." In their stead we propose a different myth, the mathematical myth of the calculus, first worked out in metaphysics by Leibniz. In place of an absolute dichotomy, he offered the notion of a universal continuum.

14. PHILOSOPHICAL AND SCIENTIFIC SUPPORT FOR A SPIRITUAL CONTINUUM

Analogical support for salvation as a continuum is found not only in mathematics, where every number is infinitely divisible, and in metaphysical theory such as in Leibniz's monadology, but also in organic evolution, where the differences between chronologically adjacent species tend to diminish with the progress of research. For instance, the study of intelligence, communication, and social ethics among animals is steadily narrowing the gap between their world and man's. And the discontinuity between living and non-living matter is being bridged; at least it is becoming increasingly difficult to identify the dividing point between them, or even to agree on what we *mean* by "life."

170

In support of a continuum joining life to non-life, the testimony of biologists is paramount. According to Paul Weisz, "any structure that metabolizes and self-perpetuates is alive."[1] But this metabolism must be controlled metabolism. Such control involves "steady state control" (self-feeding, self-adjustment, locomotion, self-repair, self-replacement); "reproduction" (development, growth, division); "adaptation" (sex, heredity, and evolution).[2]

Beginning in 1952, Stanley Miller and, later, others brought together the non-organic raw material of a supposed "primeval atmosphere" and earth (methane, ammonia, hydrogen and water), and by subjecting the mixture to high frequency discharges of electric sparks, or their energy equivalents, produced amino acids, formaldehyde, sugars and other organic molecules.[3] In 1957 Kornberg, mixing non-organic raw materials in a test tube, produced unusual organic molecules of DNA which, once made, reproduced themselves.[4] Both experiments knocked the props "from under the comfortable assumption of mankind that 'life' is inherently different from 'non-life'."[5]

The virus parasite seems to be a sort of link or borderline entity between life and non-life, for "when a virus is away from its host cell it has no detectable living functions whatsoever. It does not metabolize . . . it does not react in any positive way with its surroundings. . . . In this state it is commonly referred to as a 'resting virus.' But when a virus encounters a suitable host, suddenly it takes on the attributes of a living thing . . . . It reproduces with a well-defined life cycle . . . . The virus in this living, reproducing form is commonly referred to as 'vegetative'."[6]

> Viruses are essentially DNA with a protein coat, and that coat is primarily protective. So if viruses are alive, couldn't one say that DNA molecules are alive, too—even artificial ones? Kornberg's artificial DNA's can reproduce, and presumably can evolve.

But Kornberg's artificial DNA's were made from "purely chemical matter," compounds that were inert until
he put them together. Perhaps there is something hidden in them, a vital force unique to these particular
compounds? If so, couldn't one say that adenine, thy-
mine, guanine, and cytosine nucleotides are alive?

But they are composed of various arrangements of
elemental atoms .... Physicists have done experiments
that have "created" the elements step by step, from
hydrogen. Are hydrogen atoms alive?

As you can see there is no logical place to break the
chain: hydrogen—the elements—chemical compounds
—nucleic acids—proteins—viruses—bacteria—higher
organisms .... Any definition of life must necessarily
be arbitrary ... *In the continuum of being* [italics ours]
is there a boundary between life and non-life?

The question remains unanswered. But one is tempted
to believe that science has made the question meaningless.[7]

Turning from the testimony of biologists, let us consider the principle of this continuum from a philosophical
perspective. Michael Polanyi writes that "the beginnings of
life do not sharply differ from their purely physical-chemical
antecedents,"[8] and "living beings form a hierarchy in which
each higher level represents a distinctive principle that har-
nesses the level below it while being itself irreducible to its
lower principles .... This is not to say that the higher levels
are altogether absent in earlier stages of evolution. They
may be present in traces long before they become
prominent."[9]

Whitehead puts the matter succinctly. "Science is taking on a new aspect which is neither purely physical nor
purely biological. It is becoming the study of organisms.
Biology is the study of the larger organisms, physics the
study of the smaller organisms."[10] The ultimate organisms,
of course, are those not decomposable into others. Such,

Whitehead terms "primates," and tentatively identifies them with electrons and protons[11] This surprising classification of subatomic particles is echoed in J. S. Haldane's epigram, "If physics and biology one day meet and one of the two is swallowed up, that one will not be biology." The philosophy of organism seems to be the synthesis of the two. And Needham, being impressed by "the vast complexity of chemical structures, and the unbroken line of sizes reaching from the subatomic levels to the particles of virus molecular size," continues, "Only in the light of the conception of organic levels can the saecular gulf between morphology and chemistry be bridged."[12]

Coleridge saw the bridge of organic levels as a process of individuation.

> I define life as the principle of individuation, or the power which unites a given all into a whole that is presupposed by its parts. The link that combines the two, and acts throughout both, will of course be defined by this tendency to individuation. Thus from its utmost latency, in which life is one with the elementary powers of mechanism . . . to its highest manifestations . . . there is an ascending series of intermediate classes, and of analogous gradations in each class.[13]

Whitehead offers two descriptions of life: "The characteristics of life are absolute self-enjoyment, creative activity, aim,"[14] and "the teleological introduction of novelty with some conformation of objectives."[15] Hence every individual actual entity or occasion of experience is a bit of life—a process by which data of the antecedent world are felt by it and synthesized with selected, but till then unrealized, novel potentialities into an organic whole.[16] "This is the doctrine of creative advance whereby it belongs to the essence of the universe, that it pass into a future."[17]

Whitehead's philosophy is thus explicitly a philosophy of organism, a sort of panpsychism stressing the subjective feeling aspect of thing-events rather than their objective behavioral aspects. Each event-atom or actual occasion of experience is an organic process: it is born, grows, feels, has subjective aim, is self-directive and self-creative by incorporating new possibilities into its given actualities; it dies, and thereafter lives not in itself but only as an influence on succeeding event-atoms which it helps to generate —which are in a sense its reproductions with the addition of novel features.

Hartshorne, after praising various features of Whitehead's metaphysics, approvingly summarizes his continuum as a "generalization of comparative psychology and sociology downwards to include physiology, biology, chemistry and physics as studies of the more elementary types of sentient individuals and societies."[18] And elsewhere Hartshorne supports this generalization by asking some pertinent questions about the relevancy of feeling in entities lacking a nervous system.

> What anthropomorphism it is to suppose that the human way of feeling is anything like the only way. How does a bee feel? One thing seems sure: in no way closely similar to any human mode of feeling . . . . All argument from the necessity of nerves for feeling is a mere vicious circle. Our feelings require human nerves, a dog's feelings require doggish nerves, all vertebrate feelings require vertebrate nerves; but a "protozoan feeling," by definition, could not require separate nerve cells, since there can be no separate cells in the case . . . . Go further down. Does not an atom behave, respond, organize its parts, and under stimulation reorganize them, act also without external stimulus (when radioactive at least)? Moreover it is no mere odd fact of science that the parts of "inert matter" are not themselves inert.[19]

Summarizing the foregoing testimony of biologists and philosophers, we can state that the axiom of biological evolution that there is a continuum of protoplasmic substance undergoing structural change toward increasing complexity of organization, specialization of newly differentiated parts and ability to exploit its environment can now, in the opinion of the best scientific thought, be extended to include the chemical constituents and antecedents of the protozoa.

Concurrently with this structural and life continuum one can trace a continuum of "intelligence," which has been variously specified as "adaptive behavior" and "problem solving." And this "mental" development can be traced from the smallest single cell and its non-cellular antecedents, which survive only by "unconsciously" selective, immediate reflex responses to environmental stimuli, to the verbalized conceptual reasoning of the most sophisticated philosophic thought.

Thorndike observes that intelligence in animals "can be explained by the ordinary associative process without aid from abstract conceptual, inferential thinking,"[20] such as characterizes man, and which exists among reptiles, fishes and insects.[21] However, as over against the lower animals, the "primates display a vast increase of associations and a stock of free swimming ideas."[22] Nevertheless, when Thorndike says that animal association is homologous only "with a certain limited form of human association,"[23] he does not mean "any denial of continuity between animal and human mentality."[24]

If adaptation of means to ends be a primary mark of intelligence, one can point to tool using as a trait linking man with the lower animals. It is a commonplace observation that chimpanzees in captivity can pile boxes on top of each other to reach suspended fruit, and gorillas in the wild have been observed to lick up otherwise inaccessible water by thrusting straws into water-filled crotches between diverging tree branches. Nature has provided the anteater with a long (rod-like proboscis adapted for insertion into the narrow apertures of the anthill. But a species of Finch in the Galapagos Islands, not having a long enough beak for the purpose, breaks twigs or thorns from bushes to use as tools to pry grubs from the burrows in rotten wood.

Another species of bird has been observed to pick up and drop stones on the eggs of other birds to break them open for eating, just as men use hammers to crack out nut meats. Tools are extensions of an animal's limbs whether they be the simple straws, twigs, stones or boxes used by birds or monkeys, or the complicated tools known as shot-guns, wheat harvesting combines or irrigation systems used by men. The intelligence required for tool using is thus a continuum joining man and beast.

Thorndike continues on this subject:

> Let us not wonder at the comparative absence of free ideas in monkeys, much less at the absence of inference or concepts. Let us not wonder that the only demon-strable intellectual advance of the monkeys over the mammals in general is the change from a few, nar-rowly confined, practical associations to a multitude of all sorts for that may turn out to be at the bottom the only demonstrable advance of man, an advance which in connection with a brain acting with increased delicacy and irritability, brings in its train the functions which mark off human mental faculty from that of all other animals.[25]

In fact, observes Scott, "many results suggest that the rise of 'reason' or verbal thinking in human beings is not as frequent as is commonly supposed and that in many prac-tical instances people may make use of the more primitive kinds of behavioral organization found in animals."[26]

Thorndike concludes that man's

> inborn tendencies . . . show throughout marks of kin-ship with the lower animals . . . . His intellect we have seen to be a simple though extended variation from the general animal sort . . . . Among the minds of animals

that of man leads, not as a demigod from another planet, but as a king from the same race.[27]

The nature of communication being an expression of intelligence, it also reveals a continuum linking man to the lower animals. The distinction between animal signals and human symbols is of course readily recognizable. The animal can signal its feelings and desires by physical sounds and gestures, which are then signs to other animals and evocative of appropriate behavior in them. But such animal "language" is restricted to its expressive-emotive and motivational-directive meanings; its signals have no referential or syntactical meanings.[28]

Thus the animal which is communicating cannot dissociate itself from the immediate concrete situation of place, time, feelings and wants. Its signals cannot refer to past or future events, to hypothetical situations or to experiences at variance with its actual feelings and motives at the moment of giving the signals. The gorilla cannot utter the scream of rage when it feels tenderly affectionate nor the cry of hunger after having eaten well. Whereas with a man there is no necessary agreement between his words and his feelings when he feels in a certain way. And of course the most intelligent animals—chimpanzees, dogs and dolphins *et al.*—have no written language, no system of arbitrarily chosen, visible marks to serve as a permanent storehouse of their meanings.

But is there then no continuum spanning this gap between animal and human communication media? The answer would be more decisive if we could observe the linguistic behavior of both primitive man and his closest primate relatives. Such a comparison being impossible we have only various theories of the origin of language to go on. Of these theories, perhaps "interjectionism," a kind of communication restricted to emotive expressions and imperatives, comes nearest to filling the gap.

However, if we grant the recapitulation theory, that ontology repeats phylogeny, an infant's earliest cries and other noises are significant, for they are exclusively expressive-emotive and motivational-directive and seem to differ not at all from the speech of the most intelligent subhuman animals. By analogy, the language of civilized man is to that of his prehuman forbears as the language of a human adult is to an infant's language; that is, it is a matter of degree of development. Between the speech of the most advanced subhuman and that of the least advanced human there would seem to be not an uncrossable abyss but a natural bridge.

Paralleling the already considered continua of life, intelligence and speech, one could also establish a continuum of morality ranging from maximum egoism and minimal altruism to minimal egoism and maximal altruism. One could point out steps or stages in this gradient: the "ethical" entelechy that brings independent electrons together to form atoms, individual atoms together to form molecules and cells, individual cells to form cell colonies;[29] such colonial organization to form social systems like those of the bee and white ant;[30] among animals, increasing parental concern for offspring; tribal or in-group protective cohesiveness vis-à-vis threatening out-groups; the extension of parental risk-taking protectiveness to include members of out-groups, thus triumphing over ethnocentrism; and, at the individual personal level, the sacrifice of self for a principle, an ideology, an enemy or a religious faith.

In the foregoing sections of this chapter we have attempted to demonstrate the existence of a continuum joining "non-living" to living matter, animal reasoning and speech to human intelligence and language, egoistic self-concern to altruistic social concern. If this has been demonstrated, it should a fortiori be much easier to prove that such a gradient exists joining all members of the more homogeneous *homo sapiens* group, whether savage or civilized, with respect to their degree of intelligence, esthetic appreciation, inter-personal sensitivity, moral discrimination, social responsibility, philosophical comprehension and religious experience. And with respect to the last mentioned, we are proposing that "salvation" or "spirituality" is a continuum uniting all men according to their degree of ethico-religious capacity and behavior. Accordingly the difference between Jesus and other men would not be an absolute difference but only a difference in degree as the evidence offered in chapters two, three and four sought to demonstrate. If the gap between Jesus or Gotama Buddha on the one hand and their cultural predecessors on the other seems so wide as to violate the principle of the continuum, one can by analogy to biological evolution explain the emergence of these two great personalities as ethico-religious mutations. On such a basis, heaven and hell become theoretically opposite aesthetic limits for human experience. A calculus-like gradation is provided from one to the other, a continuum applying to life and death alike, with or without the dimension of reincarnation. From this point of view, every human being, whatever his religion, is always more or less saved in heaven and more or less lost in hell; and he may find himself higher or lower on the continuum according to the degree of his spiriutality.

15. THE UNIVERSALITY OF SAVING GRACE

That saving grace is found "outside" Christ is authenticated by the universality of religious peace and brotherly love. But it should be emphasized that such universality is quite consonant with biblical faith, in spite of Kraemer's strictures. There is biblical evidence that God sows his grace widely. Thus we have Jesus' statement that "many will come from east and west and sit at table with Abraham, Isaac, and Jacob in the kingdom of heaven";[31] his picture of the last judgment wherein nations are saved on the basis of their deeds of love;[32] and his affirmation that "Whoever does the will of God is my brother, and sister, and mother."[33] And we have Paul's assertion that the Gentiles are justified by keeping the divine law written on their hearts,[34] and Peter's testimony that "God shows no partiality, but in every nation anyone who fears him and does what is right is acceptable to him."[35]

That the universality of such saving grace may follow the pattern of a continuum, according to the degree that men accept or reject it, is reflected in the widespread belief in degrees of reward and punishment in levels of heaven and hell among various faiths.

In Hinduism's post-Vedic times it was conventional to list seven heavens rising from the earth and seven nether regions descending from it. "In the seventh heaven, which is 1,848,000,000 miles above the earth, is the world where the immortal beings live."[36] Later Mahayana Buddhism developed descriptions of eight great hells, each of which had sixteen auxiliary hells. It provided also for multiple heavens: six of sensual enjoyment, thirteen to eighteen worlds of form, and four formless worlds.[37] In later Zoroastrian thought, "Hell . . . had several levels. . . . Heaven, on the other hand, presented ascending levels."[38] In Judaism, "rabbinical and apocryphal literature speaks of seven or ten heavens. . . . In the third of the seven or the seventh of the ten heavens paradise was placed."[39] And from Judaism belief in multiple heavens seems to have "passed into Christian and Gnostic teaching."[40] Islam recognizes levels of paradise: "The Qur'an . . . clearly tells of the differences in Paradise between the doers of good who have attained a high degree of perfection and those who have committed some degree of misbehavior."[41]

Such distinctions also seem consonant with biblical faith, for one finds clear evidence of them in the New Testa-

ment. Paul accepted the current Jewish view of seven
levels of heaven, declaring that he had himself ascended
as high as the third one, Paradise.[42] Jesus certainly taught
that rewards and punishments hereafter for conduct in this
life will be proportional to the ability, fidelity or knowledge
of the persons involved.[43] He also spoke of degrees of great-
ness recognized in heaven when he said that he who is
humble and childlike "is the greatest" there,[44] and whoever
relaxes one of the least of the commandments "shall be
called least" there.[45] When he said to a scribe, "you are not
far from the Kingdom of God,"[46] he implied the existence of
degrees of distance from heaven in an abode excluded from
heaven. If this was hell, then there are degrees of hell.

Ireneus reflects this view of the after-life in his
statement:

> Those who are deemed worthy of an abode in Heaven
> shall go there, others shall enjoy the delights of para-
> dise, and others shall possess the splendor of the city
> . . . . This is the gradation and arrangement of those
> who are saved, and that they advance through steps
> of this nature.[47]

16. THE LOGIC OF THE CONTINUUM

Now it is only a simple exercise of moral logic to join
heaven and hell in a single continuum with the least degree
of punishment and the least degree of reward impinging
upon each other at a midpoint. The Roman Catholic doctrine of purgatory suggests that such an interpenetration
of opposites, of forgiveness and punishment, acceptably
links the two sides. With such a continuum, the reward or
punishment, the saved or lost condition of each person, becomes measurable according to the actualization of his spiritual potential, the degree of his religious peace and brotherly love. And all the religions of the world can be placed
along the continuum according to the effectiveness with
which they cultivate such attributes. Once this continuum

myth is adopted, it follows that every human being is now
enjoying his own particular degree of salvation depending
upon his positive response to that measure of God's grace
which he has apprehended.

Tillich reflects this view of the degrees of salvation in
his doctrine of degrees of "essentialization," or fulfilment
of one's potentiality:

> The telos of man as an individual is determined by the
> decisions he makes in existence on the basis of the po-
> tentialities given to him by destiny. He can waste his
> potentialities, though not completely, and he can fulfill
> them, though not totally. . . . It can be a reduction to
> smallness; but it also can be an elevation to greatness.
> . . . Small and great . . . are relative evaluations. Be-
> cause they are relative they contradict the absolute
> judgments that appear in religious symbolism, such as
> . . . "being lost or being saved."[48]

> "Heaven" and "Hell" . . . express states of blessedness
> and despair. . . . They point to . . . the amount of
> fulfilment on non-fulfilment which goes into the indiv-
> idual's essentialization . . . and can be used as meta-
> phors for the polar ultimates in the experience of the
> divine.[49]

It also follows that any given time certain "heathen" may
be more fully saved than some Christians.

As Tillich has expressed it, pagan and other non-Christian groups

> . . . may represent the Spiritual Community better than
> the churches, at least in some respects. They may be-
> come critics of the churches in the name of the Spiritual
> Community, and this is true even of such anti-religious
> and anti-Christian movements as world commun-
> ism. . . . It is most important . . . to consider pagans,
> humanists and Jews as members of the latent Spiritual
> Community and not as complete strangers who are in-
> vited . . . from outside.[50]

But the universality of salvation may refer not only to

the fact that all men will find some degree of salvation in all the faiths, but also that all men whatsoever will finally be fully saved; i.e., reach the upper limit of the continuum whatever that may be. The latter meaning is affirmed by most schools and sects of Hinduism and Buddhism, by late Zoroastrianism and the Christian universalism of the Unitarians and Protestant liberals generally. Conditional salvation—that is, salvation contingent upon holding a particular ethnic faith or attaining a certain degree of goodness or metaphysical development, with all non-attainers being either annihilated or eternally damned by God, is taught chiefly by Christian and Islamic orthodoxies.

Now if salvation is a special privilege conferred arbitrarily on some of his creatures by a dictator God, as in deterministic Islam and Calvinism, then many, if not most, are doomed before birth. But if it is a cosmic process through which a loving creator seeks to bring all his creatures from minimal to maximal consciousness, freedom, self-realization, and fellowship with himself, then all without exception are being saved progressively, both here and hereafter. And if there be a final, completed state of salvation, they will all in God's infinite time attain it. To insist that the Creator cannot save all his creatures because he's given each the power to resist salvation, is to make it problematical whether he can fully save any. That is, it is to doubt that God is the supreme power; that he can preserve what he has created. It is to doubt that the persuasive power of God's truth and love can woo and win over at last all his ignorant, fearful, and self-centered creatures. Jesus himself said, "For men it is impossible, but not for God; to God everything is possible."[51] Radhakrishnan states the faith in universalism quite simply: "The light within is universal. Every man has it. . . . All those who consciously obey the light are saved. Those who do not are the world yet to be saved; they are not lost."[52]

Consequently, on the basis of salvation as a continuum, the Church's motive for Christian missions will no longer be the frightening need to rescue men from annihilation or endless torture at the hands of an unforgiving deity. Rather, it will be the same as Jesus' motive: "that men may have life and may have it in all its fullness,"[53] and "to preach the good news to the poor . . . to announce to the prisoners their release and to the blind recovery of their sight, to set the down-trodden at liberty;"[54] to teach them to love each other, including their enemies, as God loves them —that is, unconditionally.[55] It will be to share with them the spiritual riches it has found in Christ, and its material and cultural resources as well. In very simple words, it will be to befriend and love them as fellow-children of God.

And, as in all true love, the Christian will be moved not only to give and teach the other, but also to be open and eager to learn and receive from him.

17. SOME OBJECTIONS TO THE CONTINUUM CONSIDERED

To return to Kraemer: holding as he does to an absolute "saved-lost" dichotomy, he rejects the idea of salvation as a universal continuum. For he does not accept either religious peace or loving behavior as definitive evidence of salvation. He disagrees with the writer of First John that since "God is love," whoever loves "is born of God and knows God."[56] Kraemer does grant the presence of what appear to be Christian virtues in non-Christian people, but for theological and exegetical reasons he denies their rootage in the indwelling Spirit of God; this in spite of Paul's insistence that love is a distinctive evidence of the presence of the Spirit.[57] In his *De Carne Christi* Tertullian depreciates any goodness outside of Christianity by declaring that heathen virtues "can only be looked upon as splendid vices." Kraemer's cynicism is even deeper: "The most sincere representation of the most impressive form of piety or quality of life may happen to be furthest from the Kingdom of God."[58] Jesus taught that "you will know them by their fruits,"[59] but Kraemer rejects such a criterion of true religion; he prefers to judge its actual fruits according to its theoretical roots, to discount indubitable goodness when it is rooted in a theology the truth of which he doubts.

Professor Callaway shares Kraemer's skepticism. He devotes an entire book to the discrediting of Buddhist virtues because they are exhibited by men who profess the metaphysics of idealistic monism.[60] Such an ontology, he insists, is necessarily a solipsism which precludes interpersonal relations and makes morality impossible. Japanese Buddhists of the Zen, Shin and Nichiren sects possess no genuine virtues because they theorize that all things are identically one and the same, thus obliterating the differences between good and evil, true and false.

While it is true that theory does tend to shape practice, it is equally true that practice has its own independent motivation and criteria, a pragmatic base which resists the encroachment of the theoretic. Northrop makes a point of this in contrasting what East and West offer to religious living. The West stresses the theoretic believing—the rational-empirical; for it, religion is primarily correct or logical believing. But the East stresses the esthetic component— the intuitive-ethical, the religion of right feeling and right action. He writes: "The esthetic factor is as primary and hence as justified a criterion of trustworthy knowledge and of the good and the divine in culture as is the theoretic component."[61]

Should we not then compare religions less by their theological systems than by the religious experiences and feelings these systems engender and attempt to explain? As between the intuitive-pragmatic and the conceptual-rational approaches to religious reality, Kraemer's approach is clearly the latter. But in taking this approach does he not defy the law of learning, which moves from experience to knowledge rather than vice-versa since knowledge (concepts) is always an abstraction from past experience or a prediction of future experience that may or may not do justice to that prediction? Is not experience the ultimate test to which conceptual truth-claims must submit for validation?

After all, feeling (pure esthesis) is the primary, intrinsic value; knowledge, is only secondary because derivative, or instrumental to it. Plato, followed by Whitehead, recognized this when he posited experience of the good and beautiful as the goal of all ideational activity. C. I. Lewis affirms it in saying that "knowledge may be, in general, a means to some more valuable end which is not knowledge."[62] And the matter has been stated poetically in Cranch's lines:

> Thought is deeper than all speech;
> Feeling, deeper than all thought.
> Souls to souls can never teach
> What unto themselves was taught.[63]

Hence the rationalist-conceptualist is the servant of the mystic-pragmatist. Although he serves as a corrective for any extravagance of the latter's imagination, he is the follower not the leader. Hence we should judge the validity of a culture's religious concepts by the richness of its religious experience, and we must not deny the validity of that experience because it may not fit into the pattern of another culture's concepts.

"Whereas I was blind, now I see," said the man healed by Jesus. The Pharisees rejected his testimony not because they doubted that the physical change had occurred, but because they doubted the formal credentials of Jesus as healer.[64] So Kraemer rejects the verbal testimony to religious peace made by non-Christians, and their observable loving behavior not because he doubts that they actually

love and are at peace, but because he doubts the metaphysical credentials of the non-Christian faiths; and he doubts
the latter because their myths differ from the Christian
myths. In Buddhist philosophy of religion the theoretic has
invaded the distinctively Eastern esthetic—but it does not
demolish it. In their skepticism Kraemer and Callaway overlook some important considerations. Even on a monistic
basis a sense of oneness or identity is as powerful a motiva-
tor to altruism as any "I—thou" obligation. In many persons, particularly lovers and mystics, it is the very capstone
of the love relation. But those whose religious experience
lacks the mystical dimension find it hard to accept this truth.

Again, a man may be both better or worse than his
ontology. Calvin and Suzuki are both morally better men
than their metaphysics would logically suggest, and Henry
VIII and Hideki Tojo were worse than theirs demanded.
Gotama Buddha himself went about doing good at the cost
of personal comfort and worldly success. If he had practiced the strict monism implicit in his *anatta* and *anicca*
doctrines, he'd never have left his meditation under the Bo
tree. It seems almost wilful blindness to call counterfeit the
vast good—the humility, gentleness, sympathy, compassion,
and self-abnegation of the millions of Buddha's followers
because some of their speculative thinkers developed a neu-
tral, monistic ontology. Such men as Asoka, Asvaghosha,
Santi Deva and Shinran were saints, not cynical recluses
or conscienceless libertines. So far as ontology itself is concerned, is there a single system which rules out all others
as false? Is there only one authorized Christian ontology?
The problem of the one and the many is not solved by
rejecting either alternative, and there are various reconcili-
ations of this paradox held by as many indubitably good
Christians.

Because evidences of divine grace outside Christianity
seriously threaten the Christian claim to a monopoly of sal-

vation, it is not strange that attempts have been made to
discredit such grace. Thus Rudolph Otto writes:

> India never knew, in the biblical sense of the world,
> *"quid ponderis sit peccatum"* (what weight sin has).
> Therefore its experience and exultant praise of grace is
> wholly oblivious of what constitutes the "glad tidings"
> in the Christian message, namely that sovereign divine
> grace is an act of reconciliation, the restoration on
> divine initiative, of an irreparably broken relationship
> between God and man.[65]

18. SPIRITUAL DEVELOPMENT VERSUS PRIMORDIAL FALL

Otto overlooks the fact that the doctrine of an original
fall and restoration, of a quarrel with God followed by reconciliation, is not the only possible description of divine-
human relations. It merely represents the Judeo-Christian
mythological version of a need for, and the attainment of,
religious peace. Surely another myth is much more meaningful today: that of "spiritual evolution"—a much older and
originally Greek myth which teaches a gradual growth
toward the divine, a steady, maturing enrichment of understanding and experience of God. But the idea of "the fall"
must be fitted into the myth of the continuum; for this myth
certainly accords better, not only with our present understanding of the cosmic process, but also with the child-parent
relationship in a good home. A monkey is not a fallen man,
a primitive is not a fallen modern, a child is not a fallen
adult; each is simply an earlier stage of the process of developing life. Children must certainly undergo parental dis-
ciplining and stormy adolescence, but in the right kind of
home they never lack the assurance of being accepted and
loved. They need undergo no "fall"—no traumatic experience of abolute separation, of being rejected and disowned
by their parents; neither must they, on their part, instigate
a rebellion which severs all home ties.

The doctrine of the "fall of man" is a Christian myth attempting to explain man's proneness to evil. It presupposes that the first man was created physically, mentally, morally and spiritually perfect; and that his first disobedience to God corrupted him and all his descendants totally, so that Aristotle could be called "the rubbish of an Adam." But if it was a fall, it was a fall upward; for it gave man a conscience, the knowledge of good vs. evil. It was a fall from instinct-controlled, non-moral, animal innocence upward to human freedom and responsibility. And who would deny that it is better to be free to grow and develop one's spiritual potentiality, even if at the risk of frustrating or wasting that potentiality, than it is to be an irresponsible puppet in the grip of instinct? In an altogether different sense, the fall of man is an accurate description of his behavior. For every time a person fails to act up to his ethical ideal, he *falls* below that ideal. But why he falls below it, why he sins, is a part of the unsolved mystery of evil in the universe.

On the basis of a single, primordial "fall," the pattern of a single redemptive and reconciling act is logical enough; Christ, the "second Adam," becomes the only savior for mankind. But on the basis of the idea of growth-maturation, the proper pattern is seen to be a creative, although frequently painful, continuous interaction with God, producing an ever greater degree of spirituality. And such a pattern extends far beyond the Christian theological circle. Ramakrishna, the Hindu saint, altogether lacked the Augustinian conviction of dreadful sin and rebellion against God, and instead felt continually enfolded in the love of his God, Kali. He saw not depravity, but ignorance and insensitivity as the barriers to the realization of God. And the dying Thoreau, when asked by a Calvinist preacher whether he had made his peace with God, replied, "We have never quarrelled." There must be many persons who share Ramakrishna's and Thoreau's experience of unbroken and ever-deepening fellowship with the divine, whose acquaintance with God has not come suddenly and catastrophically after a life of wickedness, but slowly by means of a sustained religious nurture in the home, as pointed out by Horace Bushnell, or of an ever fuller grasp of moral and religious values encountered in normal living. Perhaps this explains and justifies the lack of a vivid sense of sin in Hindu and Buddhist doctrines of grace noted by Otto. Mystical fellowship with God does not require a shattering, personal upheaval to introduce it. The religious harmony may never have been broken in the first place.

It would seem more meaningful in terms of modern Western thought forms to think of the Fall not as an aboriginal full symphony destroyed by the anarchy of the players, but rather as the discovery that an original melody, intrinsically pleasing, being in the embryonic stage of thematic development, was pitifully weak by contrast to its subsequently realized symphonic potentialities. Such harmony will in the early stages have been marred by discords due to human fumbling, but the music need never have stopped. Surely the achievement of harmony with God can be expressed in other ways than the juridical myth of rebel-prisoner-judge-sentence-proxy criminal-pardon. Surely the biblical fall-and-restoration myth is not the only description, nor necessarily the best one, of how to close the moral-metaphysical gap between man and his ultimate Ground— of how man may become more godlike.

FOOTNOTES FOR CHAPTER EIGHT

1 Paul B. Weisz, *Elements of Zoology* (New York: McGraw-Hill, Inc., 1968), pp. 14-15.

2 Cf. *ibid.*, pp. 13-14.

3 Cf. George and Muriel Beadle, *The Language of Life* (Garden City, New York: Doubleday and Co., Inc., 1966), p. 18.

4 Cf. *ibid.*, pp. 177-180.

5 *Ibid.*, p. 180.

6 Dean Frazer, *Viruses and Molecular Biology* (New York: The Macmillan Co., 1967), p. 72.

7 George and Muriel Beadle, *op. cit.*, p. 216.

8 Michael Polanyi, *"Life's Irreducible Structure,"* *Science*, June 7, 1968, Vol. 160, No. 3832, p. 1310.

9 *Ibid.*, p. 1311.

10 A. N. Whitehead, *Science and The Modern World* (New York: The Macmillan Co., 1926), p. 150.

11 Cf. *ibid.*, p. 191.

12 Joseph Needham, "A Biologist's View of Whitehead" in Paul A. Schilpp, ed., *The Philosophy of A. N. Whitehead, Library of Living Philosophers*, (Evanston and Chicago: Northwestern University, 1941), Vol. 3, p. 270.

13 S. T. Coleridge, *Theory of Life* (London: 1st edition 1848, usual edition 1885), quoted in Joseph Needham, *op cit.*, pp. 251-252.

14 A. N. Whitehead, *Modes of Thought* (New York: The Macmillan Co., 1938), p. 208.

15 A. N. Whitehead, *Adventures of Ideas* (New York: The Macmillan Co., 1933), p. 266.

16 Cf. A. N. Whitehead, *Modes of Thought*, pp. 205-208.

17 *Ibid.*, p. 207.

18 Charles Hartshorne, "Whitehead's Metaphysics" in *Whitehead and The Modern World: Science, Metaphysics and Civilization, Three Essays on The Thought of Alfred North Whitehead*, by Victor Lowe, Charles Hartshorne, and A. A. Johnson (Boston: Beacon Press, 1950), pp. 25ff.

19 Charles Hartshorne, "Religion in Process Philosophy" in J. C. Feaver and William Horosz, eds., *Religion in Philosophical and Cultural Perspective* (Princeton: D. Van Nostrand Co., Inc., 1967), pp. 259-260.

20 E. L. Thorndike, *Animal Intelligence* (New York: Halften Publishing Co., 1965, reprint of the 1911 edition), p. 20.

21 *Ibid.*, p. 240.

22 *Ibid.*, p. 154.

23 *Ibid.*, p. 153.

24 *Ibid.*, p. 189.

25 *Ibid.*, pp. 239-240.

26 John D. Scott, *Animal Behavior* (Chicago: Univ. of Chicago Press, 1958), p. 154.

27 E. L. Thorndike, *op cit.*, p. 294.

28 Cf. The general view of Otto Jesperson, *Language: Its Nature, Development and Origin* (London: George Allen and Unwin, Ltd., 1922); B. W. Kähler, *The Mentality of Apes*, trans, Ella Winter (New York: Harcourt, Brace and Co., Inc., Inc., 1925); Curt J. Ducasse, *The Philosophy of Art* (New York: Lincoln MacVeagh, 1929).

29 Cf. William Patten, *The Grand Strategy of Evolution* (Boston: R. A. Badgers, 1920), p. 33, where the theme of "cooperation or mutual service" is worked out.

30 Cf. Maurice Maeterlinck's various writings on the social insects and Peter A. Kropotkin's classic, *Mutual Aid: A Factor in Evolution* (London: W. Heinemann, 1902).

31 Matt. 8:11.

32 Cf. Matt. 25:31-46.

33 Mark 3:35.

34 Cf. Rom. 2:13-15.

35 Acts 10:34-35.

36 Radhagovinda Basak, "Hindu Concept of the Natural World," *Religion of the Hindus*, ed. K. W. Morgan (New York: Ronald Press Co., 1953), pp. 90-91.

37 Cf. *Hastings Encyclopedia of Religion and Ethics*, 1922, Vol. 2, pp. 830, 832-833.

38 John B. Noss, *Man's Religions*, rev. ed. (New York: The Macmillan Co., 1956), p. 445.

39 *The Jewish Encyclopedia*, 1904, Vol. 6, p. 298.

40 R. M. Grant, *op cit.*, p. 61f.

42 Mohammed Shahabi, "Shi'a," *Islam: The Straight Path*, ed. K. W. Morgan (New York: The Ronald Press Co., 1952), p. 210.

42 2 Cor. 12:1-4.

43 Matt. 25:14-30; Luke 19:11-27; 12:47-48.

44 Matt. 18:4.

45 Matt. 5:19.

46 Mark 12:34.

47 Ireneus, *Against Heresies*, *The Anti-Nicene Fathers* (Grand Rapids, Michigan: Wm. B. Eerdman's Publishing Co., 1950), Vol. 1, Bk. V, Chap. 36, 1, 2, p. 567.

48 Tillich, *Systematic Theology*, Vol. 3, p. 406.

49 *Ibid.*, p. 418f.

50 Tillich, *Systematic Theology*, Vol. 3, p. 154f.

51 Mark 10:27 (New English Bible).

52 S. Radhakrishman, *Recovery of Faith* (New York: Harper and Brothers, 1955), p. 17.

53 John 10:10 (New English Bible).

54 Luke 4:18 (Goodspeed).

55 Cf. Matt. 5:43-45; Luke 6:35-36.

56 1 John 4:7-8. It is true that the writer of First John speaks in sharp dichotomies: those who love and those who do not; those who are sinless and those who are not; those who have the Son and those who have him not. And each pair of contradictories means a dis-

continuity between the saved and the lost. There is no hint of a continuum joining them. But the author's contradiction — the children of God cannot sin (3:6, 9); yet they all do sin (1:8, 10) — is exegetically resolveable by noting that in the Greek the first "sin is the characteristic and perpetual sinning of one who is alienated from God, whereas the second "sin" is incidental acts of wrong-doing by one who is in a state of grace. Nevertheless, the dichotomies are all too sharp and would disappear on the continuum principle by the acknowledgement that all men show different degrees of sin, love, knowledge of God and, hence, of salvation. No man is wholly evil and totally lost, or wholly perfect and totally saved.

57 Cf. Gal. 5:22-23.
58 Kraemer, *op cit.*, p. 365.
59 Matt. 7:16, cf. James 1:26-27.
60 Tucker N. Callaway, *Japanese Buddhism and Christianity* (Tokyo: Shinkyo Shuppanshu Protestant Publishing Co., 1957).
61 F. S. C. Northrop, *The Meeting of East and West* (New York: Macmillan, 1946), p. 311. See Corroboration of Northrop in Eric Fromm, *The Art of Loving, World Perspectives*, ed. R. N. Anshen (New York: Harper, 1956), Vol. 9 Z, pp. 78-80.
62 C. I. Lewis, *Mind and the World Order* (New York: Charles Scribner's Sons, 1929), p. 145.
63 C. P. Cranch, southern mystical poet, from his poem "Gnosis."
64 John, Chap. 9.
65 Quoted in Kraemer, *op. cit.*, p. 43.

Chapter IX

MANY GUIDES TO THE ONE GOAL

IN CONCLUSION, WE may state that just as there is more than one road to New York, so there is more than one way to find peace with God and men; and there are varying degrees of such peace. In the fields of logic and mathematics we can expect and require agreement of all sane minds; but progressively less so as we make judgments in the fields of the physical, life, and social sciences; least of all in art, philosophy, and religion. For in these realms we approach the apogee of the intangibility and unpredictability of the objects of experience and of the individuality of the personal subjects of those experiences.

A basic weakness of our common human nature is its egocentric penchant for putting the straitjacket of conformity upon others, of making our own experiences prescriptive for our fellows, of forcing other minds to submit to the formulae we have worked out for ourselves. But as Professor Edman reminds us, "Individuals differ too much to have any scheme of good prescribed promiscuously for all of them."[1]

19. "THE ONLY WAY" VERSUS RELATIVISTIC SOTERIOLOGY

The neglect of this truth and the forcing of all others to lie down on the Procrustean bed of our own theology and religious symbolism ere they may rest their souls, is the chief cause of religious conflict. Yet this practice is the besetting sin of the Judeo-Christian-Islamic religious tradition and its "only way" arrogance. And writer after writer, Catholic and Protestant alike, justifies such religious arrogance on the ground that it is the nature of truth to be intolerant of what is false. Such justification, however, would be valid only if one were absolutely certain that he possessed the truth, the whole truth, and nothing but the truth. But since he lacks omniscience and objectivity, and since his truth claims are inextricably enmeshed in the ambiguities of language, man is deprived of absolute certitude. He is justified therefore only in an attitude of intellectual humility toward differing truth claims and toward those who advance them.

But the outstanding merit of Eastern religions is that they allow for individual differences of temperament, theological myth, and stages of religious development. While admitting that tolerance can be so excessive that all standards of truth and value disappear (a chief Christian criticism of Hindu and Buddhist thought), Radhakrishnan points out the rationale for tolerance in spite of this peril. He is aware with Northrop that the Western mind is so conditioned by the exactness and uniformity required for proficiency in the physical sciences that it is blind to the personal and cultural relativities of religious experience.[2] Radhakrishnan writes:

> Western forms of religion are inclined to hold that one definition is final and absolute and all others false. In India each definition represents a darsana or a viewpoint. There are many ways of viewing one experience. The different darsanas ... are pointers in the way to spiritual realization. If religious truth is seen by different groups in different ways, it is not to deny that truth is ultimately one.[3] ...

> The Hindu doctrines proceed on the assumption that the discipline prescribed for any individual should have relevance to his spiritual growth (stage of growth) .... In the *RigVeda*, in the *Upanishads*, in the *Bhaga-*

vadgita, the freedom to worship God that must appeal to us is permitted . . . . They hold that all paths lead to the summit.[4]

So for Buddhism and Hinduism, as for Plato, Averrhoes, Vaihinger, and contemporary demythologizers, there is a double truth about ultimate reality—the philosophical-metaphysical and the theological-mythological. And they recognize such broad avenues of religious apprehension as jnana, karma, and bhakti; which are appropriate for the temperamental cerebrotonic-theorist, somatotonic-activist, and visceratonic-gregarious types respectively.[5] So, also, in Hinduism we find side by side and equally orthodox; two non-theistic, five theistic, and six supertheistic systems of religious thought.[6] And in Buddhism we find non-theistic Hinayana beside theistic and polytheistic Mahayana, both of which have a supertheistic dimension, and subsects based on temperamental and philosophical preferences. Moreover, in China, we find the practice of plural religious belonging— a single individual embracing at once the social ethics of Confucius, the mystical naturalism of Taoism, and the theological salvation of Buddhism.

Each of the foregoing individual paths or their equivalents is, broadly speaking, discoverable within Christendom. But whereas, in the East, those who travel the separate paths respect each other and enjoy the fellowship of all who acknowledge a common ultimate destination, in Christendom each self-righteously despises the others or tries to get them to repudiate their own paths for his. Thus we find in sharp conflict: the atheistic systems of Humanism, Ethical Culture, left wing Unitarianism; the theistic system of main line Eastern Orthodoxy, Roman Catholicism, Anglicanism, and Protestantism; and the theistic supertheistic thought of various idealist and naturalist philosophers and mystical liberals such as Tillich, Wieman, Gerald Heard, and Teilhard de Chardin.

We have the karma marga of Roman Catholicism, seen in its salvation by sacraments, penances, and indulgences, set over against the bhakti marga of Protestantism, seen in its doctrine of justification by grace alone and expressed in the emotional fervor of such groups as the Pentecostal and Holiness branches of evangelicalism. And over against, and scorning both, we find the jnana marga rational-intellectual approach to God of the Unitarians, the Broad Church Episcopalians, philosophers, and theological liberals generally. In addition we have in Roman Catholic Mariology a Christian matriarchal Shakti cult greatly antipathetic to the monolithic, patriarchal masculinity of the Protestant Godhead; we have the virtual polytheism of Catholic hagiolatry and demonology set over against Protestantism's uncompromising monotheism; we have her magic and superstition-ridden sacramentals scandalizing Protestantism's scientific realism.

The diverse paths to God—the darsanas adjusted to the individual's temperament, power of mental abstraction, stage of spiritual development,—are all present and pursued with fervor within historic Christianity. But the devotees of each path are loath to regard the others as valid even if they are not anathematizing them. Whereas, as we have shown in the Eastern religions generally, each path is welcomed as a demonstration of the universality of the grace and wisdom of God, or in the case of non- or super-theistic systems, as proof of the orderliness of cosmic law or the rational, calculus-like structure of reality.

Kraemer objects, however, that since all other faiths are non-biblical, the salvation they offer cannot be Christian. He is quite right. Such salvation is neither biblical nor Christian. But since it is the work of God, producing religious peace and brotherly love, we must conclude that God's grace overflows the boundaries of orthodox theology and is not the monopoly of the Christian community.

Some of us are following the way of Jesus toward eternal life; others, the paths of Moses, Krishna, the Buddha, Confucius, and Mohammed. But since God invites all men to the one, ultimate destination, they ought to share their travel experience in the comaraderie of the journey. If Christians find their way good and their guide trustworthy, they ought to share with their companions the riches of God's grace in Christ Jesus. But Christians should also be glad to receive any news of divine grace which the others have found, and which still others may find in Zoroaster and Laotse and Motse, in Plato and Epictetus and Plotinus, in Nanak and Baha'u'llah and Ramakrishna. Jesus has been called "the Light of the World" and the Buddha, "the Light of Asia"; but light is good in whatever lamp it burns.

20. THE IMPOSSIBILITY OF DEMONSTRATING ABSOLUTE SUPERIORITY

But this is not to say that all religions are equally good, for then conversions would not occur. Broadly cultured and ethically sensitive persons will not hesitate to prefer Buddhism and Christianity to Voodooism; or Quakerism and Unitarianism to the snake-handler cult of Tennessee. Moreover there are various yardsticks by which to measure the value of a religion; and thus measured, each religion may exhibit some special superiority over others. If your yardstick is the practice of racial equality, Islam, historically considered, is superior to Christianity; if it is religious education, Christianity holds the edge. If your yardstick is theological tolerance, non-violence, and the life of meditation, Buddhism and Vedantism are superior to Christianity; if it is personal optimism and social responsibility, Christianity is the superior religon.

To complicate evaluation, the world's religions are undergoing constant change by mutual borrowing and historical synthesis so that they become composites of earlier or geographically contiguous religions. Within Hinduism one can trace synthetic movements toward Christian and Western thought such as the Brahmo Samaj, Theosophy and the recent philosophically reconciling writings of Radhakrishnan. To praise Buddhism is to praise the Hinduism out of which it grew and many of whose beliefs and practices it has retained. Buddhism itself exhibits a remarkable capacity to absorb aspects of other religions. Consider its easy coexistence with indigenous spiritism where it has spread, its integration with Shinto in the Ryobu faith of eighth century Japan, and its recent copying from Christianity of congregational hymn singing and youth organizations. To praise Islam is to praise Christianity and Judaism, for they are the religious parents and ethico-theological foundation on which Mohammed built his superstructure. Sikhism is a partial amalgamation of Hinduism and Islam. Baha'ism is structured upon Judaism, Islam, and Christianity and theoretically embraces any other bona fide faith.

To praise Judaism is to pay tribute to the streams of non-Hebrew belief and practice that flowed into it: Bedouin Semite rites, Egyptian circumcision, early Babylonian law, Midianite theology and judicial structure, Zoroastrian eschatology, angelology and demonology, and Hellenistic influences through Philo, the Apocrypha and Pseudepigrapha.

To affirm that Christianity is the best religion is to praise other religions from which Christianity has borrowed. For the Christian religion is an organic synthesis (not an artificial mechanical eclecticism) of Jewish ethical monotheism and apocalypticism; Zoroastrian eschatology; the Greek metaphysics of Plato, Aristotle and Plotinus; Stoic universalism, Gnostic mysticism; sacraments and cultic practices shaped by Graeco-Roman mystery religions—all of these bound together and dominated by the personality and influence of Jesus of Nazareth.

Still further to complicate evaluation, sectarian differences within a given religion may be greater than those between it and another ethnic religion. Which branch of Christianity of the two hundred fifty Christian denominations, does one refer to when he asserts that Christianity is superior to another religion; and to what branch of that other religion is he comparing it? When one asserts that Christianity is superior to Buddhism is he thinking of Roman Catholic Christianity or Southern Baptist, of Unitarian, or Christian Science? And does he have in mind Theravada autosoteric, Shin grace-of-God salvation, or atheist, existentialist Zen Buddhism? And when ranking it ahead of Hinduism is he downgrading the monistic Vedantism of Shankara, or the personal theism of Ramanuja and the Bhagavadgita?

Does not Unitarian Christianity have a closer affinity to Reform Judaism than to the Christian Jehovah's Witnesses; and aren't the Christian Quakers closer to the Moslem Sufis than to the Catholic Christian Penetentes of Arizona?

There seems to be no simple, objective standard by which to evaluate a rival religion, for each devotee will prefer the faith in which he was nurtured or some second faith whose superiority over the first has been persuasive. It has been affirmed with reason that to make a fair evaluation of the major rival faiths one would have to experience each as a practicing believer.

Such a course being impossible, it may suffice to recognize all religions not as cut-throat competitors but as men's response to the divine initiative and self-revelation through nature and human nature, as conditioned by changing cultural contexts, and each religion as mediating its own apprehended measure of the total truth and full salvation.

21. THE ONE FAITH WITHIN THE
MANY RELIGIONS

Tillich puts his finger on the common ground or core of man's diverse religions which, if perceived, makes possible their reconciliation. He writes:

> In the depth of every living religion there is a point at which the religion itself loses its importance, and that to which it points breaks through its particularity, elevating it to spiritual freedom and with it to a vision of the spiritual presence in other expressions of the ultimate meaning of man's existence.[7]

This is another way of saying that there is really only one religion: it is man's conscious relation of dependence upon, devotion to and mystical union with God—the Being describable as the originating and ultimate structurer, sustainer, and developer of the space-time continuum, and its contents, whether this Being be thought of as sub-personal, personal, or supra-personal, or some combination of the three; immanent or transcendant or both.

That there is now an implicit and may, in the future, be an explicit single world religion, is supported by a number of scientific and philosophical considerations. Consider the following areas of unanimity in human thought and experience. There is only one known universe operating under a single system of natural law. There is only one human species on this planet having a single physiological and emotional nature. All men have basically the same type of mind —which has developed in spite of cultural differences the same logic, mathematics, physics, biology, sociology. The canons of artistic expression are universal. In spite of special local emphases, all men share or can be taught to share the same moral values. Men's philosophical problems are universal and perennial—given time, the basic questions raised by thinkers in Greece, India, Europe, and Buddhist countries receive virtually the same answers by the other thinkers. An all-embracing political organization for mankind is in the offing. In view of all these agreements, why should we not expect to find agreement in basic religious truth?

The relationship of such a world religion to its many particular component religions might be compared to the relation of the bedrock foundation of a four-storied dwelling to its upper floors. The foundation, the deepest level of religious experience, on which everything else depends and in which all religious persons are at one, is the act of spiritual *worship*. Let the first floor represent *ethics*, the worshipper's sense of moral obligation to his fellows, the norm of behavior made central in Christianity as the practice of love—a norm on which the religions of mankind are practically unanimous. The second floor could symbolize *organization*, the obviously varied present social structuring of the religions. The third floor might be *theology*, men's still more widely differing mythological or rational description of the supreme religious object and his dealings with nature and human history. The fourth floor could stand for *ritual*, the tremendous variety of cultic symbols and practices whereby each religion dramatizes its beliefs and experiences under sensuous forms.

But the crucial problem is to identify the common foundation. Many attempts to do so have been made without reaching a consensus. At one extreme the foundation is too broad—viz., that it is simple existence, each religion participating in being rather than non-being. But this foundation is shared also by non-religions such as Beta particles, sulfuric acid, rats and Nero. At the other extreme the foundation is too narrow—viz., that it is the ineffable philosophical absolute or an anthropormorphic deity who created the universe out of nothing. But such foundations exclude religions such as Buddhism, Western Scientific Humanism, Jainism, Voodooism, etc.

Whatever it is, and it is complex, it seems to consist of an emotional attitude rather than an intellectual dogma, a feeling rather than a knowing. It is existential rather than rational, a mystical experience rather than specifiable cognition. The attitude expresses an ultimate concern for life's supreme value and includes in varying degree a sense of awe, humility, dependence and trust, involving communion, self-transcendance, peace, power and obligation. We have chosen to integrate this complex of feelings in the concept of "worship."

Tillich has observed what mystics of all faiths experience—that the deepest, inmost essence of all particular religions is the same, and that to the degree that this truth is realized a modus vivendi of interfaith fellowship and spiritual world unity is achievable.

Once grant a common foundation to the diverse religions, their particularities, thinks Hocking, will enrich rather than divide them. As love for their common parent will tend to reconcile children alienated from each other, so when opposing religions reconceive each other as grounded in the will of their common Creator and Preserver, they will be enabled to love each other, correct each other's faults and contribute to each other's insights and values.[8] As Professor Panikkar testifies regarding Hinduism:

> We [Christianity and Hinduism] are not self-sufficient monads, but fragments of the same, unique religion. We need one another because being one we are destined to become one.[9]

As Max Muller has summed up this truth:

> There never was a false God, nor was there ever really a false religion unless you call a child a false man. All religions, as far as I know them, had the same purpose; all were links in a chain which connects heaven and earth, and which is held, and always was held by one and the same hand.[10]

And the hand that holds it, in terms of the coming Co-
pernian Christology, is not the historical Jesus Christ of
Nazareth—culture-restricted, dated, and mortal—but a universal and eternal cosmic hand. It is that hand of God by
which he related himself to Jesus as a savior of mankind
through establishing harmonious God-man relationship with
him known as the incarnation. Called the "Logos" or
"Christ" or "Second Person of the Trinity" in the Christian
tradition, he establishes analogous incarnations, more or
less perfect, with other charismatic individuals in this and
all possible worlds as saviors of their societies. Known by
other names or even unknown outside the Christian tradition, he is yet the one soteriological center of the universe.

Even if the astronomical hypothesis which was invoked
to support the thesis of this book should prove false—viz.,
that there are intelligent beings in need of salvation elsewhere than on this planet—the other evidence presented
still justifies the conclusion that Jesus of Nazareth is not the
only way of salvation. For it is still experimentally and historically true that millions of persons, in varying degree,
find cosmic peace and live lives of faith, hope and love quite
independently of the Christian gospel.

The emergence of a single, universal religious institu-
tion for mankind, winning the highest loyalty to the Supreme Power of Good yet allowing for individual freedom
of expression and progressive revelation, is both desireable
and possible. Yet even those who deny its possibility, who
believe with David Bradley that each religion is eternally
shut up within its own circle of faith and irreducible to any
other circle of faith, so that no Christian can evaluate
circles other than his own may yet believe that if a Christian
truly understands his own faith, he "will be much less sure
that his own understanding of it is the last word or even
that Christianity is the sole possessor of salvation."[11]

The case for Christianity's monopoly of salvation is, in fact, given away by those theologians, Catholic and Protestant, who are willing to concede that God may, when he wills, save whom he will outside the Church's ministry. It is the thesis of this book to expand that grudging concession into the universal truth that all paths that lead to God are good, and all *do* lead to him by divine ordination.

In summarizing our thought on the new cosmic Christology, we can conclude: that no particular religion holds a monopoly of access to God and man's self-realization, but that each offers some degree of salvation to its followers; that no particular religion is pure, independent of and unblended with features of other religions; that the day of purely local religions is past since all particular religions are by the process of historical interaction and synthesis converging and mutually purifying and enriching each other; and that no religion, particular or universal, is final or ultimate since the ultimate is that "toward which history runs,"[12] its goal and consummation in the eternal life of God. And since finite creatures cannot observe this transhistorical goal, they cannot assert that any present, historically conditioned religion describes or contains it. We can only assert by faith that human destiny is good, and is in the hands of the Power which is drawing all creatures in all worlds by all means through many revelations, incarnations and saviors to their spiritual fulfillment.

FOOTNOTES FOR CHAPTER NINE

[1] Irwin Edman, *The Contemporary and His Soul* (New York: Jonathan Cape and Harrison Smith, 1931), p. 168.

[2] Cf. Northrop, op. cit., *passim*.

[3] Radhakrishnan, *Recovery of Faith*, p. 155.

[4] *Ibid.*, p. 156.

[5] For the best American correlation of temperament and religious apprehension, see the books of Charles W. Morris: *The Open Self* (New York: Prentice-Hall, 1948); *Paths of Life* (New York: Harpers, 1942); *Varieties of Human Value* (Chicago: Univ. of Chicago Press, 1956).

[6] S. C. Chatterjee, *"Hindu Religious Thought"* ed. K. W. Morgan, *The Religion of the Hindus* (New York: Ronald Press, 1953), Chapter V.

[7] Paul Tillich, *Christianity and the Encounter of the World Religions* (New York, Columbia Univ. Press, 1963), p. 97.

[8] Cf. William E. Hocking, *Living Religions and a World Faith* (London: George Allen and Unwin, Ltd., 1940), Lecture II, especially p. 190 f.

[9] Raymond Pannikkar, *op. cit.*, p. 22.

[10] F. Max Muller in a letter to the Rev. M. K. Schermerhorn, 1883.

[11] David G. Bradley, *Circles of Faith* (Nashville: The Abingdon Press, 1966), p. 228.

[12] Tillich, Systematic Theology III, p. 344.

GLOSSARY OF
FOREIGN AND TECHNICAL WORDS

Adibuddha — the Tantric, Tibetan name for the impersonal, primordial Buddha

advaita — literally "non-dualistic." The term which denotes Sankara's Vedantism as monistic, there being only one reality

Ahura Mazda — the Zoroastrian name for God who is Goodness and Light

alayavijnana — the Receptacle Consciousness on which the human consciousness is based in the idealistic, Yogacharya metaphysics of Buddhism

Amaterasu Omikami — the sun goddess of Japanese Shintoism

Amida Buddha — a celestial Buddha, not the historical Gotama, worshipped by some Japanese Mahayana sects as the supreme deity

Amitabha — the celestial Buddha of the Pure Realm known in Japan as Amida Buddha

anatta — literally "no soul," the Buddhist doctrine of no soul substance

Angra Mainyu — the Zoroastrian god of Evil and Darkness

anicca — literally "no substance" (matter), the Buddhist doctrine that the only reality is constant flux

apocalyptic — Jewish and Christian teachings concerning the sudden and supernatural defeat of evil at the end of the age or world

apocrypha — any religious literature not considered sufficiently authoritative to be included in the sacred Jewish or Christian scriptures

atman — the soul or real essence of man, which is identical with Brahman

avatara — incarnations or manifestations of a god in Hindu thought

207

axiological — the study of value and its criteria

Bhagavadgita — literally "The Song of the Blessed Lord." The most popular of all the Hindu scriptures. In a conversation between the warrior Arjuna and Krishna, an incarnation of the god Vishnu, the chief varieties of Hindu religion are described and approved with a preference for Bhakti theism

Bhagavata Purana — a Hindu scripture extolling the way of love and devotion to a personal god

Bhakti — Hindu sects which practice devotion to a loving, personal god

bhakti marga — loving devotion to a personal god as the road to salvation

Bhutatathata — literally "absolute suchness" (that which is such that it is because it cannot be otherwise described)

Bodhisattvas — potential buddhas, persons who though meriting it, have foresworn Nirvana to help all other persons to attain to it

Brahma — Hinduism's Ishvara (personified Brahman) particularized as the god who creates

buddha — literally "enlightened," any person who has discovered the cause of suffering and experienced its cure as taught by Gotama Buddha

darsana — any view of life inspired by the Upanishads. In general, each religion is seen by Vedantists as a darsana or viewpoint of truth relevant to its devotees' particular historical, sociological and psychological situation. But all darsanas are ways to salvation

dharma — right teaching and behavior in both Hinduism and Buddhism

Dharmakaya — the highest aspect of the Mahayana Buddhist trinity, the Threefold Body of the Buddha—its Absolute or Unmanifest nature distinguishable from the Sambhogakaya or second aspect of the Body, which is its Enlightened Mind; and from the Nirmanakaya, its earthly body, which is its third aspect

ding an sich — literally "the thing in itself," Kant's denotatation of the noumenal world of God, the self and the cosmos, which are beyond our observation and descriptive categories

DNA — deoxyribonucleic acid: a chemical whose properties make it the universal key to life. It enables the cell to manufacture specific proteins, to reproduce itself, and to undergo mutation

entelechy — the actualization of an entity's potentiality, its built-in goal

eschatology — any religious teaching dealing with the last things: the end of the world and man's final destiny

ethnocentrism — group, racial or cultural self-centeredness

Gnosticism — the thought and practice of various esoteric cults flourishing around the beginning of the Christian era, teaching a dualistic philosophy, an elaborate mythology, and salvation through knowledge intuited by an elite group of spiritually advanced souls

Hinayana — literally "the small vehicle," the commonly accepted designation for the original Buddhism of India rather than its later development when it spread into China, Tibet and Japan

Ishvara — Hinduism's suprapersonal Brahman, the Absolute, apprehended as a personal being

jnana marga — transcendant knowledge of the Supreme Being as the road to salvation

Kali — one of the chief spouses of Shiva

kalpa — a time period in Hindu thought embracing the creation and dissolution of one universe

kami — the Shinto word for "gods"

karma — literally "action," the impersonal Hindu law that all actions have inevitable moral consequences in this life and in succeeding reincarnations. One must suffer in the next life for sins committed in this.

karma marga — performance of all required duties as the road to salvation in Hindu thought

karuna — compassion or empathetic suffering with a sufferer in Buddhist thought

Kerygma — the earliest apostolic proclamation of the role of Jesus as savior-Messiah

Krishna — the most beloved incarnation of the Hindu god Vishnu

Logos — literally "word." Conceived as the rational principle of the universe by the Stoics, it became the creative function of the deity by the neo-Pythagoreans, and was still later applied to the Christ, the second person of the Christian Trinity

Logos Spermatikos — the Stoic Logos conceived as the creative source of cosmic unity and perfection. Men, having a little seed of the Logos in themselves can be described as logoi spermatikoi

Mahayana — literally "the great vehicle": the commonly accepted designation for the Buddhist schools and doctrines of the later development of Buddhism in China, Tibet and Japan rather than the original Indian Buddhism known as Hinayana or "small vehicle"

Mara — the personification of evil who tempted Gotama to give up his quest for the solution of the problem of suffering . . . the Buddhist devil or satan

maya — appearance or illusion, predicated in Hindu thinking of everything except Brahman who is the sole reality

midrash — an exposition or explanation of a biblical text in Judaism

metta — the Buddhist word for loving kindness involving sacrifice for another

monophysite — the doctrine that Jesus Christ has one nature with one will, which is both human and divine, a view considered unorthodox because in it the human nature tended to be swallowed up by the divine.

mudita — the Buddhist word for sympathetic joy in the joy of others

myth — in general the description of the new and strange in terms of the already experienced. In religion, the description of the supernatural in terms of the natural, the divine in terms of the human

Naga Kings — in the Lotus Sutra of Mahayana Buddhism they are mythological counterparts of the kings of wild tribes adjacent to India

neo-Platonism — the system of mystical pantheism erected by Plotinus on a foundation laid by Plato, holding that everything emanates from an ineffable One

neo-Pythagoreanism — a metaphysical dualism deriving from Pythagoras and Plato in which, man, sloughing off his imprisoning bonds of evil matter, may rise to ultimate union with the Good who is God

Nirvana — literally "no flame," the bliss of desirelessness, the goal of all Buddhist aspiration attainable in this life as well as after one's final reincarnation

noumenal — Kant's term denoting the reality beyond man's observation and descriptive categories; that is, God, the self and the cosmos.

One — the ineffable Absolute in the philosophy of Plotinus from which every thing else has emanated

Pelagianism — the unorthodox Christian doctrine that man can by an act of free will assist God in achieving his salvation

pseudepigrapha — apocryphal writings to which false authorship has been attached

Raja Yoga — a psychophysical self-discipline through which, by eight successive steps one gains salvation or union with the Supreme Being

Rama — the second most beloved incarnation of the god Vishnu

Ramanuja — the great Hindu champion of theism as opposed to Sankara's monism

samadhi — the final yogic state of perfect concentration, of superconscious union with the One Self or Supreme Being

samsara — the world of appearances, man's living of this bodily life

Saivite — the Hindu theistic sect offering devotion to the god Shiva

Sankara — the great monistic thinker of Indian Vedantism

Sat Nam — literally "That Name", the Sikh word for God

satori — self-enlightenment or salvation by non-verbal, non-rational meditation in Zen Buddhism

Shakti — the Divine Mother or female creative power worshipped in certain Hindu sects

Shangti — literally "Supreme Ancestor," early Chinese name for God conceived as a person

Shiva — Hinduism's Ishvara (the personification of Brahman) particularized as the god who destroys

skhandas — the five aggregates which make up the individual person in Buddhist thought: corporiality, feeling, perception, mental formations, consciousness

solipsism — the view that nothing exists except oneself

spentas — Zoroastrian personification of the various attributes of God

Stoicism — the naturalistic pantheism developed in late Greek thinking which taught that Reason is the ultimate cosmic principle and that all men contain a part of it so should govern their lives by it

sunyata — the Buddhist Madhyamika doctrine that Reality is a Void or Emptiness because it cannot be mentally grasped or described

sutra — any late piece of writing purporting to be the teaching of or about the Vedas or Gotama Buddha and held by some to be equally authoritative with the original scriptures

tabula rasa — a blank page on which nothing has been written, a comparison invoked by empiricists to combat the doctrine of innate ideas

Talmud — the authoritative body of Jewish tradition containing comments, interpretations and applications to life of the Torah made by rabbis over the years

Tantrayana — the Tantric School of Buddhism in Tibet characterized by esoteric and symbolic rites for the attainment of supreme wisdom

Targums — parts of the Hebrew Old Testament translated into Aramaic

Tathagata — literally "one who has gone thus" or followed the path of liberation, a Buddhist title for Gotama

tathata — suchness, reality which cannot be described otherwise—it is such as it is

Tao — the ineffable Way or primordial Principle of the existence and operation of all things according to philosophic Taoism

telos — the goal or end which is sought

Theosophy — a religious eclecticism combining Hindu, Buddhist, Spiritualist, and Christian teaching and practice

Theravada — The Way of the Elders, the original Buddhist thinking later widely referred to as Hinayana

Trikaya — the Mahayana Buddhist philosophic trinity of Dharmakaya, Sambhogakaya, and Nirmanakaya

Upanishads — the philosophic and speculative portion of the sacred Vedas

upekkha — equanimity or emotional detachment toward those to whom the other aspects of Buddhist love should be directed

Vairocana — the Primordial Buddha, chief object of devotion in the Japanese Shingon sect

Vaishnavism — the religion of the Hindu theistic sect whose name for God is Vishnu

Vedanta — the name given to the highest teaching of the Upanishads, upon which the system of philosophy known as Vedantism is based

Vishnu — Hinduism's Brahman personified and worshipped as the god who sustains all things

Visishtadvaita — the qualified monism of Ramanuja, yet not literally dualistic

yoga — literally "union" with God or a path leading to that union, in Hinduism

yogi — one who is seeking union with the Supreme Being by means of the disciplines of yoga

AUTHOR INDEX

Abdul Baha: 89
Abelard: 92, 161
Al Hallaj: 124
Altizer, T. J. J.: 63, 67
Amos: 116
Anaximander: 9
Anselm, Saint: 92
Aquinas, Saint Thomas: 22, 24, 72
Aristides: 161
Aristotle: 189, 199
Arius: 10
Arnold, Edwin: 11
Asanga: 51
Asoka: 187
Asvaghosha: 51, 187
Athanasius: 38
Augustine, Saint: 51, 161
Averrhoes: 22, 196
Ayer, A. J.: 52

Bab, The: 89, 125
Baha'u'llah: 10, 18, 34, 64, 89, 120, 125, 142, 198
Barth, Karl: 11, 58, 66
Bartlett, Charles N.: 19
Bayazid of Khurasan: 124
Beadle, George and Muriel: 191
Berdyaev, Nicolas: 161
Berkeley, Bishop: 74
Bernstein, Jeremy: 27
Bethe, Hans: 13
Bornkamm, Gunther: 48, 65
Bradley, David G.: 204
Bradley, F. H.: 22
Brown, William A.: 19, 72
Brunner, Emil: 11
Buber, Martin: 124
Buddha, Gautama: 18, 24, 33, 34, 50, 53, 63, 78, 109, 120, 121, 130, 142, 143, 187, 198
Buddha of faith: 51
Buddhas: 24, 52
Buddhaghosha: 158
Bultmann, Rudolf: 11, 72
Burns, Robert: 162
Bushnell, Horace: 190

Callaway, Tucker N.: 185, 187
Calvin, John: 168, 187
Cameron, Alastair: 13, 14, 27
Catos, the: 161
Champion, John B.: 19
Chuangtse: 125

Clarke: W. N.: 27
Clement of Alexandria: 21, 23, 24
Cobb, John: 37
Coleridge, S. T.: 173
Compte, August: 52
Confucius: 74, 109, 144, 196, 198
Connell, Francis J.: 133
Coomaraswamy, A. K.: 11
Cranch, C. P.: 186
Cyprian, Bishop: 146

Dante: 161
D'arcy, Charles F.: 19
Das Gupta: 11
De Chardin, Teilhard: 196
Descartes, Rene: 38, 152
Drake, Frank D.: 14

Eckhart, Meister, 74, 123, 128
Edman, Irwin: 194
Einstein, Albert: 7
Eliade, Mercea: 11
Elliott, Hugh: 73
Epictetus: 38, 74, 198
Eriugena: 24

Fosdick, Harry E.: 161
Frazer, James: 11
Fuller, Margaret: 91
Fuller, Reginald: 49, 66

Gandhi, M. K.: 89, 143, 148
Geiger: 70
Ghose, Aurobindo: 11
Goodspeed, Edgar J.: 56
Gosvami: 90
Graetz: 70
Gregg, Richard: 60
Guenon, Rene: 11

Haldane, J. S.: 173
Hamann, J. G.: 72
Haroutunian, Joseph: 161
Hartshorne, Charles: 20, 22, 36, 128, 174
Hashimoto, Hideo: 52, 155
Heard, Gerald: 196
Hegel, G. F. W.: 74
Henry VIII, King: 187
Heraclitus: 160
Herder, J. G. von: 10
Hesse, J.: 71
Hillel: 116

Hitler, Adolf: 168
Hocking, William E.: 11,
150, 203
Hodgson, Leonard: 19
Huang, Su Chu: 27
Hubble, Edwin: 14
Hume, David: 73, 152
Hurst, George L.: 70, 94
Hus, John: 89

Ignatius, Saint: 102, 104
Inchofer, Melchior: 9
Ireneus: 181
Isaiah: 116, 144

James, William: 52, 128,
139, 146
Jeremiah: 116, 143
Justin Martyr: 23, 41, 160

Kabir: 88
Kahler, Martin: 50
Kalitinsky, Andrew: 27
Kant, Emanuel: 22, 24, 45, 52
Kierkegaard, Soren: 52
King, Martin Luther: 89
King, Winston L.: 158, 159
Kitagawa, Joseph: 11
Kittel, Gerhard: 70
Klausner, Joseph: 70, 94
Kornberg, Arthur: 171, 172
Kraemer, Hendrik: 11, 150, 151,
153, 154, 155, 163, 164, 165,
166, 167, 169, 179, 184, 185,
186, 187, 193, 197
Kropotkin, Peter A.: 192
Kummel, W. G.: 48, 66

La Mettrie, J. O. de: 73
Lao Tze: 18, 50, 109, 121,
143, 198
Leibnitz, G. W.: 137
Lessing, Gotthold: 10, 161
Lewis, C. I.: 186
Lincoln, Abraham: 89
Locke, John: 165

Macintosh, D. C.: 39
Madhva: 51, 74, 90
Maeterlinck, Maurice: 192
Mahathira, Mirisse Gunasiri: 85
Mahavira: 63, 120, 121
Marco Polo: 10
Masutani, Fumio: 137, 144
McGiffert, A. C.: 28, 63, 104
McHugh, L. C.: 15

McTaggart, J. E.: 115
Mendelssohn, Moses: 10
Meynell, Alice: 16, 18
Micah: 115
Mikogami, K. G.: 91
Miller, Stanley: 171
Minhazad: 84
Mohammed: 34, 198
Montefiori, C. G.: 70, 94
Morris, Charles W.: 11
Moses: 34, 51, 71, 120, 143, 198
Motse: 74, 143, 198
Muller, Max: 11, 203

Nagarjuna: 51
Nakamura, Hajima: 85, 152,
167
Nanak: 198
Needham, Joseph: 173
Niebuhr, Reinhold: 41
Nietzsche, F. W.: 163
Nikhilananda, Swami: 11
Northrop, F. S. C.: 11, 185, 195

Olds, C. Burnell: 158
Origen: 23, 41
Otto, Rudolf: 21, 24, 45, 59, 93,
188, 190

Page, Thornton: 13, 27
Panikkar, Raymond: 42, 65, 203
Pannenberg, Wolfhart: 32, 64
Pascal, Blaise: 52
Patanjali: 88
Patten, William: 192
Paul, Saint (Teaching of) —
adoptionist christology: 106-
107; Christ mysticism: 73,
126, 127; condemnation of anger: 60; fullness of deity in
Jesus: 101, and potentially in
all Christians: 126-127: Jesus'
deity denied: 10; his subordination to God: 101, 102; his
pre-existence: 114; his resurrection: 73, 74; when sonship
attained: 106; justification by
faith: 90; valid for Gentiles:
180; Kenosis: 101; love as evidence of the Holy Spirit: 184;
love for non-believing Jews:
160; man's judgment of angels: 117; salvation as doing
work of God and man: 130,
135; multiple heavens: 181;
vision of Christ: 72

215

Penn, William: 161
Perrin, Norman: 47, 65
Perry, Edmund: 11, 32, 33,
    133, 199
Philo: 21, 100, 103
Pius XII, Pope: 72
Plato: 74, 115, 143, 186, 196,
    198, 199
Plotinus: 36, 52, 125, 143,
    198, 199
Polanyi, Michael: 172
Polycarp: 102, 104
Pratt, J. B.: 11, 161

Radhakrishnan, Sarvepalli: 10,
    11, 39, 78, 128, 183, 195, 199
Raible, D. C.: 15
Ramakrishna: 17, 88, 114, 121,
    126, 143, 189, 198
Ramanuja: 36, 74, 90, 200
Ramprasad: 128
Reimarus: 10
Rhys-Davids, Thomas W.: 11
Richardson, Cyril: 20, 22, 25, 28
Rishis, the: 51, 88, 126, 144
Roberts, Oral: 121
Ross, Floyd: 11
Royce, Josiah: 74
Russell, Bertrand: 38

Sabellius: 10
Sagan, Carl: 13
Sankara: 22, 45, 51, 200
Sansom, George: 86
Santi Deva: 79, 187
Santayana, George: 52
Saunders, Kenneth J.: 83, 96
Sayers, Dorothy: 19
Schweitzer, Albert: 54, 72, 119
Scipios, the: 161
Scott, John D.: 176
Secci, Angelo: 13
Servetus, Michael: 168
Shapley, Harlow: 14
Shinran: 155, 187
Shklovsky, I. S.: 13
Smith, D. M.: 49, 66
Smith, Joseph: 89
Smith, Joseph L.: 148
Socrates: 89, 144, 160
Soderblom, Nathan: 11
Soper, E. D.: 11, 148

Spencer, Herbert: 22
Spinoza, Baruch: 38
Stalin, Joseph: 168
Strauss, David S.: 72
Struve, Otto: 13
Sullivan, Walter: 13, 27
Suso: 123
Suzuki, D. T.: 10, 11, 52, 66,
    83, 125, 187
Tagore, Rabindranath: 88
Tai Wu, Emperor: 84
Temple, Bishop: 11
Tertullian: 184
Thoreau, David: 189
Thorndike, E. L.: 175, 176
Tillich, Paul: 11, 12, 13, 15, 16,
    17, 18, 21, 24, 26, 27, 28,
    44-46, 50, 52, 55, 57, 62-67,
    127, 142, 147, 165, 182, 196,
    201, 203
Toynbee, Arnold: 11, 76
Troeltsch, Ernst: 11, 84
Tukaran: 88

Vaihinger, Hans: 22, 52, 196
Vallabha: 90
Vivekenanda: 11

Wach, Joachim: 11
Watts, Allan: 11
Weatherhead, Leslie: 82
Weil, Simone: 65, 75
Weisz, Paul: 171
Welch, Claude: 19, 28
Wesley, John: 161
West, Rebecca: 9
White, Andrew D.: 27
Whitehead, A. N.: 36, 74, 144,
    172, 173, 174, 186
Whitman, Walt: 124
Wieman, Henry N.: 54, 196
Wise, Stephen S.: 161
Wu, John C. H.: 161
Wu-Tsung, Emperor: 84

Xenophanes: 74
Yogananda, Paramhansa: 27,
    72, 148
Zimmer, H. R.: 11, 128
Zoroaster: 18, 34, 50, 109,
    120, 121
Zwingli, Ulrich: 161

SUBJECT INDEX

Abraham: 51, 93, 115, 149, 160
Absolute, the; absoluteness: 19, 22, 24, 25, 35, 36, 44, 45, 52, 202
Adam: 101, 104, 189
Adibuddha: 16
Ahura Mazda: 52
Alaya vijnana: 16
Allah: 52, 144
Amaterasu Omikami: 52
Amida Buddha: 52, 83, 90
Amitabha: 93, 126, 137, 144
Anatta: 130, 153, 187
Ananda: 79
Anglicanism: 196
Angra Mainyu: 52
Anicca: 187
Apocrypha, apocryphal: 56, 70, 199
Apollo: 38
Apollonius of Tyana: 72
Asian faiths, distinctive emphases of: 140
Astronomy: Copernican, 9-11; *heliocentric,* 9; *Ptolemaic,* 8
Atman: 24, 126
Avataras: 32, 33, 34

Babylonian law: 199
Bahaism: 74, 199
Baptist, Southern: 200
Bedouin-Semite rites: 199
Being: 202
Bhagavadgita: 18, 24, 27, 51, 74, 78, 90, 114, 200
Bhagavata Purana: 27, 51, 90
Bhakti: 90, 93, 127, 128, 138, 147, 196, 197
Bhutatathata: 45, 126
Bodhisattvas: 22, 35, 79, 82, 83, 88, 160
Brahma: 22, 52
Brahman: 22, 24, 42, 45, 54, 77, 78, 126
Brahmo Samaj: 199
Buddhahood: 24, 44
Buddha nature: 24, 36, 42
Buddhism: the triple Trikaya, 24, 35; *Tantrayana aspects,* 16, 22, 74; *non-violence,* 85-86, 139-140, 198; *reality of the self,*
151-153; *punishment,* 167; *love,* 158-160; *monism,* 185, 187; *Hinayana* (Theravada) vs. *Mahayana,* 90-91, 127, 137, 196, 200

Calculus, myth of: 170, 197
Christ: 9, 12-13, 17-18, 23, 25, 30, 34, 37, 40, 41, 42, 43, 44, 46, 47, 50, 51, 55, 58, 63, 68, 73, 74, 81, 82, 88, 89, 93, 98, 99, 100, 101, 102, 103, 106, 107, 109, 114, 119, 120, 126, 127, 142, 143, 144, 150, 160, 161, 162, 163, 164, 166, 167, 168, 179, 189, 204
Christs, other: 9, 12-13, 15-17, 25, 205
Christianity: arrogance of, 194-195; *historical synthesis,* 199; *concept of a personal God,* 139; *distinctive emphases,* 139-140; *intolerance of,* 84, 140; *provincialism of,* 26, 141; *as the only historical religion,* 51-55; *social responsibility of,* 198
Christian Science: 114, 121, 152, 159
Christology: adoptionist, 49, 106; *absolutist,* 12-13; *Chalcedonian,* 39; *Copernican,* 7, 9-10, 13, 16-18, 26, 30, 144, 204; *cosmic,* 205; *culture-centered,* 8; *Jesus-centered,* 9; *logocentric,* 9; *monistic,* 9; *orthodox,* 8; *pluralistic,* 9, 11; *provincial,* 8; *relativistic,* 12; *theocentric,* 9
Circumcision: 141, 199
Confucianism: 158, 161
Criticism: biblical, 11, 118; *form,* 11, 50; *demythologizing,* 50, 72; *mythological,* 11; *redactionist,* 49, 51; *textual,* 50
Continuum: communication seen as, 177-178; *in doctrine of purgatory,* 181; *intelligence seen as,* 175-177; *as joining heaven and hell,* 179-183; *morality seen as,* 178; *salvation (spirituality) seen as,* 179-184; *effect of on missionary motive,* 184, *as Tillich views it,* 182; *as*

universal, 170; *joining life and non-life*, 171-172; *Whitehead's view of it*, 172-174
Cornelius: 107, 121

Darsana: 138, 195-197
Dependent origination: 152
Dharma: 78
Dharmakaya: 16, 22, 24, 35, 79, 126
Double truth: 196

Eastern Orthodoxy: 196
Ebionite: 10, 114
Eclecticism: 199
Elijah: 71, 160
Enlightenment, The: 138
Episcopalians: 197
Eschatological: 70
Ethical Culture: 196
Ethics: 202
Ethnocentric, -trism: 113-114
Extra-terrestrials: 14-18, 25

Fictions: 150-151

Gabriel, the angel: 52, 53
Gnosticism: 19, 22, 199
God: absolute-relative polarity of, 15-18, 21; *as supra-personal*, 18, 20; *Bahai manifestations of*, 32, 34; *broad definition of*, 201; *Calvinistic view of*, 139; *essence-ial nature as love*, 13-14, 18, 81-82, 184; *his judgment interpreted*, 166-167; *immanence of*, 23, 25, 142; *Tillich's definition of*; 17, 45, 52, 63; *transcendence of*, 23; *oneness with as sharing his purpose*, 101
Grace: universality of, 26, 89, 179-180, 187, 197-198; *in non-theistic terms*, 91-92

Heaven: 54, 179-183
Hercules: 161
Hiranyaloka: 16
Holiness churches: 197
Holy Spirit: 20, 25-26, 60, 73
Hubris: 154
Humanism: 196, 202
Humanist: 139

Incarnation: basic notion of, 32; *compared to avataras*, 32-33; *existentially considered*, 33; *Jesus as sole example of*, 98; *mystery of*, 38; *orthodox doctrine of*, 34; *partial in Stoicism, Greek myth, New Testament*, 38; *relativity of*, 142; *salvation through*, 81; *Tillich's concept of*, 31-32 *and criteria of*, 40; *total and manopolistic*, 34; *total and selectively pluralistic*, 18, 34; *total and universal in Vedantism, Buddhism, Plotinus, Whitehead, Hartshorne, Cobb and New Testament*, 35-37; *validation of as intuitive and pragmatic*, 141-142; *throughout the cosmos*, 142
Infallibility: Papal, 114; *of biblical revelation*, 163
Ikhnaton: 120, 143
Isaac: 93
Ishvara: 22, 24, 35, 45, 52, 77, 144
Islam: 74, 91, 114, 158, 198, 199

Jainism: 158, 202
Jataka Tales: 79, 83
Jehovah's Witnesses: 200
Jesus (the person of): virgin birth, 63; *boyhood*, 56; *carpenter*, 8; *baptism*, 58-59; *temptation*, 57, 61-62; *goodness*, 58-59; *repentance*, 58-59; *anger*, 60-61; *name calling*, 60; *discouragement*, 61; *estrangement from God*, 55-56, 61, 62; *transparency to God*, 55, 63-64; *omniscience*, 63, 98, 112; *perfection*, 56-57; *sinlessness*, 57-63, 112; *intimacy with God*, 77; *as ethico-religious mutation*, 179; *divine sonship as metaphorical*, 105, 107-108, *as spiritual*, 107-108, *as exclusivistic*, 104-130; *universalism of outlook*, 141; *crucifixion*, 82-83, 87-89; *resurrection*, 63, 69, 71, 74, 110-111; *physical return*, 63; *messianic character*, 48-49, 55-56, 57, 102, 105, 113-115, 117; *historical Jesus vs. Christ*

of faith, 46-51; *quest for Jesus of history as futile and needless*, 50
(uniqueness of teaching?): general ethical and religious, 69-71 — eschatology, forgiveness, golden rule, love of enemies, humility, non-attachment to world, selflessness, inwardness of morality; survival of death, 71-74; personhood of God, 74; fatherhood of God, 74-75; father's sacrifice of son, 75-80; salvation through death of son, 80-89; theories of atonement, 63, 88-89; salvation by grace not works, 90-93
(claims for deity): filled with God's fullness, 37; equality with or subordination to Father-God?, 98-99; "Lord" a deific title?, 99-101; self-identification *with* God alleged by others, 101-104; God's only-begotten son?, 104-106; sonship — as natural, adopted, or spiritual, 104-108, as exclusivistic or shared, 108-110; assertions of spiritual authority — light of the world, 110, brea' of life, 110, resurrection and life, 110-111, sole knowledge of the Father, 112, only way to the Father, 114, messiah, 114, no other savior, 114, preexistence, 115, authority to forgive sin, 115-117, judge of all men, 117, eternalness of his words, 117-119, monopoly of authority, 119-120; miracle-working power, 120-121; worshipped by men, 121-122, seen as idolatry, 46; mystical oneness with God, 122-130; as incarnation of God, 30-34, 40; as center of history, 12, 40; as final revelation, 12, 40

Jesusology: 46
Jiriki: 137, 138
Jnana: 93, 127, 138, 196
Joan of Arc: 89
Judaism: 74, 137, 158, 199, 200
Judaizers: 141

Kali: 22, 52
Kalpa: 16
Kami: 32
Karma: 92, 93, 127, 138, 154-155, 159, 196-197
Karuna: 112
Kenosis: 13, 79, 101
Kerygma: 49, 100
Kingdom of God (heaven): 54, 79
Koran: 118
Krishna: 17, 24, 34, 42, 78, 90, 93, 109, 142

Life, nature of: defined, 171; as linked to non-life by viruses, 171; as a continuum of being, 172, 174; in terms of panpsychism, 173
Logos: 13, 15, 17, 21, 23, 25-26, 103, 144; as spermatikos, 23, 41, 160; as universal, 41
Lord's Prayer: 70
Lord's Supper: 93
Lotus Sutra: 52
Love: as supreme ethical criterion, 157-158; as essence-ial nature of God, 18-19, 23, 81, 184

Madhyamikan: 52
Maitreya: 24
Mara: 52
Marga: 93, 127, 138, 197
Mariology: 197
Mass, doctrine of: 92
Mary, the virgin: 71
Maya: 52, 87
Meditation: 198
Metaphor: "father", "son" as examples of, 20, 150-151
Metta: 158
Michael, the angel: 52
Monadology: 170
Mudita: 158
Mystery religions (cults): 104, 109, 199
Mystical, -cism: 122-130, 187, 190
Myth: 63, 150, 170, 187; of spiritual evolution vs. fall and restoration, 188-190
Mythology, -gical: 15, 18, 52, 142, 150, 151, 188, 202

Naga Kings: 52
Neo-orthodoxy: 9, 21, 114, 163
Neo-platonic, -ism: 19, 22, 24, 45
Neo-pythagoreanism: 21, 22, 24, 100
Nero: 202
New Being: 50, 68, 111, 127
Nicea: 10
Nichiren: 85, 185
Nirmanakaya: 22, 24, 35
Nirvana: 22, 54, 74, 127, 130, 152-154
Nirvikalpa: 128, 130
Non-being: 52, 202
Non-violence: 198
Noumena, -al: 38, 45

Ontology: 185, 187

Parousia: 49
Pelagianism: 137
Penetentes 200
Pentecostal churches: 197
Poseidon: 38
Project Ozma: 14
Protestantism: 197
Pseudepigrapha: 70, 199
Purgatory: 181
Pythagoreans: 115

Quadrinity: 19, 23, 25
Quakers, -ism: 93, 198

Racial equality: 198
Rama: 34, 53
Ramakrishna-Vivekenanda Mission: 54
Reincarnationist: 72
Religion: Kraemer's view of, 164; one world religion — desireability of, 204, argument for, 201, relation to its component faiths, 202; rational vs. esthetic components of, 185
Religions of the world: common ground of, 201-203; goal of, 205; social structuring of, 202; views of non-biblical varieties, 120
Religious education: 198
Religious experience: relativity to temperamental, cultural, mythological, and theological factors, 194-197

Remythologize: 170
Revelation: as final in Christ, 12; finality examined, 40-44; Kraemer's view of it vs. religion, 163-166; relativity of, 46, 142; Tillich's view of, 44-46
Revelators, Bahai: 32
Ritual: 202
Roman Catholic, -ism: 88, 92, 137, 139, 181, 196-197
Ryobu: 199

Samadhi: 128-129
Sambhogakaya: 22, 24, 35, 79, 144
Samsara: 22
Sainthood: 111
Saints: 187
Salvation, aspects of: a continuum, 170, 184; as God's work and man's work, 130, 138; as conditional, 183; as escape from sin or suffering?, 153-154; Kraemer's unclear view of, 166-168; objective love of neighbor as criterion, 157-168, denied by Kraemer, 184, and Callaway, 185; subjective religious peace as criterion, 146-155, denied by Kraemer, 150, 184-185; theoretic vs. esthetic criteria of, 127-128; Tillich's view as "essentialization," 182; as universal, 125-126
Satan: 52, 53, 118
Sat Nam: 52
Satori: 93, 125, 129
Savikalpa: 74, 128
Self, aspects of: self-sacrifice, 79; self-denial, 107-108; as absorbed into God, 128; Buddhist analysis of, 151-153, and annihilation denied, 153
Septuagint: 99
Shakti: 90, 197
Shangti: 52, 144
Shin sect: 52, 90, 91, 185, 200
Shingon: 74
Shintoism: 74, 158, 199
Sikhism: 74, 91, 199
Skhandas: 152
Snakehandler cult: 198

Spentas: 25
Spiritual leaders as colleagues: 143
Stoic, -ism: 74, 114, 199
Saddharma Pundarika Sutra: 27
Sufis: 200
Sunyata: 22, 24, 45, 52, 79
Supertheistic: 196, 197

Talmud: 70
Tanha: 154
Tao: 45, 52, 91, 92
Taoism: 91, 158, 196
Tao Teh King: 70-71
Tariki: 137
Tathata: 24
Telemachus: 89
Temperamental types of believers: 196
Tendai sect: 86
Theology: Midianite, 199; *as mythological,* 52, 202
Theosophy: 72, 199
Thomas (Jesus' disciple): 102
Tojo, Hideki: 148, 187
Tolerance: 198
Torah: 117, 137, 141
Trajan: 161
Transubstantiation: 92
Trikaya: 22, 24, 51
Trinity, -ies: as metaphysical dualities, 18, 20, 23; *biblical-traditional,* 15, 18, 20, 23; *interlocking,* 15; *social analogy of,* 18, 23, 26; *reappraisals of,* 13-25
Tritheism: 18, 20

Unitarian: 92, 196, 198, 200
Upanishads: 18
Upekkha: 158

Vairocana: 16, 147
Vaishnavism: 34
Vedantism: 19, 22, 198; *Advaita V.,* 35, 42; *Visishtadvaita V.,* 36
Vedas: 118
Virus, -es: 171, 173
Vishnu: 16, 22, 24, 52, 53, 78, 91, 144
Voodooism: 198, 202

Witch of Endor: 71
World Faith: 17
Worship: 121-122, 202

Yaweh: 24, 52, 102, 103, 144
Yogacharya: 16
Yukteswar, Sri: 16

Zen: 54, 185, 200
Zeus: 38
Zoroaster: 198
Zoroastrianism: 74, 158; *its eschatology, angelology, and demonology,* 199